# PROPERTY, BUREAUCRACY AND CULTURE

This book places the British middle classes in their historical and regional contexts in order to explain how they exercise a powerful impact in present-day British society. It develops a new theoretical perspective on the middle classes, criticising fashionable but unhelpful theories of the 'service class', and draws upon the work of Wright and Bourdieu to develop a theoretical realist perspective which is sensitive to the variety of ways in which middle-class formation takes place. It argues that the British middle class has been split between a cohesive and well-established professional middle class, and insecure and marginal managerial and self-employed middle classes.

The book argues that recent changes in economic restructuring have enabled the professional middle class to consolidate its position of domin-ance. The managerial middle classes are, however, becoming more marginal and insecure. The book explores the implications of this position by analys-ing processes of social and spatial mobility, cultural practices and political mobilisation.

*Property, Bureaucracy and Culture* arises from research carried out by the authors on economic and social changes in the South East of England. Each of the authors uses their specialist expertise in historical sociology, migra-tion, housing, and cultural studies to provide a rounded and comprehensive analysis of the middle classes today. It will appeal to readers not only interested in the sociology of stratification, but also in urban and regional studies, cultural studies, politics and social theory.

**Mike Savage** is Reader in Sociology at the University of Keele; **James Barlow** is Reader in Housing at the University of Westminster; **Peter Dickens** is Reader in Sociology at the University of Sussex; **Tony Fielding** is Reader in Geography at the University of Sussex.

# INTERNATIONAL LIBRARY OF SOCIOLOGY

## Founded by Karl Mannheim

### Editor: John Urry
*University of Lancaster*

# PROPERTY, BUREAUCRACY AND CULTURE

## Middle-Class Formation in Contemporary Britain

*Mike Savage*
*James Barlow*
*Peter Dickens*
*and*
*Tony Fielding*

London and New York

First published in 1992
by Routledge
11 New Fetter Lane, London EC4P 4EE

Simultaneously published in the USA and Canada
by Routledge
29 West 35th Street, New York, NY 10001

Reprinted 1995
New in paperback 1995

Typeset in Baskerville by Michael Mepham, Frome, Somerset
Printed and bound in Great Britain by
Hartnolls Limited, Bodmin, Cornwall

*British Library Cataloguing in Publication Data*
A catalogue record for this book is available from the British
Library

*Library of Congress Cataloguing in Publication Data*
A catalogue record for this book is available from the
Library of Congress

ISBN 0–415–03773–5 (hbk)
ISBN 0–415–13009–3 (pbk)

# CONTENTS

# FIGURES AND TABLES

## FIGURES

## TABLES

# PREFACE

## WHY WE WROTE THIS BOOK

The 1980s might be seen as the decade when the middle classes came into their own. Alongside 'yuppies', 'dinkies', 'career women' and other stereotypes came official support for the values associated with the enterprise culture, homeownership, and the prevalence of upward mobility. But what is the reality underlying this rhetoric? Is there a homogeneous middle class? If not, how many middle classes are there? How have the middle classes been changing in the context of economic restructuring, the growth of owner occupation, and a decade of Conservative hegemony? This book holds the answers to these questions.

This book arose piecemeal from a series of different, though overlapping, research projects based at the University of Sussex in the mid–1980s as part of the ESRC-funded research programme on 'Economic Restructuring, Social Change and the Locality'. An interest in the nature of social change in the prosperous South East of England led Peter Dickens and Mike Savage to conduct a small project examining how employer strategies in a sample of Berkshire firms were affecting patterns of social division inside and outside the workplace. During the course of this we began to realise the enormous significance of the middle classes. In some of the establishments we visited, the vast majority of the workforce was professional or managerial. In most cases employers were more preoccupied with recruiting, retaining and utilising skilled middle-class labour than manual or routine white-collar labour. The middle classes mattered enormously to these employers.

We could also see that the middle classes mattered in other respects. James Barlow's research was showing how they affected patterns of housing demand, and examined their vociferous involvement in the political struggles over development and conservation in the Home Counties. Also, having interviewed a number of middle-class residents as part of a house-

ix

hold survey carried out by Peter Saunders (see Saunders 1990), we realised how much the middle classes mattered to themselves!

We were also struck by the fact that the middle classes did not seem to conform to our sociological understanding of them. They did not stay loyal to one organisation; they were highly entrepreneurial, preoccupied as much by their housing careers as by their employment careers; reluctant to move around the country at the behest of their employers; and showed a great diversity of cultural tastes and political practices. None of this seemed to tally with the arguments of those who had written about a 'service class', where the stress seemed to be on orderly bureaucratic careers, a high degree of spatial mobility, and their emergence as a steadily more homogeneous social class.

Our initial publications were concerned with arguing three things: firstly, that the middle classes (or service class as we preferred to call them at that stage) 'mattered'; secondly, that they needed to be placed in particular spatial contexts, and that migratory practices were of general importance in affecting their practices; and, thirdly, that they were changing and becoming more fragmented (Savage 1987a; Savage *et al.* 1988; Savage 1988a; Savage and Fielding 1989; Dickens 1988; Dickens and Savage 1988). Peter Dickens (1988) wrote a book arguing that the role of the service class was central to processes of economic, social and political change in Britain. Mike Savage (1988a) looked at the neglected relationship between social and spatial mobility. At this stage Tony Fielding began to use the Longitudinal Study, which linked the census records of 1 per cent of the English and Welsh population between 1971 and 1981, providing a superb resource for the analysis of social and spatial mobility as they affected the service class, and this began to produce rapid results (Fielding and Savage 1987; Fielding 1989; Savage and Fielding 1989). It was at this point that we began to write the present text, which we saw as a simple elaboration of our research findings.

However, the book has taken a rather different shape. As we progressed we encountered a series of problems which led us to reconsider our position. Part of the reason for this was practical: attempts to gain further research funding to probe the changing characteristics of the middle classes failed. Our original Berkshire research was simply not substantial enough to allow us to write an entire book on the subject, and the Longitudinal Study was not suitable for all the issues we wanted to discuss.

More seriously, the problems were conceptual. When we talked about the fragmentation of the 'service class', were we talking about new classes being formed, or an existing class being divided? What was a class, anyway? The more we looked into the literature, the more we realised that new middle classes were being discovered regularly every few years. What – if anything – was really new about the contemporary middle classes?

This problem was compounded by the fact that there is a dearth of good empirical research on the middle classes. Hence we simply lacked good comparative material by which to judge what was new and what was old about our findings. There simply were inadequate benchmarks allowing us to gauge change effectively. For a while, we did not know how to proceed. Finally, we decided to make this book an attempt to clear the way for a better analytical approach to the middle classes, by using all the available empirical and conceptual material at our disposal to develop a general argument not only about the middle classes, but also about the nature of class analysis. We begin by recognising the limitations of existing work on the middle classes, and then use this as a starting point to provide a more adequate account, which would allow us to reflect on the significance of the middle classes in contemporary Britain.

This book, therefore, should not be read as an elaboration of our earlier research. There are of course similarities, but our conceptual framework has changed in the course of writing the book – most evident in the fact that we have abandoned the concept of the 'service class' as an analytical device. And while we draw on our original Berkshire research, it is not a particularly important part of our argument.

## STRUCTURE OF THE BOOK

The definition of 'middle class' is vague but evocative. The term goes back to the early nineteenth century, where it developed as a negative term (Briggs 1960). By calling yourself middle class you distinguished yourself from those above you – the aristocracy – and those below you – the working class. But this does not indicate that different people within the middle classes actually have anything in common other than that they are not upper or lower class. As a result, the basic problem in writing about the middle classes is to find a way of going beyond the mere recognition that the middle classes are a group of otherwise diverse people who cannot be slotted into the working classes or the upper classes.

In practice three types of literature have attempted to advance our knowledge of the middle classes. Firstly, there are some abstract analytical accounts of the place of the middle classes in the class structure. These go back a long way, to the work of Marx (see Ratansi 1985) and Weber (1978), and in more recent years have been particularly evident amongst Marxists who try to elaborate the relationship between the middle classes and the capitalist and working classes (Carchedi 1977; Poulantzas 1975; Wright 1978, 1985; Abercrombie and Urry 1983). These accounts are provocative and have been consulted extensively while writing this book: however, they share the tendency of stopping once they have arrived at their chosen theoretical position. Rather than using their theoretical perspective to shed light on the contemporary world, they finish once they have 'slotted' the middle class into their theoretical schema.

The second type of literature comprises of broad descriptive overviews of work, culture and lifestyles of the middle classes (Lewis and Maude 1953; Raynor 1969). There are very few of these works, however, and no recent ones, and they do not go beyond a recital of some descriptive features of middle-class groups, usually emphasising their heterogeneity. Fair enough, but this is simply fleshing out what we knew already. It does not improve our conceptual understanding of the middle classes.

Finally, we have a greater number of studies of one particular aspect of the middle classes. The most important of these, in our view, is Goldthorpe's work on social mobility (Goldthorpe 1980, 1987); but there are many other examples – the study of sections of the middle class at work (Smith 1987a; Whalley 1986), family life (Pahl and Pahl 1971; Bell 1969; Edgell 1980), politics (Parkin 1967; Garrard et al. 1978; Eckersley 1989), housing (Smith 1987b) and so forth. These are all very valuable, and have been important starting points for our own inquiries, but they do not link up the different features of middle-class life.

In short, for all the insights they provide, existing literature on the middle classes bears all the hallmarks of what Holmwood and Stewart (1983) call 'explanatory failure'. Analytical accounts are seldom used in actual research, and are frequently of such a type that it is not clear how they *could* be used in practical research. Descriptive accounts do not help advance analytical understanding. Ritual incantations of middle-class fragmentation and diversity mark the end, rather than the starting point, of research. It is not clear how the activities of the middle classes in some social practices relate to their activities in others.

The first task, then, is to attempt to provide a way that might allow us to provide a better alternative. This forces us to think about the nature of class analysis in general, to enable us to find a way in which theoretical and empirical research can work together. The aim of Chapter 1 is to provide a (relatively!) accessible account of how the middle classes can best be conceptualised. Although our ideas developed out of a long, and at times tortuous, engagement with stratification theory and class analysis, we have not included an abstract discussion of the nature of class analysis in this chapter in order not to discourage those readers whose prime interest is in the middle classes, not stratification theory. Our views on the status of stratification theory and research are confined to Appendix 1, where they can be consulted by interested readers.

Chapter 1 argues that social classes are best understood as *social collectivities* rooted in particular types of *exploitative relationships*. We argue that class analysis should take place within a realist framework, in which the analysis of the causal properties of differing forms of exploitation to give rise to social collectivities should be distinguished from a study of the sorts of contingent, contextual conditions that might allow these causal powers to be realised.

Chapter 1 indicates our key arguments here. To anticipate and simplify, we see middle-class formation as being based around three causal entities: property, bureaucracy and culture. These are not symmetrical in the properties they possess, and indeed much of our argument rests upon the differences between these three assets: organisations do not convey the same degree of security as cultural assets, while cultural assets can only be effective in allowing exploitation when used in organisations or enterprises. Property assets, however, are more robust in conveying exploitative potential.

However, it is central to the realist argument that causal properties are only activated in certain contingent conditions. We cannot assume that, because there are three different assets affecting middle-class formation, people can be neatly slotted into one of three middle classes, each with different attributes. Classes are only formed in particular historical and spatial circumstances, and an elaboration of these is vital to show how middle classes actually emerge as distinct social collectivities. Here it is important to recognise that two contingent conditions are of particular importance in indicating how three class assets may or may not give rise to distinct class collectivities. These are the role of the state and the significance of specific forms of gender relations. These factors help determine how the three assets actually lead to distinct types of middle class. Our elaboration of this argument takes place in Chapter 2, where we indicate the sorts of contingent conditions in which a 'service class' might emerge.

In Chapter 3 we begin our analysis of the British middle classes by considering their historical formation. Our main argument is that while, in some capitalist nations, organisation and cultural assets were fused to produce a unified 'service class', in Britain this did not happen. A distinct, cohesive, professional class emerged in the course of the nineteenth century. We argue that the role of the state was of particular importance in ensuring the distinctiveness of the professional middle classes, and when managerial workers began to be employed from the turn of the century they developed as very much a subordinate middle class, particularly dependent upon their largely capitalist employers.

The remainder of the book can be seen as falling into two parts. Chapters 4, 5 and 6 are primarily concerned with how the salience of the three assets of property, bureaucracy and culture have changed in the recent past. Chapters 7, 8 and 9 are more concerned with the issue of middle-class formation: about how differing groups within the middle classes are forming as collectivities in view of the changes we discussed earlier.

In Chapter 4 we indicate how contemporary patterns of economic restructuring are changing the historical patterns identified in Chapter 3. We place particular emphasis upon the changing structure of organisations, which we believe is undermining the position of those who rely upon organisation assets alone – industrial managers in particular. We argue that the restructuring of private enterprises, by increasing the demand for specialists and contractors, is increasing the scope for the deployment of qualified workers, and so enhancing the role of the professional middle class. We also point to the growing role of the self-employed, and the growing entrepreneurial behaviour of sections of the middle class. The implications of these findings are to stress the growing significance of cultural assets in middle-class formation, and we argue that the professional middle class is becoming ever more distinctive in its social and political behaviour – a point we develop in the remainder of the book.

Having considered the declining salience of organisation assets we turn, in Chapter 5, to changes in the housing market to examine whether the significance of property assets has increased as owner-occupation has grown. We consider whether the expansion of owner-occupation has allowed a greater role for middle-class entrepreneurial behaviour. We discuss whether this is leading to the creation of a 'housing career' which, in some respects, is as significant as an employment career. This argument is shown to have some relevance, and it is clear that the operation of the housing market does affect middle-class formation.

In Chapter 6 we consider the nature of cultural assets in contemporary Britain by reporting the results of a survey on spending and consumption. We show how different groups within the British middle classes have distinctive cultural tastes, and use this to elaborate in more detail our arguments about the significance of cultural capital in the process of middle-class formation. We see once again that the managerial middle class emerges as undistinctive in its cultural tastes, while the professional middle class is the pioneer of cultural distinctiveness.

The last three chapters elaborate the sorts of boundaries and divisions that exist within the middle classes. Chapter 7 returns to one of the main areas of orthodox sociological inquiry: social mobility. Our aim here is to show how our arguments connect with those developed by Goldthorpe, who argues for the pertinence of the 'service class'. We take issue with Goldthorpe's discussion of social mobility, as it affects the middle classes, and use data from the Longitudinal Study and the British General Election Survey to argue that the three assets affecting middle-class formation have differing potential for allowing career mobility and the inter-generational transfer of class privileges. We then suggest the crucial role played by the education system in reproducing the dominant role of the professional middle class, and point to the growing role of household structure as a determinant of middle-class formation.

Chapter 8 takes us into less familiar territory: spatial mobility. This is a much neglected topic within contemporary class analyis, and we argue that since class formation develops in particular places, it is necessary to examine how spatial mobility affects patterns of class formation. Here we use the Longitudinal Study to provide a comprehensive account of spatial mobility and its association with social mobility. We point to the role of the South East of England as an 'escalator region' for the middle classes, and point to the historically vital role of inter-regional migration as a facilitator of social mobility into the middle classes.

Finally, in Chapter 9 we consider the crucial issue of how the patterns of middle-class formation that have been uncovered actually affect political change. Here we once again argue against those writers who consider that the service class has distinct political patterns, showing instead that there is a major political cleavage between professional and managerial groups, and that one of the most important changes in the past decade is the radicalisation of the professional middle class.

To some extent the later chapters can be read as specific debates with the work of the most original and interesting writers thinking about key issues concerned with class formation. Thus Chapter 5 is in part a debate with Peter Saunders; Chapter 6 with Pierre Bourdieu; Chapter 7 with John Goldthorpe; Chapter 8 with Doreen Massey and Nigel Thrift; and Chapter 9 with Anthony Heath, Gordon Marshall and John Goldthorpe. Nonetheless, we would like to encourage readers to read the book as a whole. It develops an argument chapter by chapter, and leads to a set of general points which we develop in our conclusion.

# ACKNOWLEDGEMENTS

This book would not have been written without the support and interest of many people. We hope they find the finished version something they enjoy arguing with! First and foremost the Centre for Urban and Regional Research at the University of Sussex has proved a stimulating place to launch our research and many of the ideas discussed in this book owe much to our colleagues, especially Mark Bhatti, Susan Halford and Peter Saunders who have provided stimulating discussions. Our initial interest in the middle classes owed much to Nigel Thrift's inspiration in the early days. John Urry also encouraged us to develop our ideas, and was responsible for commissioning the book.

Many thanks to those who helped with our research. The ESRC funded the programme on 'Economic Restructuring, Social Change and the Locality' in which our work began. It has also funded James Barlow's research on flat conversions, European growth regions, and housing and labour markets. Thanks also to Anthony Evans for analysing the survey of housebuilders which we use in Chapter 5. The British Market Research Bureau made available to us (free of charge) the data on which Chapter 6 is based: Lawrence Bruce of BMRB also donated a lot of his time. We would like to thank Angus Stewart, Kathy Kiernan and Angela Dale at the City University for helping us access the Longitudinal Study, which we use extensively in Chapters 7 and 8. Cathy Sayer helped us access the British General Election Survey, which we report in Chapters 7 and 9, and Anthony Heath gave us advice on its analysis. Paul Collis gave advice on computing at Keele University.

We have learned a great deal from discussions with other people. First and foremost, many of the main arguments concerning the nature of class analysis and the significance of gender relations on the middle classes emerged from collaborative research between Mike Savage and Anne Witz. Hopefully, this book is now Weberian enough for Anne's taste!

Roger Burrows kept reminding us not to forget about the petite bourgeoisie. Although we may still have forgotten about them more than he might have liked, they are now an important part of our story. At a crucial moment Gordon Fyfe drummed home the importance of Bourdieu's work to our arguments. John Law forced us to think through some of the issues concerning the concept of exploitation, while Vincanne Adams failed to let us get away with a number of misconceptions. Rosemary Crompton has provided comments on various papers and drafts with remarkable enthusiasm, and Alan Warde has provided astute (and prompt!) comments. Anthony Heath's comments on an earlier manuscript were of great value in helping us organise the book properly.

John Allen, Simon Duncan, Andy Miles, Paul Watt, Sarah Whatmore, John Seed and David Vincent have all passed judgement on drafts of various chapters: their advice is much appreciated. Mike Winstanley and Paul Bagguley alerted us to important references. Peter Abell has always shown a lot of enthusiasm for our work (though he would no doubt have preferred more statistical modelling), and we have learned a lot from working with Sara Arber. John Goldthorpe will no doubt disagree with much of what we have to say, but his interest in our research and his readiness to respond to our queries have been of great value.

It goes without saying that we are responsible for all the remaining mistakes.

*Universities of Keele and Sussex*
*January 1991*

# 1

# ARE THE MIDDLE CLASSES SOCIAL CLASSES?

Social scientists have puzzled over the middle classes for well over a century. At the most general level the reasons for this are straightforward. Most concepts used to analyse social divisions are simple, binary ones: that is to say, they divide people into two groups along a single axis. A great variety of concepts have been used in this way: society has been divided into the propertied and propertyless; exploiters and exploited; powerful and powerless; those functional for society and those non-functional, and so forth.

Such concepts can be readily applied to groups that are clearly at the extremes of any of these poles, such as a 'ruling class' or 'establishment' on the one hand, or a working class on the other. But they run into problems when applied to those who do not instantly appear to fit either of the binary terms used: that is, those who are not particularly powerful, but who are not excluded from power; and who do not appear to exploit anyone in a particularly obvious way, but who do not seem to be exploited either. The middle classes, because they are in the middle, do not readily fit into the types of binary concepts so widely used in social science.

Classical social theory has left three ways of 'coping' with this problem. The first tendency is to squeeze them into binary oppositions by positing a set of links between the middle classes and either the dominant or subordinate social group. The second tendency is to adopt a more descriptive approach and to abandon any clear attempt to explain the specificity of the middle classes. The third – and in our view most promising – avenue has been to explore how the middle classes might actually be social classes in their own right. This has, in British work, centred around discussion concerning the argument that some groups within the middle class can best be seen as a 'service class'.

Before passing on to consider the debate on the service class, let us briefly assess the limitations of the other two approaches. The attempt to link the middle classes to other groups involves finding a mechanism by which the interests and concerns of the middle class can be attributed to a

1

different – dominant or subordinate – class. The most common linkage used here is a functional one, where a certain middle class grouping is seen as functioning, or performing a particular service, for a dominant social group or for 'society' as a whole.

This view of the middle classes is explicitly found in functionalist sociology, where the position of any group can be seen as a reflection of its functional importance for society as a whole. But it also surfaces in a more interesting way within both Marxist and Weberian accounts of social stratification. For Marx the dominant and organising principle in capitalist society is that of capital accumulation. When one class of people own the means of production they can employ the propertyless and by the exploitation of their labour, can extract profit for themselves.

This crude account involves the type of binary opposition characteristic of much social science. Initially, there seems little place for a middle class within it at all, since it envisages a capitalist class opposed to a working class. And, indeed, some Marxists have argued that the middle classes are a chimera, who will at some stage be 'proletarianised' so that they join the rest of the working class. Braverman (1974) argues, for instance, that capital tends to deskill labour by breaking and simplifying the labour process so that labour can be made more productive. Braverman considers that this process tends to reduce even 'middle-class' or white-collar occupations to the level of working-class ones, and tends to argue that the middle class is becoming less distinctive as property becomes centralised (see Abercrombie and Urry 1983: 56–60 for discussion).

Braverman also refers, however, to the separation of conception from execution: the way that within capitalist production the 'thinking' work is taken away from the actual production process and hived off to specialist workers, leaving manual workers simply to execute – carry out – instructions given by others. This separation of conception from execution, which Braverman sees as an essential part of the deskilling process, has also provided a theoretical criteria for Marxists to distinguish a distinctive middle class responsible for the conception of work.

This latter approach is followed in rather different ways by Wright (1978), Carchedi (1977), Abercrombie and Urry (1983), Carter (1985), and Ehrenreich and Ehrenreich (1979). We shall not go into the rather different ideas developed by each (see for discussion Abercrombie and Urry 1983; Lockwood 1988; Goldthorpe 1982), but note that within this perspective the middle class is best understood by the functions it performs for capital, or the capitalist class. For Carchedi this involves the supervision and surveillance of labour; for Wright it involves the control over the physical means of production, control over labour power and control over investment. The important point to note here is the way in which the criteria for determining the role of the middle class is derived from an analysis of its functional importance to capitalism.

Two points stand out here. Firstly, as a result of their theoretical perspective, Marxists can examine managers much more easily than they can professionals, administrators or the self-employed. The most important Marxist works on the middle class have focused on the role of managers, and especially managers in private industry (e.g. Wright 1978; Carter 1985; Braverman 1974). Professional workers are less easy to categorise since they are less centrally involved in the manufacturing process, while the self-employed petite bourgeoisie is often assumed to be of declining significance. Secondly, the effect of relating the middle class to the capital accumulation process is that the role of this class is strongly related to the process from which it is derived. Virtually by definition, it is not possible to see this class as having any independent social and political effectivity.

These criticisms of particular Marxist approaches are not especially novel (see, e.g., Lockwood 1988). The same theme also emerges in Weberian work, however. The characteristic stress here concerns how the middle classes are functionaries for the processes of domination, which Weber sees as pervasive throughout all societies. In modern societies it is the role of the middle classes as bureaucrats that is given greatest emphasis. Weber saw bureaucracies as the embodiment of an impersonal, rational authority, in distinction to traditional or charismatic authority based on personal characteristics, which is characteristic of older societies. The middle classes have a distinct role as functionaries within bureaucratic processes. Weber himself drew attention to the purely passive role of the middle classes within this framework.

> In the great majority of cases (the professional bureaucrat) is only a small cog in a ceaselessly moving mechanism which prescribes to him an essentially fixed route of march. The official is entrusted with specialised tasks, and normally the mechanisms cannot be put into motion or arrested by him, but only from the very top.
>
> (Weber 1978: 988)

As in Marxist work the focus is on how the middle classes serve others and hence do not interfere with the 'pure' workings of a given social process.

The same stress arises in subsequent Weberian work: for instance, in C. Wright Mills in his study *White Collar* (1951). For Mills the dominant trend in the USA in the decade following the Second World War was the growing bureaucratisation of society. The old, independent self-employed middle-class strata were giving way to the large corporations: 'the organizational reason for the expansion of white collar occupations is the rise of big business and big government, and the consequent trend of modern social structure, the growth of bureaucracy' (Mills 1951: 68). It was this dominant trend which allowed Mills to argue that different middle-class groups were being subject to this force for bureaucratisation.

3

The general stress is to see the middle class as a lieutenant class, performing certain functions for other classes or groups. Hence its members are not important in their own right, but only as the functionaries for others. Such a perspective, we would maintain, disables any serious inquiry into the nature of the middle classes from the start. It not only assumes a degree of middle-class passivity which is counter-intuitive to anyone with experience of middle-class life but also acts to morally absolve the middle classes. Since the real villains of the piece are the dominant classes, the middle classes are largely exempted from having to scrutinise their own actions as possible causes for social inequality or division.

The second legacy of the classical tradition is, in some ways, more useful. Its main emphasis is descriptive – an attempt to draw out the empirical variety of social groupings and testify to their distinctiveness – and Weberian writers have led the way here. Weber himself recognised the diversity of people in intermediate social positions, and suggested that there were four distinct social classes: between the working class and capitalist class was a petite bourgeoisie and a class of propertyless intelligentsia and specialists (Weber 1978: 302–7). Weberian writers ever since have specialised in producing other class schemas, many of which emphasise the diversity of intermediate social classes and groups.

The problem with such work is simply that it does not explain why these descriptive groupings have emerged. Much Weberian writing in this area shelters behind extended definitions and descriptive categories rather than providing a rigorous attempt to explain processes of social class inequality. The exception to this, within the Weberian tradition, is among those who have attempted to develop Weber's theory of 'social closure' to give a fuller understanding of the processes by which groups might be able to achieve a specific position in society through processes of exclusion and inclusion (Parkin 1979; Murphy 1988). Social closure works through one group restricting access to a certain prized good or service, so enhancing its own position at the expense of other social groups.

Parkin's advocacy of the idea of social closure has led to a considerable interest in the processes by which certain groups may carve out privileged positions for themselves. However, its explanatory value remains more doubtful. This is because it is not clear why some groups are able to engage in successful social closure and others are not. Why are doctors typically able to engage in effective struggles to close their profession from outsiders, but school teachers, for instance, are not? Insofar as this question can be addressed within closure theory the usual response is to examine the types of resources which specific groups can bring to help their closure strategies. Anne Witz, for instance, has shown how medical men were able to draw upon patriarchal gendered resources in order to enhance their professional projects in Victorian Britain (Witz 1991). This sort of argument, however, soon begins to deploy explanatory concepts that are outside the remit of closure theory itself – in Witz's case, the concept of patriarchy, for instance.

Social closure may then be a useful way of showing how specific groups are able to achieve middle-class positions, but it is not especially helpful in showing why they are able to do so. It offers no systematic way of explaining why certain people are able to achieve middle-class position. We therefore turn to the third legacy of the classical tradition, which argues that the middle classes are best seen as distinct social classes in their own right. This, we argue, is the most helpful way to proceed out of the impasse left by classical theory.

## WHAT ARE SOCIAL CLASSES?

The third legacy of classical stratification theory argues that the middle classes should be seen as social classes in their own right, rather than as simple functionaries, or intermediate groups. The precise status of the claim that a particular group forms a social class is, of course, hotly contested, since the concept of social class is one of the most controversial in the social sciences (e.g. Calvert 1982; Furbank 1985). Our view on this matter is presented and defended in Appendix 1, which can usefully be consulted at this point by any reader wishing to discover the more general theoretical orientation of our work. Since, however, the primary concern of this book is to throw light on the middle classes, and because the debate on class analysis has become so esoteric and purely technical that it is now largely only of interest to specialists, we content ourselves here with presenting only the basic features of our approach.

In our view social classes are first and foremost stable social collectivities. They are groups of people with shared levels of income and remuneration, lifestyles, cultures, political orientations and so forth. This is why they are interesting to social scientists, since by being social collectivities they are able to engage in social action and so have an impact on social change. The concept of social class is not, therefore, best seen as a classificatory device by which people are slotted into specific social classes on the basis of a given trait such as occupation, but is primarily concerned with the issue of class formation.

This formulation does, however, beg one crucial question. There are usually lots of social collectivities in diverse walks of social life, but not all of them can usefully be seen as social classes. Boy Scouts, for instance, are a social collectivity with shared cultures and lifestyles, but it hardly seems appropriate to regard them as a social class. In order for a social collectivity to be regarded as a social class it has to have its roots in a process of exploitation.

The concept of exploitation is itself problematic. It has its origins in Marxist analyses of social stratification, in which one class exploits another if it appropriates labour from that class. This, however, is rather restrictive and is economically deterministic, arguing that exploitation is only an economic process. More recently other Marxists, such as Erik Olin Wright, have preferred a less specific, more general notion of exploitation, in which 'one person's welfare is obtained at the expense of another' (Wright 1985: 65). The particular case of the extraction of surplus labour is one – extremely important – example of this, but there are others. For instance the concept of 'deleting the labour' developed within symbolic interactionism (Star 1991), where a particular person's contribution to an activity is concealed or hidden, is another variant. When an academic man writes a book that draws upon his wife's labour as typist, copy-editor, researcher, general discussant, or provider of domestic labour, but where only his name appears on the cover, her labour has been deleted.

The important point here is that the concept of exploitation specifies a relationship between classes: an exploiting and exploited class. Hence, it shows how a social class differs from another sort of social collectivity because it inherently stands in opposition to other social groups or collectivities. It is this which gives it historical importance, since the ensuing (latent or manifest) conflict between these classes may well be of major importance in shaping social and historical change.

The most difficult conceptual problem here is how the relationship between specific types of exploitative relationships and particular social collectivities can best be formulated. A deterministic account, where exploitative relationships always give rise to full blown social collectivities, is wrong, since in some cases people may be involved in exploitative relationships without forming wider social collective ties to others who are also involved in these relationships. In our view, theoretical realism, as developed by Bhaskar (1975), Keat and Urry (1975), Sayer (1984) and Outhwaite (1987), offers the most useful way of resolving this problem. Realists begin by thinking about the causal powers of specific natural or social entities. People, to give a trite example, have the power to speak, or work, by virtue of the fact that they are people. However, these causal powers may only be manifested in specific contingent circumstances: people do not speak if they are gagged, nor do they work when sleeping.

Applied to the study of social class we first need to think about the types of causal power involved in differing types of exploitation. Of crucial importance here is the way varying types of exploitation have the differing causal potential to give rise to stable social class collectivities. The best way of thinking about this is by considering *how easy is it for the exploiting class to store the gains it has won from the exploited class*. Only if they can be stored can they be transmitted to others, moved to different places, or accumulated. If they can be stored it is far more likely that they will give rise to stable social class collectivities. This is the point developed by Offe and Wisenthal (1980), who show that because capital can be stored and accumulated (in

6

the forms of stocks and shares, property and so forth) it is much easier for capitalists to organise than it is for workers. Since labour power cannot be stored outside the individual bodies of workers, the working class remains more fragmented and divided, and is less able to develop cohesive class identity and action.

This analysis of the causal properties of specific forms of exploitation must, however, be supplemented by an examination of the sort of contingent conditions that might allow these varying causal powers to exercise their properties. In periods of economic recession, for instance, capitalist class formation might be hindered because of competition between firms. In liberal democracies working-class formation might be enhanced because of the potential strength of their relatively large numbers in influencing voting patterns.

We have now set out the rudiments of our approach. The claim that the middle classes are social classes involves showing that they have been formed as cohesive social groups, which are linked to specific types of exploitation.

## THEORIES OF THE SERVICE CLASS

In the 1930s the Austrian Marxist Karl Renner argued that there was a growing 'service class' of professionals and managers in contemporary capitalist societies. Although his ideas were taken up by Dahrendorf in the 1950s, it was not until the 1980s that debate on the possible existence of a service class really took off. In the USA a similar set of debates emerged around consideration of the idea of a 'new class' (Gouldner 1979), or a 'professional–managerial class' (Ehrenreich and Ehrenreich 1979). Yet the debate has been enormously confused, largely because the proponents of the 'service class' idea have very different ideas of what social classes actually are. The idea of the service class has been used in at least six different ways in existing literature, but it is common for the same writer to use the concept in several different ways, without acknowledging possible contradictions between uses. We need to begin by unpacking the different meanings of the 'service class', since in our view some of these are useful, but others less so. Some of them follow in the classical tradition we have criticised above, while others take the debate onto more fertile ground.

Initially the concept of the service class, which began with Karl Renner in the 1930s, shares a similar problematic to that of the classical tradition we have criticised above, in which the service class is functionally related to capitalism. Renner saw the emergence of the professional manager and the decline of the owner-manager as an indication that 'the functions of capitalists appear sub-divided in a steadily growing number of salaried employees of the very highest and of high and of lower rank' (quoted in Dahrendorf 1959: 94). Since capitalists can no longer carry out all their activities personally they delegate them to groups of people, and it is these managers, professionals and administrators who form the service class, to collectively carry out the functions of capital.

This functional argument also surfaces in more recent work, for instance by Goldthorpe (1987), or Urry with various collaborators (Abercrombie and Urry 1983; Lash and Urry 1987; Bagguley *et al*. 1990). Lash and Urry thus refer to the service class as occupying

> those places (which) are located within a set of interlocking social institutions that service capital through meeting three functions: to conceptualise the labour process; to control the entry and exercise of labour power within the workplace; and to orchestrate the non-household forms under which labour-power is produced and regulated.
>
> (Lash and Urry 1987: 162)

This view of the service class does not indicate why it should be seen as a social collectivity, or how it is involved in exploitative relationships. It is unclear what advantage we gain in calling professionals and managers a class, rather than a group, of functionaries. Lash and Urry's formulation is especially weak, since it is unclear why we should see one 'service class' rather than three, each serving one of the functions they specify. It is not that this functional account is necessarily wrong, but simply that in and by itself it is not adequate in specifying how service-class formation might come about. So let us proceed to the second meaning.

In a second sense the service class is a descriptive grouping of managers, professionals and administrators who occupy a similar work and market situation. It can be also be seen as a development of the classical tradition: in this case the descriptive Weberian initiative. Goldthorpe sees the distinctive market and work situation of the service class in the following terms: 'what (upper service class) positions have in common is that they afford their incumbents incomes which are high, generally secure and likely to rise over their lifetimes, and that they are positions which typically involve the exercise of authority and/or expertise' (Goldthorpe 1987: 41). The same point surfaces in Urry's various writings, where he notes the distinctive market and work situations of the service class (e.g. Abercrombie and Urry 1983: 122ff).

This seems initially a more valuable approach, since it may well indicate a certain commonality of economic interest around which social-class collectivity may develop. There are two problems, however: (a) as a descriptive account it fails to specify any axes of exploitation; (b) even at a purely descriptive level the argument fails to convince. On virtually all criteria the service class – as Goldthorpe defines it – has a remarkable *diversity* of market and work situations: it includes employers and employees, managers and managed, credentialled and uncredentialled workers, millionaires and those earning below average salaries (nurses, for instance). We are unconvinced that, even in Goldthorpe's own terms, the service class enjoys the commonality of work and market position which he suggests it does. Goldthorpe does indeed recognise that he is skating on thin ice here, and his usual response – after suggesting that some of these differences are more apparent than real (e.g. Goldthorpe 1987: 41) – is to claim that the members of the service class are united in terms of their common 'service relationship' with their employers.

We can see this reference to a distinct 'service relationship' as a third way of specifying the service class. Goldthorpe explains the privileged work and market situations which the service class enjoys by arguing that professional, managerial and administrative employees,

> being typically engaged in the exercise of delegated authority or in the application of specialist knowledge and expertise, operate in their work tasks and roles with a distinctive degree of autonomy and discretion; and in direct consequence of the element of trust that is necessarily involved in their relationship with their employing organisation, they are accorded conditions of employment which are also distinctive in both the level and kind of rewards that are involved.
>
> (Goldthorpe 1982: 169)

Goldthorpe focuses upon trust as the key unifying element, which explains why those with expert knowledge and those in managerial jobs might have a similar basis for class formation. The members of the service class serve their employers, but the relationship is ambivalent. Employers are forced to grant superior conditions to these employees because of their special skills and significance.

Yet this emphasis upon 'trust' is problematic. Goldthorpe seems to assume that some – service-class – occupations have to be filled by people who need to be trusted, but it seems much more plausible to argue that 'trust' is constructed in a much more fluid way, and that it is never the case that people in senior jobs are always trusted, and those in routine jobs are not. It is inherent to the capitalist employment relationship that the employer only hires labour power rather than actual finished labour, and therefore all forms of job require a certain 'wage-effort bargain'. This is not to say that there are not important differences between jobs, in the way suggested for instance by Fox in his distinction between jobs of 'high trust' and 'low trust' (Fox 1974). However, it is a difference of degree rather than of kind, and is subject to negotiation and re-evaluation and does not appear to offer a useful basis to define a clear service class. Some 'high trust' jobs are manual jobs, particularly in craft work such as building, handicraft or engineering. In such jobs employers are often forced to trust workers to carry out certain tasks, and they may also work with considerable autonomy, yet Goldthorpe does not label such groups as 'service class'.

Other, high-status jobs have very little trust: Marshall (1987) shows that airline pilots, for instance, are heavily scrutinised in the course of their work by air traffic controllers and the like.

Hence we do not feel that the previous three meanings for the service class get us very far. However, in more recent contributions conceptual progress has been made.

Fourthly, there is Urry's stress on the notion that the service class is an active historical force with important social effects. While Goldthorpe is primarily concerned to defend the concept as a classificatory tool for understanding social mobility (and social stratification more generally), and he is therefore forced to use it as a device to classify occupations and to discuss where appropriate boundaries should be drawn, Abercrombie and Urry (1983) are less interested in this 'boundary problem', and are more concerned to argue that this class forms an active social force in advanced capitalist societies.

Urry (1986) illustrates this general argument in a paper suggesting that the development of scientific management in the USA from the turn of the century was not a result of the imperatives of capital accumulation alone, but was produced by the actions of service class managers and professionals struggling to secure a role for themselves in the production process. This emphasis is taken further by Lash and Urry (1987). These writers argue that there has recently been a transition from organised to disorganised capitalism in modern western societies. It is difficult to summarise briefly what Lash and Urry mean by these terms but, very crudely, organised capitalism, dominant from around 1900 to 1950, was characterised by a high concentration of capitalist production, strong linkages between the economy and the nation state, and the centrality of the capital–labour social cleavage. The contemporary phase of disorganised capitalism involves the declining link between the nation state and the economy, the growth of 'Post-Fordist' economic patterns, for instance those replacing mass production by flexible specialisation, and the declining centrality of the capital–labour cleavage.

The crucial point here is that Lash and Urry refer to the service class's role in causing this transition. They argue that the service class developed under organised capitalism, and then expanded and attained a highly visible position in disorganised capitalism. Lash and Urry argue that the service class is the prime agent behind the development of disorganised capitalism. They argue that 'the service class, which is an effect or outgrowth of organised capitalism, is subsequently, largely through its own self-formation, an important and driving factor in capitalism's disorganisation process' (Lash and Urry 1987: 11). The service class is here seen, in an active sense, as a leading force behind economic and social change. It de-skills workers, it creates heavy demands for state support leading to political conflicts, and it has profound effects on culture and education.

This is a very useful attempt to consider the service class as a distinct social collectivity, able to engage in social action and hence affect historical change.

Yet Lash and Urry seem to neglect the fact that this stress rather problematises their earlier conceptualisation of the service class as functionally related to capital. If the service class is an active social force, it is a contingent matter whether its actions service capitalism or not. But if the service class is functionally derived and is forced to 'serve' capital, then it would appear that there are some sorts of limits on the social action it can pursue. Further, Urry gives us a series of *examples* of the way in which different professional or managerial groups have a social impact, and he does not indicate why we should see them as rooted in a common class basis, as opposed to each group having their own specific social identity based around their own particular occupational group. We can accept that industrial managers, for instance, struggled to introduce scientific management in the USA and hence had an important historical effect, but this gives us no explanation as to why we should see them as part of a wider service class that includes welfare professionals, civil servants and so forth. By not relating his account to a concept of exploitation, Urry cannot, at the end of the day, establish that service-class formation, rather than 'professional formation' or 'managerial formation', is the correct way to develop his argument.

Fifthly, we have the argument developed by Dahrendorf. He uses the concept to argue for a clear distinction between two groups of workers who should be allocated to different social classes. Dahrendorf argued that 'a fairly clear as well as distinct line can be drawn between salaried employees who occupy positions that are part of a bureaucratic hierarchy and salaried employees in positions that are not' (Dahrendorf 1959: 55). The former he placed in the service class, and the latter he assigned to the working class. Dahrendorf's view retains the Weberian focus on bureaucracy, but begins to allow us to think about how relations of power and authority within bureaucracies might also be used to sustain the position of superordinates within the organisation – the service class.

Dahrendorf's account has influenced some writers, and there are echoes of it in Abercrombie and Urry (1983: 119), who state that 'one of the most significant features of the position of the service class is that most of the places of the class are located within bureaucracies'. Goldthorpe also refers to this bureaucratic basis of the service class. In our view this stress is useful because it begins to allow us to think about how exploitation may be based upon organisational hierarchies. Bureaucracies and organisations allow superordinates to 'delete the work' of subordinates, and hence they provide assets which may be the basis on which class formation develops. Doctors, managers and civil servants do have a common, superordinate organisational position which allows us to see them as an exploitative social class in their own right. We shall develop this point below.

Finally, however, there is another meaning of the service class, as developed by Crompton (1986). Here the argument is that the service class is a gendered class, defined in terms of its male characteristics. Crompton develops this argument in two ways: first by showing how the male service class depends on routine, ghettoised female white-collar workers – a point also made by Abercrombie and Urry (1983); and, secondly, they rely upon the domestic servicing work offered by their wives and female kin.

This perspective is also a helpful one. It suggests that the middle class is formed, at least in part, through gendered processes (for an elaboration of this argument, see Savage and Witz 1991). It is also consistent with the stress on organisation, evident in Dahrendorf's account. As recent feminist scholarship has demonstrated, organisations are gendered, with men dominating senior positions and women being employed in subordinate jobs (Pringle 1989; Kanter 1977).

The concept of the service class is in itself unconvincing, but begins to point to some more promising ideas. It confuses and misleads as an attempt to suggest that professional, managerial and administrative employees are in the same class because of some trait they possess (whether this be trust or a common market and work situation or their functional relationship to capital). But Urry's development of the concept shows how groups within the middle classes cannot be written off as mere functionaries of capital, and Dahrendorf's formulation begins to point to the salience of organisational hierarchies as axes of exploitation and hence class formation. It is precisely this issue that has been elaborated by Erik Wright.

## ERIK OLIN WRIGHT

The class theory developed by Erik Olin Wright in the mid-1980s (Wright 1985) has been heavily, indeed almost universally, criticised (G. Marshall *et al.* 1988; Crompton 1989), not least by Wright himself in his more recent work (1989). While there are undoubted problems in his argument, we shall show that it offers a far more useful base to think about the nature of middle-class formation than his critics seem to suggest. This is because Wright's initial starting point, arguing that classes must be related to the possession of assets that allow one class to exploit another, directs our attention to what we believe to be the most important issue in class analysis: a consideration of the sorts of axes of exploitation around which class formation might take place.

For Wright there are three main types of exploitative assets around which classes are based: property (or economic assets), organisational position, and skill. The use of property relations as a basis for exploitation is not especially novel, and follows the basic Marxist principle arguing that class is based around the ownership of the means of production. In this, Wright clearly establishes a conceptual space for the distinctive exploitation of the bourgeoisie and the petite bourgeoisie. These classes, not being deprived of the ownership of the means of production, have a distinctive asset which allows them to exploit others: in the case of the bourgeoisie, other workers; in the case of the petite bourgeoisie, members of the family. This aspect of Wright's argument is not controversial, so we shall now focus on his other claims.

The second and third types of asset constitute Wright's claim to conceptual novelty. Wright explicitly uses the concept of organisation asset to point to the significance of power relations within organisations as a major axis of class formation. He states that organisations are in themselves productive resources:

> the asset is organisation. The activity of using that asset is co-ordinated decision making over a complex technical division of labour. When the asset is distributed unequally, so that some positions have effective control over much more of the asset than others, then the social relation with respect to the asset takes the form of hierarchical authority.
>
> (Wright 1985: 80)

Hence, managers and administrators might be said to form a class by the way they use their hierarchical bureaucratic position to secure a privileged position for themselves in relation to their subordinates.

This is not unlike Dahrendorf's view of the service class. Organisations are vehicles for exploitation. In this respect Wright's arguments can be related to those developed in radical organisational theory (Clegg *et al.* 1986), which also see organisations in this light. The crucial theoretical step here is to abandon the Weberian stress on the instrumental nature of bureaucracies. For Weber, bureaucracies were important as the most 'technically efficient' forms of organisations in modern capitalist society. Clegg (1989, 1990) argues, however, that bureaucracies should be seen as the vehicles of power struggles and relationships. Rather than being seen as the 'natural', efficient way of organising, they have developed as an embodiment of power inequalities, and the people in superordinate positions within these hierarchies reap the benefits. Once this has been established, it is possible to argue that bureaucracies are an axis around which exploitation takes place.

Wright does not, however, simply refer to the significance of organisations, but also adds another asset to the picture – that based around skill. These assets exist where workers are able to gain advantages because of the scarcity of prized skills. Wright argues that this takes two main forms: (1) credentialism limits the number of people able to exercise particular skills and forces the employer to increase wages in order to recruit such a person; (2) if a person has a particular natural talent, this can be used to secure increased income (or 'rent' in Wright's terms). Wright uses this concept to argue for the singular position of skilled professional workers who would appear to rely upon skill assets as their privileged position relies upon the demand for their skills, incumbent on its restricted supply.

It is clear that Wright's arguments have rather different implications for middle-class formation compared with theories of the 'service class' (see also G. Marshall *et al.* 1988: 33–8). The most important point is Wright's emphasis that organisational assets and skill assets are different bases on which exploitation takes place, and hence the putative 'service class' is in fact divided along two different axes. In the realist terms which Wright occasionally uses, there are two different causal entities affecting class formation of middle-class employees. Wright indirectly, and probably unknowingly, considers how his theorisation of class relates to that offered by Goldthorpe when he considers the possible existence of 'strategic jobs', where employees are given privileged positions since they cannot easily be monitored by their employers (Wright 1985: 94). In the end Wright emphasises that this account must be discarded since 'we cannot derive any clear class relations from the analysis of strategic jobs as such: the incumbents of such jobs have no intrinsic relation to incumbents in non-strategic jobs' (Wright 1985: 94).

We have presented Wright's account in a positive light so far. However, there are a number of problems with Wright's work which mean that it cannot stand unchallenged as an account of middle-class formation. Some of these problems are of minor importance and can, in our view, be easily remedied, but others are more fundamental.

The first, relatively minor point is that Wright wrongly operationalises his class categories. Because he attempts to justify his class theory by showing the strength of the correlations it has with other social phenomena, through various types of statistical modelling, he reaches for empirical indicators for his types of class assets in an unconvincing way (for a longer discussion see Appendix 1). In particular, he assumes that people with credentials (educational qualifications) rely on skill assets, while those in a supervisory or decision-making position within organisations rely on organisation assets. Yet neither of these may be true: a worker with a credential might not be in the type of job where this asset means anything. On the other hand, a worker in a managerial post may be there because he or she is credentialled. It is theoretically possible that an individual who carries out decision-making functions may rely on skill assets, while a worker with credentials may rely on organisation assets. Hence Wright's empirical research is, we feel, not well designed to test his own theoretical approach, and it comes as no surprise that it fails to hold up well in quantitative testing (G. Marshall *et al.* 1988). This point is not especially serious, however, since we believe that it can be overcome by greater theorisation of the nature of the assets concerned, before empirical indicators are used in the research process.

However, more importantly, what about the conceptual status of the distinction between skill and organisation assets, which is his main contribution to theories of the middle class? It is simply very difficult to separate the two assets in most contexts: does a doctor, for instance, rely upon assets of skill or organisation? He or she works in a bureaucratic organisation in a superordinate role, belongs to a powerful organisation defending his or her position (the British Medical Association), but is also highly credentialled. Also, isn't it the case that most credentialling bodies are organisations?

This, however, is not a crucial objection, since we are not bothered about mapping people to classes: at this stage we are more concerned with establishing the respective 'causal powers' of different class assets. And here an important point can be established. We have stated that Wright is correct to argue that organisation assets involve a particular form of exploitation. They allow superordinates to exploit subordinates, which allows revenues to be appropriated by those in senior positions within organisations. Hence they can be seen as a potential basis on which class collectivities might form, but – and this is the crucial point – they are very difficult to store. This is the point made by Val Burris in her critique of Wright, when she states that, 'the asset of organisation cannot be owned in the same way as property and skills: it has no existence apart from the positions within which it is exercised and cannot be transferred by its owner from one use to another' (Burris 1989: 163). Organisations allow superordinates to exploit others, but this exploitation is context specific and ties the exploiter to the particular organisation involved. Hence, because the asset cannot be stored outside the organisational context, it does not allow class formation as readily as in the case of the ownership of property.

The concept of skill assets, on the other hand, is a major theoretical weakness in Wright's account. The problem is that while it is possible to see how an owner of capital exploits those without capital, and to see how a superordinate in an organisation exploits subordinates, it is less clear how a person with skill assets exploits the unskilled (Wright 1985: 95; 1989). In his most recent formulations Wright argues that since skilled workers are employed, it makes more sense to suggest that these workers can use their skills to allow them to be exploited less by capitalists, rather than to suggest that they exploit the non-skilled. This recognition is linked to a wider failure in Wright's account, which is unable to see systematically how professional workers exploit others. As Wright accepts, 'experts and professionals of various sorts constitute the category which has caused me (and others) the most persistent problem in formulating a coherent Marxist class structure concept' (Wright 1989: 331).

Wright's problem here is identical to that faced by Weberian writers (on

Wright's closet Weberianism, see Marshall and Rose 1986). It is difficult to see skills as axes of exploitation since it is the *process* which defines a particular occupation as skilled – and not the skill itself – which is the key causal entity at work here. In order to show how skills might be seen as forms of exploitation it is therefore necessary to consider what sorts of causal entities define skills. It is in this context that the concept of 'cultural capital', developed by Pierre Bourdieu, can be fruitfully applied.

## PIERRE BOURDIEU

Bourdieu offers a very different approach to class analysis to that used in the more quantitative British and American work. For Bourdieu classes are not collections of occupations but are primarily based around differing types of capital. Capital, for Bourdieu, refers to 'the set of actually usable resources and powers' (Bourdieu 1984: 114; see also Bourdieu 1990: 117–18). Occupations are simply the product of the interplay of different types of capital. He basically sees two types of capital, one based around the classic Marxist principle of relationship to the means of production ('economic capital'), the other based around relationship to cultural distinction ('cultural capital'). For Bourdieu, 'to attempt to map taste purely in terms of income is to miss the dual principles in operation, for cultural capital has its own structure of value, which amounts to convertibility into social power, independent of income or money' (Bourdieu 1984: 62).

Bourdieu sees the creation of cultural capital as being based around the contested legitimation of cultural forms (e.g. Bourdieu 1984: 70), and through the processes of 'symbolic violence' which are the result of social struggles between different classes (Bourdieu and Passeron 1977). In this sense culture can itself be theorised as a form of exploitation in its own right, since the process of making one's own culture legitimate is to discredit the culture of others. Culture is not to be understood as concerned with how a predefined social group develops a set of tastes and values; rather, it is a process through which mutually antagonistic classes are formed as each attempts to legitimate its own culture.

This theoretical step allows us to see how skills are defined – the very problem to which Wright had no answer. Skills can be seen as defined in relationship to a cultural 'field' in which certain types of activities are valued more than others. Skills themselves are not the axes of exploitation; the axes are the cultural fields that define and legitimise those skills. Hence, Wright's stress on skill assets is best changed to an emphasis on what we shall term cultural assets.

Further points flow from this observation. We have seen how organisation assets cannot be easily stored. Cultural assets, on the other hand, are much more easy to store, in what Bourdieu calls the habitus, or set of internalised dispositions which govern people's behaviour. Cultural assets

16

are stored physically in people's bodies and minds: the body itself materialises class taste. They can be reproduced through the passing on of cultural tastes to offspring: Bourdieu himself first developed his account of cultural capital as an attempt to explain educational inequality, where the children of 'cultured' parents were able to convert their inherited cultural capital into educational qualifications. Whereas it is difficult to pass on organisational position to children, cultural dispositions, like property, can be stored and transmitted, so facilitating class formation.

There is, however, one crucial weakness of cultural assets, compared to property and organisation assets. As we have seen, cultural assets are defined in a cultural field, and do not in themsleves involve the appropriation or control of other people's labour. Hence, in order to use cultural assets to achieve material rewards – in the forms of high income, security of employment and so forth – these assets have to be extended and applied to the labour market. They are hence forced to compete with the two other assets in an employment field colonised primarily by property owners and organisations.

We can now begin to piece together the respective causal powers of the assets underlying middle-class formation. Organisation assets allow superordinates to control and exploit the labour of subordinates but cannot be stored easily. Cultural assets can be stored more readily, through the 'habitus', but in order to reap economic rewards have to be deployed in other fields in which their value has to be established, rather than assumed. In this respect cultural assets are almost the mirror image of organisation assets. In order for cultural assets to become axes of exploitation of labour they need to be applied, often in organisational contexts. Hence, those with cultural assets often have to acquire organisation assets or property assets in order to transform them into assets that allow them to exploit others. On the other hand, those with organisation assets often have to transform them into cultural assets or property assets in order to store them and hence transmit them. This dynamic is the central feature of middle-class formation, and the way in which this evolves in any particular society will lay the foundations for patterns of middle-class formation.

## CONCLUSION

We have now specified three assets which affect the actual processes of class formation. These are property assets, organisation assets and cultural assets. But these must be seen in realist terms as social entities, rather than as descriptive classificatory devices. Any particular individual may draw on a number of these assets, and one of the main tensions we wish to emphasise is the dynamic relation between them, where people attempt to convert one type of asset into another type of asset.

Furthermore, it is essential to recognise that these assets are not symmetrical, and they offer differing potential for class formation. Property assets offer the most robust bases for class formation, since they allow other people's labour to be readily exploited, and also can be readily stored as capital. But the situation is different for organisation and cultural assets. Organisation assets allow superordinates to exploit subordinates, but they cannot easily be stored. Cultural assets can be stored and transmitted – though not as effectively as property assets – but need to be translated into other contexts in order to actually produce material rewards. Hence, middle-class formation is crucially concerned with the way in which cultural and organisation assets relate to each other.

So far we have examined the salient social entities at work in middle-class formation. But we have also insisted that this is simply a preliminary stage, and it is necessary to consider the types of contingent conditions under which forms of exploitation may give rise to actual social class collectivities. The actual nature of middle-class formation is an empirical matter, and we need to see how the dynamic between the three assets takes place in any particular time and place.

This argument does not mean that we have to retreat behind empirical description. It is possible to illuminate the most significant factors that are likely to shape the contours of middle-class formation. This is the task we turn to in Chapter 2, where we show how the complex interplay between cultural and organisation assets may give rise to separate middle classes, but can, in certain contingent conditions, give rise to a more unified group of middle-class employees which might usefully be seen as a 'service class'.

# 2

# THE DYNAMICS OF SERVICE-CLASS FORMATION

In Chapter 1 we have criticised theories of the service class for failing to demonstrate that a service class of professionals, managers, and administrators is a stable social collectivity, based upon specific forms of exploitation. This chapter will, however, take a rather different tack, arguing that in some cases a service class might exist as a recognisable social collectivity in situations where the fragmenting tendencies of organisation and cultural assets are offset by other factors. For this reason the existence of a service class is an empirical matter, which depends on the existence of specific contingent conditions. This chapter will illuminate some of these.

We begin by elaborating our account of how the dynamic relationship between organisation assets and cultural assets is likely to fragment the ranks of middle-class employees. We argue that there is much to be learned from older sociological literature exploring the relationship between professionalism and bureaucracy. The causal properties of these two assets is likely to fragment middle-class employees, but in the second part of our chapter we discuss three tendencies which might counter this and help establish a more unified 'service class'. These are, firstly, the role of the state; secondly, the significance of gender divisions and, finally, the role of social and spatial mobility.

## PROFESSIONALISM vs BUREAUCRACY

We saw in the last chapter how cultural and organisation assets have rather different causal powers. It is the respective weaknesses of each of them which lead to people drawing upon them to attempt to pursue particular strategies to strengthen the insecurities offered by each. This leads to a dynamic tension within the ranks of middle-class employees which finds its strongest expression in the division between professionals and bureaucrats.

The distinction between professions and bureaucracy has been extremely pervasive in sociological work. At the most abstract level it is seen as the

concrete embodiment of a conflict between two opposing social imperatives: the impersonal, routinising world of conformity to bureaucracy on
the one hand; and the creative, dynamic role of 'knowledge' which
depends upon professional 'autonomy' on the other. A distinction of this
sort can be found in the writing of Parsons (Scott 1966, see also Davis 1983)
who argued that professions were 'altruistic', while bureaucracies were
self-interested. The distinction also informs C. Wright Mills' work, in
particular his stress that the independent professions would increasingly
be subjugated to bureaucratic forces in modern capitalism, and similar
ideas informed the work of Merton (1961) and Gouldner (1957–58). By
the 1960s this common recognition of supposed antinomy between the two
opposing principles led to considerable research focused upon the 'anom-
alous' position of professionals in organisations (e.g. Harries-Jenkins
1970). The essential supposed differences were summarised by Scott
(1966). He argued that whereas a professional has special training, is
socialised into a group of equals, carries out entire tasks, and does not seek
further promotion, a bureaucrat on the other hand is trained on the job,
is supervised, carries out specific tasks, and expects a career within the
organisation.

This distinction has also been incorporated into theorising the middle
class, nearly always as an attempt to explore bases of internal differentiation. For Giddens (1973: 186–8), professional groups are distinctive in
being able to use professional associations to increase their market capacity.
Goldthorpe (1982) distinguishes between 'professional' and 'managerial'
situses, the first gaining their structural advantages through their employers' reliance on their 'expert knowledge', the second through their
role in exercising delegated authority. Abercrombie and Urry (1983: 121)
also note that 'there is ... a potential conflict between professionalisation
and bureaucratisation in respect of the work situation of the service class',
and see the former as more likely to strengthen the service class *vis-à-vis*
capital.

Yet the use of this antinomy to explore middle-class (or 'service-class')
fragmentation is problematic given the severe critiques that have developed since the 1960s. The critiques have taken a variety of forms. At
the most abstract level it has been argued that it depends upon a misleading
Weberian view of bureaucracy, and upon a stereotyped view of professions
which uses the 'old' independent professions such as law and medicine –
where practitioners are characteristically self-employed – as the benchmarks of professionalism more generally. Furthermore, Larson (1977)
shows that professionals, far from being undermined by large organisations, have often been employed in them, and she argues that the
emergence of professionalism has been closely related to the modern
organisation, both in the state and in the modern business company. She
stresses that there was 'an organic relationship of professionalism ... with

the two large central structures of the social order, namely the large business corporation and the state' (Larson 1977: 144). Professions and bureaucracies are able to control and organise work in complementary ways (see also Friedson 1986).

Yet what is striking about all these critiques is that some sort of distinction simply will not go away. Notwithstanding the thrust of her argument, Larson continues to see organisations and bureaucracies as different – though complementary – ways of organising and controlling work. In specifying these differences she draws out the different types of knowledge they use: in the case of bureaucracies the knowledge is vested in the organisation, while for professionals knowledge is internalised into individual practitioners (Larson 1977: 206). This is very much the distinction we drew in Chapter 1 between organisation assets and cultural assets. Elsewhere she clearly distinguishes those professions that are able to develop a 'cognitive base' before the emergence of modern organisational forms, and those cases where a cognitive base is created subsequent to *and dependent on* a prior position in an organisation. Thus, she argues that social work and school teaching were only given a formal training after the occupation emerged in bureaucratic settings, where, as she puts it, 'the professional project depends first on (the employing) organisation' (Larson 1977: 184). She also distinguishes between those professions which emphasise work autonomy within organisations, and those which participate more fully in organisational decision making (e.g. Larson 1977: 195, Table 2).

One finds much the same line of argument in another recent critic. Rosemary Crompton (1990a), having first disputed the salience of the professional–bureaucrat distinction, talks in another paper about the two patterns of regulating expert labour: one being '"professionalism" which is articulated largely at the level of the occupation', the other being 'organisational corporatism or the "clan form"' (Crompton 1990c: 12). In the former, moral regulation goes along with being a practitioner of a particular occupation, while in the latter the organisation itself regulates the practitioner.

So, what is the theoretical status of the distinction between professionalism and bureaucracy? What the recent contributions point to is the fact that the central distinction refers to ways of regulating work *within* organisations, rather than to differences *between* occupations. The idea that people in professional occupations can be clearly distinguished from those in managerial occupations is mistaken. Instead, the crucial difference is the way in which occupations are organised, so that they are linked to specific types of knowledge and cultural competence.

The crucial point here is the role of knowledge, or what Larson refers to as a 'cognitive base', in affecting the control of occupations. Professionalism is an attempt to establish 'structural links between relatively high levels of formal education and relatively desirable positions and/or rewards in the social division of labour' (Larson 1990: 30). By making this link those with cultural assets, who hence tend to gain the best educational qualifications, may be assured of desirable employment, so allowing their cultural assets to lead to material rewards. As well as providing links between credentials and desirable forms of employment, professionalism also attempts to defend the cultural distinctiveness of particular forms of knowledge, thus ensuring the perpetuation and reproduction of cultural assets themselves. The crucial issue is to find ways of deploying skills so that they can lead to economic rewards, without having these skills downgraded or routinised in the process, which would undermine their value as distinct assets. Professionalism can therefore best be understood as an attempt to translate cultural assets into material rewards. It involves the maintenance of an independent 'cognitive base', linked to institutions of higher education, which allows qualified groups of professional workers to retain their autonomy from any particular employing organisation, thus ensuring the continued distinction of the skills they profess.

This is not to say that workers with organisation assets do not have skills, or knowledge. The crucial point for these workers is that because their knowledge is organisation specific it offers no real prospects for security. This point is brought out very well by Whitley (1989) in his attempt to think through the specific nature of managerial knowledge. Whitley argues that managerial work is distinctive because of its 'interdependent, dynamic and contextual nature' (Whitley 1989: 215). As a result, 'because tasks are quite interdependent and embedded in particular contexts, general problem-solving procedures which treat them as isolated problems will be less useful than methods and approaches that take account of their contextual nature'. While managerial skills are context dependent, professional skills are established outside any one organisational base, and hence retain a measure of autonomy.

This having been said we need to recognise that professional knowledge at its most abstract and refined, needs to be transformed in the work situation to become useful practical knowledge. Friedson (1986) emphasises that while professionals are important as 'agents of formal knowledge', this knowledge has to be transformed to become useful in particular employing contexts. 'While each profession may be said to represent a particular discipline or formal body of knowledge, that knowledge is used selectively and transformed in the course of its use' (Friedson 1986: 217). But, as abstract knowledge becomes more specific to organisational routines and contingencies, the potential always exists for the routinisation of professional skills. As Whitley and Larson suggest, however, the crucial mechanism preventing professionals' cognitive base from being diluted lies in the fact that individual professional employees claim to have sole prerogative in deciding how professional knowledge can be applied in specific contexts.

This point allows us to conceptualise the idea of professional autonomy more precisely. Rather than seeing it as linked to types of employment – where professional self-employment is regarded as the ideal – or due to professional socialisation, we can suggest that it is linked to the nature of cultural assets as such. The claim to professional autonomy is the claim that the individual worker can decide how his or her professional knowledge should be transferred to any particular context. It is hence a claim that only the individuals concerned can know how to apply particular sorts of knowledge, and hence it preserves the distinction of cultural assets as vested in particular people. It indicates the 'em-bodied' nature of cultural assets. To contextualise forms of knowledge, to root them entirely in the practices of any particular organisation, would immediately run the risk of downgrading the security offered by having an independent cognitive base.

What this discussion points to is the dynamic character of the relation-ship between organisation assets and cultural assets. Because organisation assets cannot be easily stored outside the organisation they need to be transformed into other assets – either property or cultural – in order to facilitate class formation. But because cultural assets do not themselves appropriate other people's labour, they need to be translated into skills that can be used to earn material rewards, but in this process there is the danger of these skills becoming routinised and hence losing their distinction. Hence while unqualified workers in organisations pursue 'professional projects' to allow them a more secure base to perpetuate or develop their advantages, workers with cultural assets pursue 'organisa-tional projects' in order to find employment in specific organisations which allow their skills to earn rewards. And in this context their claim to professional autonomy can be seen as an attempt to preserve the distinc-tiveness of their skills.

The tension that results from the interplay between organisation assets and cultural assets is hence played out not between pre-given occupations but by people drawing upon different forms of these assets in the course of their careers. The career, rather than the occupation, is the correct focus for class analysis, as we elaborate below.

## MIDDLE-CLASS CAREERS

We have argued that the difference between professionalism and bureau-cracy is not occupational, but dynamic, relating to the relationship between organisation and knowledge. But this is still rather imprecise. The crucial way in which these tensions might actually lead to forms of middle-class fragmentation is through their effects in structuring middle-class labour markets and career strategies.

It has been argued that the careers of middle-class employees are of one type. Weber argued that orderly career advance was one of the defining characteristics of bureaucratic structures: 'the official is set for a "career" within the hierarchical order of the public service. He expects to move from the lower, less important and less well paid, to the higher positions' (Weber 1978: 963). High-level posts within bureaucracies are filled from junior positions where the workers have been trained to administer effectively the organisation's business – a process called 'bureaucratic succession' (Levenson 1961) or 'occupational succession' (Warner and Ableggen 1959). This stress on the orderly progress of middle-class workers is shared by Abercrombie and Urry (1983: 119), who argue that 'bureaucracies function as internal labour markets ... to be employed in a bureaucracy at a certain level implies the possession of expectations of increasing income, control and responsibility', and Goldthorpe also places the bureaucratic career at the heart of his analysis.

It is, however, clear that there is no one type of middle-class career corresponding to the Weberian stereotype. Studies of organisational labour markets clearly reveal the significance of a basic division between organisational and occupational internal labour markets. In the first extended discussion of the concept of internal labour market, Doeringer and Piore (1971) distinguish between firm internal labour markets (FILMs) and occupational internal labour markets (OILMs). In the former workers move only within organisations, while in the latter they may move between different employers, but stay within the same occupation. The same distinction is taken up in the best analytical account of internal labour markets (Althauser and Kalleberg 1981). They define internal labour markets as involving the existence of job ladders – entry to the organisation only at the bottom, and vacancies filled by promotion – and follow Doeringer and Piore in emphasising the difference between FILMs and OILMs.

It is true that both types of career involve skill acquisition and moving through to jobs with greater organisational power. Brown emphasises that both 'organisational' and 'occupational' career strategies are 'for those who seek a career with advancement in work on the basis of skills, qualifications and experience' (Brown 1982: 126). They do, however, relate closely to the dynamic relationship between knowledge and organisation that we developed above. Althauser and Kalleberg (1981) make the important point that in FILMs the acquisition of skills is dependent on the job and the organisation, and that the ability to learn skills depends on organisational position and is hence context specific. OILMs, on the other hand, are possible where occupational groups have a 'cognitive base' outside any particular employer, and so can move between jobs as the individuals concerned are responsible for transforming formal knowledge into practical knowledge within an organisation.

The important point to emphasise here is that the distinction we are drawing is not an occupational one, since individuals in the same occupations may be involved in different internal labour markets, according to how any particular employer manages the tension between organisation assets and cultural assets. Thus, Snape and Bamber (1985) argue that managers may operate in four different types of labour market: at one extreme, FILMs; at the other extreme, OILMs. Smith (1983) showed that the football and baseball coaches in the USA could be divided into two groups: one characterised by internal promotion; the other based around high labour turnover between employers.

The same point arises within 'professional' occupations. Not all of these occupations are characterised by OILMs with high occupational mobility between employers. Wholey (1985), for instance, showed that lawyers in the USA tended to become partners in law firms by being promoted from associate status, not by being externally recruited. And organisations may choose to prefer to rely on OILMs rather than on FILMs. Pfeffer and Cohn (1984) examined the existence of internal labour markets (ILMs) in 309 organisations in the San Francisco Bay area and showed that there was considerable variability in the presence of ILMs. They were more likely to be present where the organisation was a branch unit, where unions were weak, and there was a personnel department; but even so, most of the variation in the presence of ILMs remained unaccounted for (they obtained an $r^2$ of only 0.19 in a regression equation testing the existence of ILMs in manufacturing plants against a range of economic and organisational variables). The same emphasis on variablity is found in other research in this area (Baron *et al.* 1986).

The structure of the middle-class labour market is itself the product of the dynamic tension we have been referring to. And this in turn leads to, and is affected by, the various strategies used by middle-class employees. This recognition of different career strategies goes back to the work of Merton (1961) and Gouldner (1957–58), who noted a distinction between 'cosmopolitans' and 'locals'. The 'locals' have high loyalty to their employing organisation, have low commitment to particular skills, and have a reference group centred on the organisation (Gouldner 1957–58). The 'cosmopolitans', however, have low loyalty, are committed to particular skills, and have a reference group based outside the organisation. This distinction, which has informed sociological research ever since, relates closely to Larson's distinction between those whose cognitive base is independent of a particular organisation, and those whose cognitive base is not.

This polarity has been repeated constantly since Gouldner, even among those not drawing on his work. Hall (1975) distinguished four main types of career. Two of these are defined by the enterprise and are similar to Gouldner's locals. These are either early ceiling or late ceiling careers. The former do not permit much career progress beyond a certain point while the latter do. More interesting from our point of view are the careers which Hall describes as 'colleague defined'. In these careers workers have transferable skills which allow them to move between organisations and to develop their career in the process. These can be either jobs that do not allow progress beyond a certain point (such as technicians), or jobs that do. These careers are characteristically of people who are highly skilled and have reached a considerable qualification level.

Gouldner's typology is again taken up and refined by Brown (1982). Brown distinguished between three career strategies. 'Organisational strategies' involve workers working steadily up an organisational structure. 'Occupational strategies' are similar to those which Hall calls 'colleague defined', and involve moving between employers to better and better jobs within the same occupational grouping. Finally, there is what he calls 'entrepreneurial strategies', where workers attempt to set up in business on their own account.

Each of these career strategies relates to the sorts of assets we have already discussed. Organisational strategies are those used by workers with organisation assets, where the knowledge and skills they acquire in the course of their work are specific to the organisation that employs them, and hence prevents them from moving outside that particular organisation. Occupational strategies can be used when there is such an independent cognitive base, facilitating movement between employers, but here there may be a problem in finding ways of moving to better jobs. And, finally, entrepreneurial careers exist when workers try to maximise their property assets through self-employment.

These differing career strategies and prospects in turn relate to wider issues about middle-class work cultures. The experience of the organisational labour market is conducive to patterns of dependence and insecurity, while the occupational labour market is conducive to frustration. There is a considerable literature on the strains of 'organisation man' (Whyte 1957). In his well-known polemic, Whyte rails against the 'organisation man' whose life is filled by conformity, 'belongingness' and 'togetherness' to the organisation. 'What they ask for', he claims, 'is an environment in which everyone is tightly knit into a belongingness with one another; one in which there is no restless wandering but rather the deep emotional security that comes from total integration with the group' (Whyte 1957: 32). Whyte sees the organisation as a hungry beast, sucking the executive into its work routines at the expense of family, leisure and cultural interests: 'one of the few secrets many an executive manages to keep from his wife is how much more deeply he is involved in his job than in anything else under the sun' (Whyte 1957: 147). Company loyalty is sacred.

Whyte's work is not detached social science research, but many of his insights have surfaced in other work. Presthus (1979), in his analysis of the 'upward mobile' type of worker, writes, in terms reminiscent of Whyte, that 'the organisation tends to resemble a church, which needs champions to endorse its values and increase its survival power ... the organisation's values are internalized by the upward mobiles and thus become premises of action' (Presthus 1979: 151). He amplifies this by arguing that 'political opinions, patterns of consumption, of work activity and so forth tend to fall into the bureaucratic net' (p 161). Presthus argues that this dependence leads to insecurity, quoting a president of a large firm on this issue: 'fear is always prevalent in the corporate structure. Even if you are top man, even if you're hard, even if you do your job – by the slight flick of a finger your boss can fire you. There's always the insecurity' (Presthus 1979: 154). Presthus argues that this problem leads to a variety of possible solutions: individuals can work harder, or they can 'withdraw' and treat work purely instrumentally.

Merton's account of the bureaucratic personality makes similar points. He refers to the fact that

> the bureaucratic structure exerts a constant pressure upon the official to be 'methodical, prudent, disciplined'. If the bureaucracy is to operate successfully it must attain a high degree of reliability of behaviour, an unusual degree of conformity with prescribed patterns of action.
>
> (Merton 1961: 52)

The image of the conformist to the organisation once more stands out.

If workers who rely on organisation assets are dependent and insecure, professionals relying upon cultural assets are permanently frustrated. This is because no employing context can ever be the perfect vehicle for the exercise of cultural expertise, since by their very definition cultural assets are forms of distinction which gain their powers by being defined in the 'cultural field', and in opposition to the practical and everyday. As a result, any form of employment, for those with cultural assets, is some sort of compromise which runs the risk of downgrading the particular cultural assets concerned. Anthony Smith (1982a) develops this argument in his account of nationalist politics. He argues that professional frustration at the instrumental use of their labour by the state is an important factor behind their activity in nationalist politics, where they can hope to create a new and better set of state structures, more in line with their cultural outlook.

We can see then that the two distinct assets can give rise to considerable fragmentation within the ranks of middle-class employees. Rather than occupational differences, however, the crucial effects will be on career patterns, labour markets, career strategies and work experiences. It is therefore possible that two fundamentally different middle classes may develop if these tensions are particularly prevalent. However, we have only seen one side of the story. There are ways by which such centrifugal forces can be overcome. Particular employers may be able to integrate the two opposing tendencies and help produce a more cohesive class. Thus, in France, where entry to senior managerial jobs within organisations is dependent on educational credentials, there is a much smoother process where cultural assets can be used to acquire organisational position, so producing a distinct class of 'cadres' (Boltanski 1985).

So far we have considered forces leading to differentiation among middle-class employees. However, there are also tendencies towards unification. We first consider the role of the state before going on to consider the significance of patriarchal gender relations and spatial mobility.

## THE STATE AND MIDDLE-CLASS FORMATION

The state plays a vital role in middle-class formation. It can serve to reinforce the divisions between professional and managerial workers or it can, in other circumstances, help to undermine them. The precise character of any given nation state will have important repercussions on the contours of class formation and on the resulting tensions and conflicts.

This is because the state is of major importance in structuring cultural and organisation assets. Bourdieu, in his analysis of cultural capital, is notably silent on the way in which the state plays a crucial role in legitimating cultural forms. Corrigan and Sayer (1985), however, in their book *The Great Arch*, show how the process of state formation is a cultural process in which 'states define, in great detail, acceptable forms and images of social activity and individual and collective identity: they regulate, in empirically specifiable ways, much – very much by the twentieth century – of social life' (Corrigan and Sayer 1985: 8).

One indication of this general point is the very close link between the state and professionalism. Until the past decade, it was generally assumed that the professions stood in opposition to the state, and that the ideal of professional autonomy was premised upon non-interference by the state. This particular version of the alleged tension between professionalism and bureaucracy has been shown to be largely false, however. Following Johnson's (1982) demonstration of the close link between the structure of nascent legal profession and the imperial state in Victorian Britain, it has become clear that the state plays a vital role in sponsoring professional projects, securing cultural exclusiveness, and – through its role in educational provision – the transmission of cultural capital itself. Burrage (1990a) has demonstrated how the differing types of professionalism in France, England and the USA can be traced to the differing political processes in each country. The French Revolution, with its demolition of corporate structures, prevented any powerful professional associations from ever forming again. In Britain, the slow process of state formation allowed organised professionals a major degree of autonomy and privilege.

The state is also, however, an organisation: indeed it is *the* organisation above all others. When Wright developed his concept of organisation asset he believed that most state bureaucrats relied on such organisation assets. 'The state becomes the central arena for organising the organisations, for managing the organisation assets of the whole society' (Wright 1985: 122). The way the state is related to the professions is therefore of major significance in determining how professions and bureaucrats inter-relate. As Torstendahl (1990) suggests, in some countries professionals are incorporated into the centre of the state decision-making processes: in such countries professionals may well be integrated into a wider bureaucratic élite. In other countries professionals may be recognised by the state as semi-independent bodies of experts, whose expertise may be drawn upon by the state, but who are kept at arm's length from central decision making. In such circumstances the fragmenting tendencies between professionals and bureaucrats are likely to be enhanced.

The former case, Torstendahl suggests, is found in France, a country where the distinction between professionals and managers does indeed seem relatively weak. In France the élite class of 'cadres' encompasses both professional and managerial groups (Boltanski 1985), and so a more unified 'service class' does exist.

Perhaps the most crucial single area in which state intervention is likely to affect middle-class formation is the state's role in educational provision. We have already shown how cultural assets are reproduced through the passing on of specific cultural dispositions to children, who will then be able to convert these into educational qualifications. However, the specific type of educational provision is also of major importance in determining the degree to which other groups will be able to gain qualifications. Halsey et al. (1980) show that in Britain social-class background is not the sole explanation of educational attainments, since the type of school a child attends also has an important impact on educational provision, independent of the effect of social class. For this reason, some types of educational system may be more conducive to the reproduction of the culturally dominant classes than others. Halsey et al. (1980) argue, for instance, that within the tripartite system of education that existed in Britain between 1944 and the 1970s, it was possible for children attending grammar schools to obtain good qualifications whatever their own social-class background. In that case, the children of managers and of the working class who managed to pass the 11-plus and attend grammar schools were able to gain educational credentials, so undermining the exclusiveness of the professional middle class.

We can see that the state may serve to offset any fragmenting tendencies evident in the tension between organisation and cultural assets, but that is not the only important force here. Patriarchal gender relations may have a similar effect.

## GENDER AND THE MIDDLE CLASSES

It is striking that most historical accounts of middle-class formation give great weight to the way in which gender relations are centrally involved in the formation of middle-class identities. This argument is most clearly developed by Davidoff and Hall (1987) in their account of early nine-teenth- century Britain. They argue that the development of middle-class culture in this period cannot be extricated from the new types of gender relations that developed. As Hall summarises, 'the middle class (partly) defined itself through the establishment of new cultural patterns and new institutional forms. Central to its culture was a marked emphasis on the separation between male and female spheres' (Hall 1990: 94). The distinc-tion between (male) public and (female) private was of particular significance here. Much the same stress is evident in American historical studies. Blumin's (1989) study of American middle-class formation argues that one of the crucial sites of change was in the family and household:

> middle-class formation was a phenomenon that went beyond the re-alignment of work, workplace relations, incomes and opportuni-ties. Events on the other side of the retail sales counter, and in the 'separate sphere' of domestic womanhood, were influential, perhaps even crucial in generating new social identities. To this extent middle-class formation was woman's work.
>
> (Blumin 1989: 191)

These writers point to the unifying effects that common patriarchal gender relations might have on a class otherwise divided along the axes we have sketched above. The dynamic tension between cultural and organisation assets, which we have suggested may lead to fundamentally differing career patterns and identities among middle-class employees, may be offset by a common, shared, set of gender-based practices.

The point we wish to develop is that men using cultural assets and men using organisation assets may have convergent interests in supporting the subordination of female labour. A considerable amount has been written on the way in which professional groups employ various closure strategies. Witz (1990, 1991) shows how professional men have engaged in gendered strategies of exclusion and demarcation. In the former, women are removed altogether from professional forms of employment, while in the latter, women are confined to subordinate occupations where they 'service' male professional expertise. The medical profession, with divisions be-tween 'medical men' and women in subordinate occupations such as nursing or midwifery, offers obvious examples of the latter. It is notable that throughout most of the nineteenth century women were legally excluded from most institutions of higher education, which, as Larson shows, are the key sites where the professions' cognitive base is derived.

The creation of professional expertise is hence a gendered project linked to the subordination and exclusion of women.

A very similar pattern of female subordination can be detected in organisations as men with organisation assets seek to exclude women from promotion prospects in order to ensure their own privileged position. Kanter (1977) indicates how in organisations one result of this process of internal closure is that women are, by definition, regarded as being unsuitable for promotion, and hence the work done by women is defined very largely by the fact of their gender, not by its objective job content. She shows how secretarial work does not fit any clear notion of bureaucracy which emphasises the 'rational' nature of job structures. Secretaries derive their status not from their job, but from their boss's position. The bosses have total – not codified – discretion over the secretaries, and expect total loyalty from them, in a way that Kanter characterises as 'patrimonial'.

Similarly, though we have emphasised the differences between organisational and occupational careers, the very idea of a progressive work career has been defined in male terms, because the work career is isolated from personal and household life, and is seen as a thing in its own right, which should not be interfered with by 'personal' factors (Gallos 1989; Marshall 1989). Hence, the differences between the two types of career we have discussed above, while important, should still be seen as based upon a common process whereby men's energies are devoted to career development, and their domestic servicing – including the 'emotional labour' they demand – is provided by female relatives.

This indicates that the gendered processes behind class formation do not stop at the level of the labour market. The relationship between work and home, with the wife being confined to the home while the husband works in the labour market, is also an arena in which such commonality may be created – and this is given central emphasis by Davidoff and Hall, and by Blumin. It is, indeed, notable here that all standard accounts of the sociology of the family talk generally of 'the middle-class family' and do not specify any important distinctions within it. In particular, the functionalist theory of the family – developed in the 1950s by Parsons (1959) and in a different vein by Goode (1963) – tends to assume the middle-class family as the norm. The patterns of social and spatial mobility exhibited by the middle classes tended to make the role-divided nuclear family the best 'fit' in Goode's terms for these groups. Normally the distinction made is a broad one between working class and middle class, and does not correspond in any clear way to the types of class asset we have developed.

The functionalist theory of the family, in which the sex roles of women and men are seen as being separately defined, has in recent years come under strong criticism by feminist writers. One of the most salient points here is the rejection of the emphasis that women are confined to a separate 'expressive' world within the family. Rather, as Finch (1983), drawing on

31

the conceptual ideas of Delphy (1977), argues, the most useful way of investigating family structures is to examine modes of women's incorporation into men's work through the institution of marriage.

Finch (1983) shows that, in most families, far from men being concerned with the instrumental world of paid work and women being confined to emotional and expressive roles, women are in fact incorporated into men's work. At the most basic level this may simply take the form of performing domestic labour and giving 'moral support', but it also involves a whole range of tasks which directly contribute to the husband's work: entertaining work friends, taking messages, acting as a proxy if the husband is unavailable, keeping the books, typing work and so forth. Finch notes that

> by the capital she brings to a marriage, by making direct and indirect contributions, and by her performance of domestic labour, a wife facilitates her husband's performance as a worker, thus enhancing his present performance and future potential.
>
> (Finch 1983: 117)

Finch argues against any strong class basis to this pattern: for her, as for Delphy, the institution of marriage is the key factor behind women's incorporation into men's work. She does, however, recognise one significant pattern, that the wives of the self-employed are particularly prone to be incorporated into their husbands' work, to which we have referred above (Finch 1983: 131).

Finch also considers the relationship between wives' incorporation to both professional and bureaucratic careers. Although she notes that there are many aspects about these types of jobs (especially the significance of geographical mobility) which may promote especially intense forms of incorporation, she resists ideas that it is necessarily connected to these sorts of careers. However, other writers suggest a rather different pattern in which middle-class employees do have distinct ways of using their wives in their work. Kanter (1977) discusses the significance of 'office wives'. She argues that, in the corporation she examined, the wives of executives had careers alongside those of their husbands. She argues that as the man moves into a managerial career the wife is increasingly involved in professional socialising, and she quotes Levison's observation that 'when a man has a responsible leadership post, for all practical purposes both he and his wife are employed' (Kanter 1977: 116). When the manager becomes a public figure his wife is also forced to follow suit, by getting involved in charities, entertainments and so forth. Some of the instances Finch gives correspond closely to this type of activity: in particular, where she discusses the ceremonial activities of diplomats' wives, which is similar to the activities of managers' wives in what Kanter refers to as the 'institutional phase' of their careers. Very much the same pattern can be found in professional marriages (Rueschmeyer 1981).

The stronger the subordination of women within the family, the more likely it is that the dynamic tension between organisational and occupational careers will be offset by the shared patriarchal practices of middle-class men. Finch (1983) makes especial note of the significance of spatial mobility here: in the course of their careers men move while their wives and children are forced to follow. Women's subordination is hence reinforced by the problems women consequently have of building up contacts and resources in any one place.

## SPATIAL MOBILITY AND THE MIDDLE CLASSES

Class formation does not take place on the head of a pin. It occurs in specific spatial contexts. Hence the nature of spatial mobility – migration – is of crucial importance in affecting patterns of middle-class formation. There are a series of broader issues here which also need airing in order to demonstrate the importance of this point. Most generally, it is vital to recongise that middle-class formation is frequently retarded by the wide spatial scale in which middle-class workers exist. While working-class formation may well be reinforced by the propinquity of work and home, and the closely formed cultures which develop on the basis of the resulting shared experiences, this is far less likely to occur for the middle classes.

Embedded in the very notion of the middle-class person is the expectation that the relationship of that individual with that place or region of residence is a contingent one. Both occupational careers and organisational careers require a knowledge of, and ability to handle, non-locally-based information – codes, rules and systems of thoughts and actions. Information and experience which is to a high degree locally rooted is totally inadequate as a basis for responsibility in employment – whether this be knowledge of an organisation's activities in different sites or attempts to keep in touch with professional developments outside a particular place of employment.

Hence, middle-class migration, and the types of domestic and social life such migration tends to produce, presents another way by which any tension between cultural and organisation assets can be offset. Workers using organisation assets and cultural assets both tend to be highly geographically mobile: the former as they are posted to different sites within organisations, the latter as they move between employers located in different areas. The experience of migration and, hence, the possible solidarity that might arise from common patterns of domestic life based upon migration, may be factors serving to unify these employees into a more cohesive whole.

It is evident from the considerable literature on this issue that both professional and managerial workers tend to be spatially mobile. Whyte (1957) was drawing on an already well-worn theme when he referred to the high numbers of 'organisation' men who were 'transients'. He argued that upward social mobility was tied to geographical mobility and that 'high school records show that roughly 25 per cent of the graduating class do not return to Newburyport but instead go off to join the organisation world, and in many cases this geographic movement represents social movement as well' (Whyte 1957: 272).

The basic argument is straightforward enough. In order to gain access to a promising career – either through organisational or occupational strategies – the aspiring workers often need to leave their home towns either to gain a good education or to gain a promising job. Further spatial mobility is often required in order to gain promotion since the aspirant will be posted to different sites within the organisation. The end result is a process of overlapping spatial and social mobility, a process called 'spiralism' (Watson 1964). Watson sees this process as characteristic of both managers and professional workers. He was borne out by a detailed British study, by Johnson *et al.* (1974), who carried out a detailed survey of migrants in High Wycombe, Chatham, Northampton and Huddersfield in the 1970s and showed that migration for job reasons was common and that this frequently involved promotion. They observed that 'labour migration for job reasons was therefore a very positive agent for spiralism for the middle classes' (Johnson *et al.* 1974: 212; see also the discussion in Savage 1988a).

This pattern can be contrasted with that typically found among the petite bourgeoisie, who tended to be less spatially mobile. Watson (1964) referred to these as burgesses and argued that they comprised people who were 'shopkeepers, owners and managers of small-scale industries, and other small capitalists, whose limited scale of operations usually restricts them to a specific local community' (Watson 1964: 149). It is clear that these groups of people are the types of workers who have 'property assets' and pursue entrepreneurial careers. These types of workers often rely on local resources in order to develop: they need local contacts, local credit, customers, workers, etc., and so are unlikely to move to a strange place to set up in business.

## SUMMARY

The operation of the causal properties of the three class assets we have identified depends on a number of contexts and contingencies. It is a mistake to assume that because there are three class assets, there are 'three middle classes'. In certain situations, where there are strong nuclear patriarchal families for instance, the causal powers of organisation and cultural assets may be offset and a more homogeneous 'service class' may emerge.

This point is particularly pertinent in relationship to occupations. As Chapter 1 showed, much research on social class uses aggregates of occupations to measure class. However, as we have seen in this chapter, this is at best a very crude measure, since the causal powers of organisation and cultural assets cannot be neatly divided between occupations. Professional workers, for instance, rely on cultural assets but also usually work in organisational settings. An examination of the differences in labour markets, career patterns and strategies can provide a more accurate method of distinguishing the different assets in various contexts.

A further point follows. In order to understand the contemporary dynamics of middle-class formation it is necessary to be clear about the historical processes by which particular assets have affected patterns of labour market division and how, in turn, this might affect the occupational order. Only in the light of such a historical analysis is it possible to begin to see how actual patterns of middle-class formation have developed. This is the task of Chapter 3.

# 3

# THE HISTORICAL FORMATION OF THE BRITISH MIDDLE CLASSES

We have argued in the last chapter that the way in which social class collectivities form is dependent upon a range of contextual factors which affect the respective causal powers of differing class assets. In this chapter we show how, in Britain, each of the three assets we have enumerated has in fact given rise to a distinct social class. We show how there has been a deeply entrenched division between a professional middle class on the one side, and a petite bourgeoisie and managerial middle class on the other. The state has played a crucial role in the formation of the professional middle classes, and in the effectivity of cultural capital as a whole. The process of state formation – a process which Corrigan and Sayer (1985) show stretches back over many centuries – is of vital importance in forming the British middle classes and giving the professional middle class a pivotal position within the middle classes as a whole. As a result of this early link, the other middle-class groups have historically been much less cohesive and well organised. And this, we contend, has left a historical legacy which exerts a powerful influence today.

## THE PROFESSIONAL MIDDLE CLASS IN HISTORICAL PERSPECTIVE

Interpretations of modern British history tend to stress either (a) the dynamic changes brought about by the early development of capitalism during the period of the Industrial Revolution (e.g. Hobsbawm 1968; Thompson 1965; Perkin 1968), or (b) the remarkable stability and persistence of the old aristocratic order. In the eyes of Perry Anderson (1963) the ability of the British landed aristocracy to hold to the levers of privilege and power well into the Victorian period had given British social development a distinctive course, characterised by unrevolutionary and pragmatic political change. In the past decade the latter interpretation has held sway, bolstered by accumulating evidence of the slow and unrevolutionary character of British economic growth in the period of the 'Industrial

Revolution'.[1] The work of Anderson (1963, 1987), Beckett (1986), Thomson (1963), Cannadine (1980), Stone and Stone (1984) and Joyce (1980) have all explored different dimensions of aristocatic persistence.

This debate has, however, had the unfortunate effect of drawing attention largely to divisions within the propertied classes alone. For the facts of the matter are quite plain: whatever the social divisions between aristocrats, merchants, financiers and industrialists, they all drew upon property assets to secure their dominant positions in British society – usually as a means of securing rentier income. The extensive researches of Rubinstein (1981) have demonstrated that the leading group within this class were aristocrats and – increasingly as the nineteenth century progressed – financiers (see also Ingham 1986). The economic position of the industrial bourgeoisie was much more marginal.

The divisions between these respective groups should not be exaggerated. There was a fair degree of social movement between their ranks. Many of the larger industrialists came from a landed, aristocratic background (see Foster 1974). Erikson (1959) shows that almost 90 per cent of leading steel magnates were drawn from the upper class between 1850 and 1925. Honeyman (1982) shows that the more secure the industrial sector, the higher proportion of landed classes that moved into it. Very few successful industrialists rose from humble origins. Miles (1990) demonstrates that only 18 per cent of people in the 'Independent' class of wealthy property owners between 1839 and 1914 came from non-middle-class backgrounds.

In short, it is clear that a small, highly cohesive propertied class, comprising primarily wealthy landowners and financiers, but including some of the more successful industrialists, dominated British society throughout the nineteenth century and into the twentieth. But the significance of the other middle classes has been overlooked by the concentration on the dominant class alone – in much British social history the middle classes have at best figured as shadowy presences lurking off stage (see Gunn 1988). The non-propertied classes continue to be seen largely as a passive offshoot of these more 'basic' conflicts.[2]

Two more specific historical orthodoxies have helped sustain this view. The first is the acceptance of the orthodoxy laid down by Carr-Saunders and Wilson in the 1930s which argues that the professions were basically a product of the Industrial Revolution. The second is the tradition – originating with Dicey, and culminating in MacDonagh's famous argument about the 'nineteenth century revolution in government' – which neglects the significance of the state before industrial development, and which sees the growth of a state bureaucracy as a product of a nineteenth-century 'administrative revolution' which replaced a *laissez-faire* polity with a collectivist one.

These two orthodoxies carried the clear implication that the professional middle class and the public sector middle class were a product of industrial growth, and hence they were dependent on the economic activities of entrepreneurs and an essentially capitalist class. These writers based their case on the relationship between educational credentials and the middle class. Although Carr-Saunders and Wilson were aware of the existence of professions before the Industrial Revolution, they argued that 'a profession can only be said to exist when there are bonds between the practitioners, and these bonds can take but one shape – that of the formal association' (Carr-Saunders and Wilson 1933: 298). Hence the true emergence of professionalism had to wait until the development of qualifiying associations after 1800 (see also Millerson 1965) and the related process of relying on educational credentials as a criterion for membership of professions. For MacDonagh – the leading exponent of the idea that there was an administrative revolution in early Victorian Britain – the rise of the qualified expert and the decline of patronage in the civil service were crucial features of the revolution. Perkin (1968) emphasised the way in which patronage ensured that nascent professionals continued to be dependent upon the landed classes.

In the past decade both these orthodoxies have been seriously undermined (see Burrage 1990b). The work of Holmes (1982), and Prest (1987) has shown that recognisable professions existed well before the nineteenth century, and exerted considerable power and influence. Holmes argued that by 1730 at the latest, a large number of professions had formed as distinctive occupational groups, and he estimates that there were 55,000 professional workers by 1730 (1 per cent of the population – even by 1971 this had only increased to about 4 per cent of the population). Against Carr-Saunders and Wilson's argument (followed by Perkin 1989, Larson 1977; Waddington 1984) that the professions were weakened by the small market for professional services, and were hence forced to rely upon powerful patrons thus reducing their autonomy, Prest (1987) argues that there was an extensive market for services and that distinct occupational identities could develop.

The second error, which sees the pre-industrial role of the state as minimal, has recently been criticised in the pathbreaking account of state formation developed by Corrigan and Sayer (1985). They argue against the modern state being a late product of capitalist development in the nineteenth century: instead, they point to 'the singular capacity of the English state forms to accommodate substantial changes whilst appearing to preserve an unbroken evolutionary link with the past' (p. 17). They point out that state regulation of social life goes back into the medieval period, and that 'state formation ... entailed the early development of lay, as well as ecclesiastical, clerks in the business of ruling routines' (p. 23). Recognisable career structures existed in the Treasury, for instance, from as early as 1400 (p. 21).

These two re-interpretations also link together since this early state formation was closely related to the early development of professional occupations, though this point is not fully recognised either by Holmes or Prest, or by Corrigan and Sayer (but see Burrage 1990a). Holmes only discusses the state's role as a direct employer of professional labour, which in fact was not inconsiderable by 1730; he notes that the professional civil service and army were entirely public employees, and so were many doctors and lawyers. He neglects the state's wider role, however, in structuring those professions whose members were not actually public employees – a role which increased as time wore on. The Church of England remained a state church, while the legal profession by definition developed to administer and police the law: Duman (1982: 13) notes that 'by the early nineteenth century, the leaders of the bar both in fact and in official precedence were the law officers of the crown ... These officers were political appointees ... ' Peterson (1978: 122ff) shows how state employment was prized by medical men in the nineteenth century.

Most of the early professions hence developed in some sort of relationship to the state. This is the point developed by Johnson (1982) in his account of how the structure of the legal profession – especially the division between barristers and solicitors – developed in relation to state procedures. It is also germane to Corrigan and Sayer's emphasis upon state formation as a cultural process. Many professional occupations were engaged in the sort of moral regulation that they place at the heart of English state formation.

The crucial changes evident in the nineteenth century did not involve the novel formation of professions, but rather they created the structural links between professionalism and cultural capital, educational credentials, gender segregation and the state which came to mark out the singularity of British middle-class formation. They marked the development of a close association between cultural assets and professionalism: an association of far-reaching historical significance.

The development of a distinctive cultural capital linked to professional position became an increasing feature during the nineteenth century. Cultural artefacts which had formerly been concerned to display aristocratic power and munificence in ceremonial, convivial settings, became objects invested with objective meanings which could only be appreciated by the properly educated. This shift was related to the privatisation of cultural consumption – a process which Davidoff and Hall (1987) shows was integrally tied to middle-class formation and new gender relations based upon the division between male public and female private (see also Wolff 1988). The value of cultural artefacts was now deemed to rest in their objective, interior meaning – which could be appreciated in the serenity of the home – rather than their role in lavish display. As Fyfe (1990) shows, this process was also related to the emergence of the modern Museum and Art Gallery, which helped develop the notion of the artist as creator.

Two specific points are important here. Firstly, women had an ambiguous role in the development of cultural capital. They were largely excluded from the public realms of cultural production: the Literary and Philosophical Societies, Athenaeums, and so forth (Wolff 1988). However, their role as 'homemakers' – as well as their prominence in the teaching profession – gave them a distinctive place in disseminating new cultural forms privately. As a result, women occupied a key place in the transmission of cultural assets – in contrast to property, from which they were legally barred until the twentieth century.[3] This meant that cultural assets were the prime way by which women could enter the middle classes on some terms. We return to this vital point below.

Secondly, the emergence of cultural capital entailed a problematic relationship with aristocratic culture. On the one hand it broke from its character as conspicuous display, but in another sense it continued to draw upon aristocratic values. This was particularly evident in the field of education, and the changing character of 'liberal education'. In the eighteenth century this was concerned to cultivate a 'civilised' outlook – based on the learning of 'great truths' from classical learning – among the gentry (Rothblatt 1976). The resulting notion that education should not be vocational or instrumental was also vital to the new cultural outlook, since, as we saw in Chapter 2, the value of cultural assets lie in their independence from any particular instrumental use. As Rothblatt shows, the new 'liberal education' was concerned to teach 'the truth', based on detail and research (see also Engel 1983: Ch. 1). While this was a departure from older aristocratic traditions, there were still many points of contact – there was still a role for classical learning, for instance – and, as a result, ties with aristocratic culture continued.

But what is significant here was the way in which this new cultural capital was explicitly drawn upon by the professions. Many of them demanded that their practitioners be versed in liberal education. Peterson (1978) recites, for instance, how the medical professionals demanded that liberal training should be an essential preliminary for all medical practitioners. Engel (1983) shows how the very creation of the professional academic was based on the notion that the new dons should be 'students of truth, not practitioners for gain' (Engel 1983: 29).

This professional association with cultural capital was nowhere more apparent than in another crucial development – the growing professional concern with formal credentials. Before the nineteenth century professions had only a very loose relationship with the education system. Most professionals were trained through 'apprenticeships' and very few professions had qualifying associations before 1800. As Peterson (1978) points out in her study of the medical profession in London, it was common for direct occupational inheritance to be practised. Even in the nineteenth century over a quarter of apothecaries were apprenticed to relatives (Peterson 1978: Ch. 2). In legal work, on the other hand, professional skills were passed on by working as a legal clerk, where 'since no formal syllabus existed ... the student who wanted to learn the principles of the law had to rely on advice provided by established barristers' (Duman 1982: 37). Skills could be passed on directly, and hence professional identities could rest on this basis alone.

This situation changed dramatically in the course of the nineteenth century as professions demanded more formal qualifications. In medicine apprenticeships, training through simple observation and informal family education was replaced by a rigorous system in which candidates had first to have undergone 'general' education to provide an appropriate cultured background, and then a supervised medical training which included large amounts of course work (Peterson 1978: Ch. 2).

The best documented use of credentialism was in the civil service. Here recruitment, which was previously based around patronage, began to switch towards a form of credentialism, and explicitly looked to the universities, especially to Oxford and Cambridge, for their intake. The Northcote-Trevelyan Report of 1854 advocated appointment dependent on passing civil service exams, and also claimed that 'the staff would be recruited for life and constitute a distinct profession' (Gowan 1987: 10). This report was not implemented immediately, but by 1870 it was decreed that all clerks needed a 'certificate of fitness' (indicating that they had passed an entrance exam) from the Civil Service Commission.

Much time has been spent examining the implications of these changes for an understanding of the social composition of the British civil service. Writers such as Kingsley have seen these as an indication of growing middle-class presence. Gowan (1987) and Anderson (1987) argue differently, seeing these reforms as an attempt to reconstitute gentry control over the civil service, since recruitment via Oxbridge would benefit the sons of the gentry who studied there. 'The (Northcote-Trevelyan) Report gave a concrete answer to the haunting issue of how to defend the propertied classes in the face of ever-growing pressure for democracy' (Gowan 1987: 33).

In fact, the older interpretation is correct here. Gowan commits the error, brilliantly exposed by Rubinstein (1986), of assuming that those educated at public schools and Oxbridge were by definition from the landed classes. But, in fact, by the late nineteenth century only a minority of Oxbridge students were from the gentry, and those who were academically outstanding – that is, those who were liable to pass Civil Service Exams – were not at all likely to be from a landed background. Becher (1984) shows that while 31 per cent of Cambridge students between 1800 and 1849 had gentry fathers, the fathers of the academically outstanding 'wranglers' between 1830 and 1860 were predominantly drawn from professional ranks: only 7 per cent definitely came from gentry or titled backgrounds. And, Kelsall's (1955) study of the social origins of civil servants shows that in 1929 – the earliest date for which figures are available – only 8 per cent of senior civil servants were from a landed background, a point echoed in Rubinstein's (1986) study of the social background of senior civil servants.

Very much the same picture emerges elsewhere. The growth of credentialism was related to growing professional self-recruitment, and declining entry from the landed classes. Peterson points out that virtually no medical professionals had any aristocratic connections, and many came from medical or other professional backgrounds (Peterson 1978: Table 9). Sixty per cent of nineteenth- and twentieth-century Anglican bishops (Morgan 1969) were from professional backgrounds; by the end of the nineteenth century, 47 per cent of Oxford Dons had fathers who were either clergymen or professionals (Engel 1983); only 8 per cent of barristers were from landed backgrounds by 1850–75 (Duman 1982); and even in the army the landed gentry were a minority by the mid-Victorian period (Otley 1970).

The new professions, relying upon credentialled workers, claimed to be meritocratic, but in all cases it appears that they had become overwhelmingly self-recruiting. The crucial mechanism assuring such a situation was the way in which the reformed educational system served to advance the interests of the professional middle classes. This process has been most illuminatingly elaborated by Simon (1987), who argues that the crucial period of educational reform was 1850–70, where the state was responsible for a series of Commissions which re-evaluated educational provision for the middle classes. The Schools Inquiry Commission argued that there should be three types of school: a first-grade school aimed at the sons of professionals and businessmen; a second-grade school for the sons of mercantile and trading classes to prepare their sons for the medical and legal professions, civil engineering, and business and commercial employment; and a third-grade school for sons of farmers and tradesmen. The reformed public schools were used as the first grade, and the previously declining grammar schools were used as the second grade. These reforms established clear routes by which the sons of the various social classes could be provided with appropriate education and then could be directed to future jobs.

Professional middle-class reproduction began to take place via the educational system. The important point to recognise is that this reform happened largely independently of changes to the capitalist class. Bourdieu and Boltanski (1982) argued that the emergence of educational provision as a key institutional site for the reproduction of class dominance was related to changes in the capitalist economy: with the decline of the family firm and the rise of the large joint stock company, a son could less easily inherit a business from his father, and hence a key process of class reproduction was endangered. However, by making entry to cadre jobs within the new large companies dependent upon educational qualifications, and ensuring that the sons of existing owners tended to have the best education, the practical reproduction of the capitalist class could be ensured. However, in the British case the rise of the joint stock company post-dates the key educational reforms and, as Simon (1987) emphasises, the industrial bourgeoisie were not important supporters of the educational reforms that were put through. There is, on the other hand, considerable evidence of the role of the professional middle class in developing higher education. Dennis Smith's account of educational reform in Sheffield and Birmingham picks out precisely this point: 'in both cities the leading part was played by professional men' (Smith 1982a: 216). It hence seems more sensible to see the process as one which attempted to create an organic link between cultural capital, educational provision and professional employment.

The distinctive place of the professional middle classes also rested upon gender segregation in employment. By hiving off ancillary work to women, qualified male entrants could be rushed through to senior positions early in their careers. This strategy can be found in the Northcote-Trevelyan Report which criticised the existing practice of using qualified men for routine clerical work; they hence advocated a division between 'intellectual' and 'mechanical' work (Drewry and Butcher 1988). The increasing employment of women from 1870 (Zimmeck 1988) hived off this (female) mechanical work from the (male) intellectual work, and it proved exceptionally difficult for even qualified women to move into senior positions within the civil service (see also Martindale 1938; Sanderson 1990). In the medical professions Witz (1990, 1991) has shown how professional men engaged in strategies of closure in which women were confined to subordinate jobs within a hierarchical division of labour. The rising status of the male medical professions was hence dependent upon the subordination of women in organisational hierarchies. As early as 1911, 63 per cent of lower professional workers were female (Perkin 1989: 80). The almost universal use of female domestic servants by middle-class households further showed how the middle-class position was buttressed by women's subordination.

How is this relationship between cultural capital and professionalism to be explained? Firstly, it would appear that the changes were linked to the growing organisational structures of professional employment. In the pre-industrial period professionals worked in self-employment and practices could be passed on within families, but the growing scale of employment in organisations made such previously informal procedures unworkable. The significance of this is brought out very well by Peterson (1978) who shows how the rise of the hospital as an employing organisation problematised the traditional tripartite divisions between physicians, surgeons and apothecaries and overlay it with one based around consultants and junior doctors. The Medical Reform Act of 1858, which created a General Medical Council in which all the medical professions were represented, was a mark of the growing salience of the new division of labour. The growing scale of employment made it imperative for new mechanisms of selection to occur, and credentialism was a clear option.

The credentialist route was also favoured since other ways of recruiting professionals – e.g. patronage – were under heavy political attack, especially in government employment. The employment of professionals through patronage created severe problems of legitimacy in the face of early working-class radical movements which culminated in Chartism, all of which were directly antagonistic to 'Old Corruption'. Gowan (1987) shows how Trevelyan was haunted by fear of the 1848 revolutions, and sought to reform the state to avoid any direct attack in the future. This interpretation is close to that of Corrigan and Sayer, which argues that they were partly a response to the political challenge to the state in the 1840s and that they helped to secure the position of civil service administrators against outsiders (Corrigan and Sayer 1985: 160–1).

Our point, then, is that by the nineteenth century a highly cohesive male professional élite had been formed with very close links to the state, educational provision, and cultural capital. To see this class as somehow under gentry or aristocratic patronage misses the point entirely.[4] One index of its strength was its remarkably closed nature, with the majority of recruits to most of the professions coming themselves from professional, not landed, backgrounds. Perkin (1989: 89–90) shows that from as early as the 1880s most top professional men had been born into professional, rather than to landed or capitalist, families (see also Rubinstein 1986). It is clear from Andy Miles's work – the most systematic attempt yet to examine patterns of social mobility in nineteenth-century Britain – that the professional middle class were more closed to outsiders than any other social class in Victorian Britain, excepting only the dominant capitalist class. In Miles's sample of over 10,000 men who married between 1839 and 1914 (Miles 1990), 41 per cent of professionals had professional fathers, and only 6 per cent came from outside the middle classes. It was well established not simply in individual private practices, but also in organisational hierarchies, and the early use of female subordinate labour by the state was of particular importance.

If the cohesive class formation of these groups was secured through credentialism and gender segregation, it was reinforced by its distinctive spatial bases. The professional middle class developed as a London élite. Any number of points could be mentioned here: almost one-half of British barristers between 1730 and 1875 came from the South East, and over one-quarter came from London (Duman 1982: Table 6). Offer (1981) calculates that in 1900 one-third of the country's 16,000 solicitors were working within 10 miles of the Central Post Office in London. Sixty per cent of medical degrees for entrants to the Royal College of Physicians were from Oxbridge or from London universities by the 1880s (Peterson 1978: 67); and 'London became the locus of power, international prestige, and wealth for the (medical) profession by the early Victorian era' (Peterson 1978: 3). The most striking figures, however, come from Rubinstein (1987), who shows that 44 per cent of middle-class income was based in London in 1911, even though it only contained 14 per cent of the population.

There are two exceptions to this: (1) the Scottish professional middle class retained its distinctive identity, based on a strong university system that provided 20 per cent of medical degrees in the 1880s; and (2) to a lesser extent, a professional middle class also existed in the North West, where professional middle-class culture thrived (Seed 1988). Together these three spatial arenas – the South East, Scotland and the North West – accounted for around two-thirds of British middle-class income in 1911.

The professionals were also a distinctively urban class. They were found in London, Edinburgh and Manchester. There were relatively few in the Home Counties, or other rural areas. As a result, professional middle-class formation was both helped and hindered. On the one hand, its association with particular urban milieux allowed it to develop a distinctive presence in the burgeoning institutional life of the cities – in the case of London, the Academies, the Museum complex in South Kensington, and so forth (Fyfe 1990). But it also led to a split between the Londoners and the provincials which divided them on a spatial basis.

By the mid-Victorian period at the latest, the professional middle class had developed a distinctive presence in British society. Its presence was significant in shaping the overall contours of British social development. Indeed, by reproducing and forming itself it disorganised other social classes, thus helping to ensure the overall legitimacy of capitalism. Thus, by ensuring that distinct educational routes were open to their own children – which would allow them entry to certain professions – they were also ensuring that other less advantaged educational routes were open to the working class. By spreading professional services to a growing market, relations of professional power and dominance overlay those already present in the capitalist workplace.

## THE BRITISH PETITE BOURGEOISIE

It is against the backdrop of the cohesive class formation of both a propertied ruling class and a professional middle class that the social significance of organisation assets and petty property assets should be understood. The central point to establish here is that the tightly formed relationship between the state, the education system and the professional middle class had considerable implications for the formation of other middle classes that developed as subordinates.

In Britain the powerful hold of the dominant propertied classes created a particularly strong division between them and the petite bourgeoisie. The incorporation of the few successful large entrepreneurs into the dominant class meant that petty property owners – including minor capitalists and small employers – developed as a subordinate, excluded group. Small and medium-sized employers were a notoriously unstable grouping since business instability and the boom/slump cycle meant that very few survived over a long period of time.

The self-employed petite bourgeoisie was, however, a persistent and significant force in urban environments. It has been assumed that the petite bourgeoisie is the oldest of the middle classes, and that its position steadily declined with the onset of industrial capitalism (see the discussion in Bechhofer and Elliot 1976; Scase 1982). It might be argued in the British case, however, that the petite bourgeoisie only emerged as a distinct class during the course of nineteenth-century capitalist development, and – as Scase (1982) and Bechhofer and Elliot (1976) suggest – have retained a distinctive place ever since.

The British case is singular. The process of agricultural enclosure – often seen as directly related to the consolidation of landholdings – has a very long history, and a recent estimate suggests that nearly half of England's land was enclosed by as early as 1500 (Wordie 1983). It is very difficult to be precise about the numbers of self-employed farmers after this date. Conventional accounts suggest that they were virtually non-existent. For Hobsbawm (1968: 98), 'England was a country of mainly large landlords, cultivated by tenant farmers, working the land with hired labourers'. Beckett (1984) shows that the small, independent, landowning farmer began to decline from 1680, but it is not clear if the small landowners he refers to were employers of labour. Some of these older interpretations have been criticised. Reed (1984) argues that significant numbers of independent family farmers remained, but these tended to be confined to 'marginal' agricultural areas – especially in some of the upland regions – and they were a small minority of the agrarian workforce.

If the rural petite bourgeoisie was of only relatively small importance in the British rural class structure – compared to continental Europe at least – the position of the urban petite bourgeoisie became more important as the nineteenth century progressed. They were a diverse set of people: at one end of the spectrum were the nascent capitalists, whose businesses expanded to the extent that they became employers of labour. At the other end of the social spectrum were what Benson (1982) refers to as 'penny capitalists': people making a marginal living by selling anything they could lay their hands on. Self-employment, in its different forms, continued to be important even in new sectors of the economy. Foreman-Peck (1985) has shown that in the inter-war years there was a continued increase of small firms in building, motor repairing, timber and furniture trades, and there was also a strong move into self-employment in the service sector.

Two distinct interpretations of the urban petite bourgeoisie can be found. Many historians stress their marginality and instability: many of the self-employed were workers, whose turn to self-employment was simply a last resort in the face of under-employment in the wage labour economy. Mayhew (1971), Thompson (1963) and Benson (1982) chart the descent of skilled, employed, tailors into 'slop tailors' as evidence of the marginality of these groups of self-employed. On the other hand, Bechhofer and his colleagues argued that the self-employed were – at least by the mid-twentieth century – a cohesive class, set apart from other groups. Bechhofer and Elliot (1976: 185) stated that

> from generation to generation, the petit bourgeois reproduce themselves, sometimes simply handing on land, real estate, diverse business or entrepreneurial skills from parents to children, at others, recruiting 'outsiders' on the basis of ideological as well as material factors.

Despite a considerable turnover among the ranks of the self-employed, Miles's work shows that by the Victorian period the petite bourgeoisie had formed into a reasonably cohesive class. The movement of workers into self-employment was not especially significant, at least between generations: around 35 per cent of small businessmen had come from working-class backgrounds (Miles 1990), while 41 per cent came from small business backgrounds. The level of self-recruitment was even higher among farmers, where 78 per cent of farmers came from farming backgrounds. There was, admittedly, a fair degree of mobility of the sons of the self-employed into the working class – slightly over 50 per cent moved into manual work, but this might have been a temporary step, before inheriting the family business at a later date.

It would seem then that Bechhofer and Elliot's stress on the ability of the self-employed to become a cohesive social class is indeed correct. The crucial vehicle allowing this was the ownership of petty property, allied to the specific exploitation of family labour (Delphy 1977; Whatmore 1990). Finch (1983) has shown how the wives of 'self-employed' men are characteristically forced into providing a considerable degree of unpaid labour within their enterprises – and this set of patriarchal relations provided important resources allowing the continuation of petty enterprise.

The two most important groups within the urban petite bourgeoisie were shopkeepers and private landlords. Winstanley (1983) argues that shopkeepers were able to establish a distinct urban presence as early as the 1820s, and in later periods they were notably active in local politics

(Hennock 1973). However, the crucial point to emphasise is that the formation of this class, around the axis of property, led frequently, though not inevitably, to resistance to the very state intervention from which the professional middle classes benefited. The hostility of the petite bourgeoisie to public expenditure is a well-known theme in urban history (Hennock 1973), though, as Winstanley points out, there were exceptions. In particular, the self-employed hoteliers often supported municipal provision of facilities for tourism which they felt would benefit the tourist trade (Walton 1983). But, on the whole, the class formation of the petite bourgeoisie was set in a direct opposition to the processes that the professional classes used to establish their position, so leading to a major tension.

This tension increased during the course of the twentieth century as the development of working-class associational practices – notably the Co-operative movement – together with centralisation of capitalist retailing and the development of multiple stores, combined with growing state restrictions placed on private renting and the transmission of property, led to the self-employed being marginalised from the first part of the twentieth century. This is not to say that they declined in numbers: indeed, Table 3.1 shows that they increased slightly in the inter-war years. Winstanley rightly points to the persistence of the self-employed shopkeeper after 1900, and similar points can be made about other self-employed trades. Rather, it would appear that while self-employment was a frequent recourse for the unemployed in this period, it became more difficult to pass on the businesses. The security and cohesiveness of this class declined.

Table 3.1  Occupational groupings in Britain, 1911–71 (per cent of workforce)

| Year | Employers | Professionals | Self-employed | Managers | Others |
|------|-----------|---------------|---------------|----------|--------|
| 1911 | 4.1 | 4.1 | 5.1 | 3.3 | 83.4 |
| 1931 | 3.5 | 4.6 | 5.5 | 3.5 | 82.9 |
| 1951 | 2.0 | 6.6 | 5.4 | 4.5 | 81.2 |
| 1971 | 2.5 | 11.1 | 4.0 | 8.0 | 74.4 |

Source: Derived from Routh (1980), Table 1.1.

The petite bourgeoisie hence has a persistent presence, and the self-employed continued to make a vital contribution to the British economy well after industrialisation, and indeed, as Foreman-Peck has shown, well after the rise of corporate capitalism after 1914. The only way it could establish a reasonable degree of class formation was through the inheritance of property, yet this route became increasingly problematic in the twentieth century as property became regulated and taxed. It was not until the 1970s that this marginality began to change.

# THE DEVELOPMENT OF THE MANAGERIAL MIDDLE CLASS

We have so far investigated the significance of class formation arising around the axes of property and culture. The rise of managerial workers, dependent upon organisation assets, is however one of the great mysteries of British history. There are no historical studies which focus directly on this theme. The reasons would appear to be that it is assumed that either no managerial groupings emerged or if they did they were professionalised.

The former idea is implicit in those accounts focusing upon the survival of the family firm in British industry and the slow, or partial, development of the modern capitalist corporation (e.g. Elbaum and Lazonick 1986). The latter, more prominent, view is implicit in the Chandlerian tradition of economic history, where the rise of the large corporation is seen as causing the rise of the modern 'professional' manager. For Chandler, at least in some of his writing, the rise of the career manager is tied to the emergence of the large managerial firm, which is economically more effective than the smaller one. Chandler argues that with the development of mass markets and technological innovation, firms which could replace the 'invisible hands' of the market by internalising functions (such as marketing, financing, etc.) could gain economic advantages and could produce more effectively than smaller firms. These large firms depended on a managerial hierarchy, since managers had to actively carry out the sorts of co-ordinating activities previously left to the market. Hence the rise of the large firm was linked to the creation of career managers, which in turn succeeded because of the economic advantages that such firms possessed in the age of mass markets, mass transits, and advanced technology. These career managers became increasingly professionalised. In Chandler's words, 'the careers of the salaried managers who directed these hierarchies became increasingly technical and professional' (Chandler 1977: 8). In this view the rise of the managers is part of a wider process of professionalism in society (see Perkin 1989 for a particularly strong statement of this view).

In fact, both these views are wrong. A distinct managerial grouping did emerge, but far from professionalising, it remained weak and subordinate, and no marked degree of class formation ensued. Managers continued to be dependent on their capitalist employers for position and advancement – a point we have seen to be characteristic of organisation assets – crucially weakening their social significance. We shall discuss this at some length, since it is vital to understand the structure of the managerial class before the 1960s in order to put more recent changes into perspective.

To start with, there can be no doubt about the increasing numbers of managers employed after 1900 (see Table 3.1). Even in 1911 there were nearly as many managers as professionals, and the percentage of the workforce who were managers increased from 3.3 per cent in 1911 to 5.4 per cent by 1951. And, as Raynor (1969) shows, managerial incomes also increased rapidly in this period. Managerial income rose 925 per cent between 1913 and 1960, compared with 255 per cent for civil servants (Raynor 1969: Table 18). Indeed, the rate of increase for managerial incomes was faster than for any other occupational grouping in these years (Raynor 1969: Table 20).

Part of this reflects the late development of managers in Britain, but it also relates to the wider trends in the British economy. There is in fact no question that the significance of large firms in the British economy did increase considerably after 1900: Hannah's (1976) figures suggest that the 100 largest firms accounted for 15 per cent of manufacturing output in 1909, but 26 per cent by 1930. The merger wave from the 1880s onwards also saw the development of a number of large companies such as ICI, Courtaulds and GEC, all of which testified to the growing corporate presence in the economy. What is in doubt, however, is the social significance of these structural changes. The mere growth of managerial occupations related to growing firm size does not in itself tell us very much about the possible formation of a middle class based on organisation assets.

In the British case, managerial workers *did* expand but not in the way elaborated by Chandler. The best initial indication of career patterns can be derived from a short survey of managerial recruitment carried out in 1952 (see Acton Society Trust 1956). This survey is often regarded as the first systematic analysis of managers in British industry, and its findings are often quoted as a point of comparison with later surveys (e.g. Lee 1981). The most striking findings have rarely been commented on, however.

The survey was not representative of British industry: it deliberately chose to focus on the largest firms in Britain, and had a remarkable response rate: 44 of the 65 private firms in Britain employing over 10,000 people co-operated, and a further seven firms were included, employing between 7,000 and 10,000. These firms gave full details on recruitment and training, and a supplementary survey of 3,327 managers employed in 27 of these firms was also analysed. Altogether the 51 firms surveyed had 1.6 million employees: one-sixth of the manufacturing workforce.

Given this bias to large company the results of the survey are even more remarkable. They indicate first and foremost the existence of a large group of managers inside the leading industrial firms. There is no question that managerial groups did exist in large numbers inside British industry.

Secondly, there is also no doubt about the significance of the 'organisational career' for these managerial workers. Sixty-three per cent of managers had either worked at their present company all their lives or had joined it under the age of 25. Of the 46 firms who gave replies to a question asking about the degree of internal promotion, 28 (61 per cent) stated that they relied on internal promotion 'entirely', 'almost entirely', or, if they

50

gave figures, that over 90 per cent of managerial jobs were filled in this way. A further 13 companies (28 per cent) stated that their use of internal promotion was either 'considerable', 'usual', 'mainly', or, if they gave figures, between 50 per cent and 89 per cent. Only five (11 per cent) had reservations about the use of internal promotion, one firm stating that it was 'policy that there should be some new blood' (Acton Society Trust 1956: App. IV).

If the dominance of the organisational career based around an internal labour market is confirmed by the evidence of the survey, what is remarkable is the means by which internal promotion took place. The overwhelming impression conveyed is a situation where promotion took place by patronage and sponsorship, rather than through a process of meritocratic selection. This is occasionally mentioned explicitly, with one firm reporting that 'each top manager is supposed to ensure his own succession', but it is more starkly revealed by the fact that internal advertising of vacancies was rare: 24 of 51 companies used them for some jobs, but only four firms stated that they used them for all jobs. Most firms only used them for foremen, or to fill jobs they did not otherwise know how to fill.

Personnel offices, where they existed, also had relatively little say in promotions. Only in 12 companies did they control promotion, while in ten others they had a consultative role, and in four they had the right of veto (figures calculated from Appendix IV of Acton Society Trust). While annual assessments or 'merit ratings' were reasonably frequent (20 companies had them), only two had appraisal schemes that allowed for dialogue between employee and the appraising official.

The overwhelming impression is of a system of managerial recruitment based on employees being singled out by existing managers in the organisation as 'promising material'. Only rarely would there be any systematic evaluation of this employee, and post-entry training was rare. The chosen employee would be slowly promoted into managerial work by a process of patronage, or sponsorship. Roper (1989) argues that managerial careers in this period often involved finding a suitable 'father figure', who would then help promote the junior worker: 'male managers do indeed perceive their own progress as having been dependent upon a male lineage ... their career accounts are narrated in terms of a passage to manhood mediated by a father-figure' (Roper 1989: 52). Managers would regard the sponsorship of an older man in the organisation as vital if they were to be promoted.

The key point is that the education system and the state more generally played a marginal role in the training of managers, and selection and promotion was based on non-credentialist criteria. As a result, managers could only rely upon organisation assets as an axis of exploitation, and this left them dependent upon the organisation in the way we have discussed above.

51

The reasons for this particular pattern are partly related to the character of British economic change. Particularly important here were the problems of ensuring a transition from the privately owned firm to the joint stock company. Chandler, referring to the USA, emphasises that the development of the managerial company over the private one was a slow process, and initially the owners of firms were concerned at giving discretion to professional managers, who they may not entirely trust. This concern, however, was lessened if the managers they employed were tried and trusted, and in this context the employment of managers who had devoted their careers to one firm seemed to offer suitable reliability. It offered a suitable basis for trusting managers to act in the interests of the private owners.

In the British case the persistence of the family-owned or controlled companies into this century is well known (Elbaum and Lazonick 1986; Tolliday 1987; Hannah 1976), and the problem of transition was far greater than it was in the USA. It is often assumed, however, that these family firms were small and could neither adapt nor expand, and that the larger firms that did exist were organised on managerial lines. But it is remarkable that many of the most successful twentieth-century British firms continued to be organised under this rubric. Indeed, only a few of the large firms that became part of Hannah's corporate economy did not still have strong family interests: Gourvish's study (1987) of ten of the largest companies in inter-war Britain found that only three (ICI, Harland and Wolff, and Midland Bank) did not have strong family interests. Imperial Tobacco, Courtaulds, W.H. Smith, Pilkington's, Colvilles, Bowater, and Kenricks – most of which were profitable, expanding concerns – were still based around family control.

These family firms were hence forced to take on managerial staff to carry out the growing range of co-ordinating activities, but the owners were concerned lest this should undermine their ultimate control. Hence the loyal, lifetime manager seemed the obvious choice. By being promoted from within the company by the owner, the manager would become loyal and dependent, and be unwilling to fundamentally challenge the owner's control.

This pattern clearly emerges from specific studies of particular firms. Moss and Hume's account of Harland and Wolff indicates in passing that the early board members of the company in 1902 were chosen by the leading figure, Lord Pirrie, on this basis: 'these were Lord Pirrie's "splendid men", who could be relied upon for their technical skills and the devotion of their service. All of them, except Carlisle, owed their promotion to him and would never have gone against his decisions' (Moss and Hume 1986: 132). Coleman's (1969) discussion of Courtaulds indicates a similar pattern, where members of Samuel Courtauld IV's board in the inter-war period were frequently internal appointees, and very few had 'significant' business connections outside the firm.

The slow move away from the family firm was a major factor in creating a patrimonial internal labour market. But even those firms that adopted a managerial capitalist structure – ICI being the outstanding instance – still developed a similar sort of pattern. ICI had more 'meritocratic' features: it employed relatively large numbers of graduates from the outset, in 1926. However, head office had little control over managerial recruitment – especially after a scheme to recruit trainees was ended in 1932 – and Reader (1975) makes it clear that ICI also had the same pattern of promotion through patronage and clientilism.

The case of ICI does, however, indicate another factor – the second on our list – behind the patrimonial internal labour market. This concerns the problems of co-ordinating large companies. In the USA Chandler shows that the 'multi-divisional' firm, with specific functions divided between semi-autonomous units under the overall command of head office, became the dominant form of the business enterprise in the twentieth century. In Britain these multi-divisional companies did not emerge until after the Second World War, and only partially even then. Instead, many British companies were organised as holding companies, with merged companies not being integrated into a coherent and unified structure, but being able to retain day-to-day autonomy. As a result, problems of the overall co-ordination of the firm were inherent.

Hannah shows that the principal device by which head offices kept some degree of control was through accounting procedures that were able to monitor the activities of the constituent units to some degree. It ensured that all the operation's short-term economic viability could be measured and assessed. But it allowed no clear way of helping the company in three main areas. The first of these was sanctions for large amounts of capital expenditure. Requests for capital expenditure from units could not easily be evaluated by head office when the only people who could effectively judge its use were already employed by the units. Wilson (1954) shows that the fixing of capital expenditure by the different operating units of Unilever was one of the most significant elements of the interchange between head office and the units.

Another factor, related to the above, was that of evaluating research when it was not carried out centrally by a research and development department – as it was in the USA – but in the constituent units of the company. It was difficult, if not impossible, for head offices to judge whether money allocated to particular divisions for research was being used well or badly. Reader (1975) shows clearly the problems of ICI in organising research spending. ICI's research was nearly all based in the particular divisions, and after 1945 a rapid acceleration in research expenditure, from £782,000 in 1938 to £6,043,000 in 1952, led some directors to show concern that there was no clear way of evaluating the effectiveness of this research. Lord Weir devised a new formula to measure the effectiveness of research spending, which found that research-sponsored developments had only produced considerable profit for two of ICI's products, polythene and perspex, while the amount of research money spent on other innovations had rarely achieved much financial comeback.

A final problem was how to manage product innovation. Constituent units were able to refine products only in their specific area of operation, and it was difficult to develop totally new products if they did not fall clearly under one unit's jurisdiction. Reader shows that ICI faced this problem acutely. 'ICI's organisation designed originally with the heavy chemical industry in mind had never really been successfully adapted to further the needs of fine chemicals, even after their importance had been grasped ... divisions were considering their own interests rather than ICI's total resources or borrowing power' (Reader 1975: 461–2). ICI was particularly slow to develop products in pharmaceuticals and plant protection.

The problem was that an accounting framework, which most holding companies used to monitor the performance of their constituent units, was simply inadequate to effectively develop new products and new business. British firms never entirely overcame this problem, but it explains why they developed an internal labour market as an interim step to attempt to prevent the managers of particular units ignoring the interests of the centre. By creating promotion links between the units and the centre, managers might be persuaded to think a little of the overall interests of the firm, rather than their own specific units. Unilever regarded the free interchange of personnel between the head office and operating units as vital, though it is not clear if this extended to promotion systems. Much of ICI's problems, on the other hand, lay in the fact that most head office managers were promoted from one division alone – Brunner Mond – and hence these managers tended to act in the interests of that division, while the managers of other divisions may have not identified with ICI at all. The patrimonial internal labour market was an *ad hoc* solution to the problem of forcing managers to think of wider interests than those of their specific operating units.

The third point of general importance is the significance of gender relations in the creation of internal labour markets. There was remarkable reluctance in many large firms to use female labour as a way of rationalising the male career, and many private firms were slow to follow the lead of public employers in recruiting women to subordinate jobs within organisational hierarchies, so 'freeing' male labour for superior positions. Even the banks, one of the most 'managerial' of the large private companies, waited until the 1920s before employing women on a large scale (see Savage 1991a). As Glucksmann (1990) demonstrates, manufacturing firms in the newer industries of electronics, consumer goods and food processing waited until the 1920s and 1930s before turning to female labour on a major scale. Even this turn can be overemphasised (see Savage 1988b), as some of the areas specialising in the new industries had below average numbers of women in the labour market until the later 1930s.

One further development grew out of the trends discussed above. Since managers tended to work for one firm constantly they were of relatively little use in allowing standardisation of procedures between organisations. As Hannah (1976) and Armstrong (1987) point out, this led to the professional accountant playing a pivotal role in many large organisations. Particularly in response to state intervention in economic management during the First World War and the need to keep tax returns, accountants had to be employed, and they often occupied key positions as mergers took place. The result was that from the time of the First World War onwards some professional workers began to move into managerial employment, leading to a growing field of employment. In this sense, rather than managers becoming professionalised, professionals were being employed to carry out managerial functions. We shall return to this issue in Chapter 4.

The point we have endeavoured to establish is that in Britain the industrial manager relied entirely on organisation assets. The potential to pursue 'professional projects' was severely circumscribed by the character of British economic development and the character of state intervention. The colonisation of the educational system by professional workers meant that relatively few managers were credentialled, and the particular type of economic change in Britain was such as to favour the long-term company loyalist as manager. And, as we have seen, organisation assets are not conducive to being stored by individuals, so facilitating class formation. This, we contend, is the crucial feature of British middle-class formation: that the rupture between professional and managerial workers is particularly deeply embedded, with professional workers relying on cultural assets and managerial workers relying on organisation assets.

## CONCLUSIONS

In 1949 Lewis and Maude, analysing the position of professionals in British society, remarked that 'the number of professions in which public authorities neither directly regulate practice nor possess a substantial influence as potential employers proves on examination to be startlingly small' (Lewis and Maude 1953: 115). They listed only dissenting ministers, senior trade union officials, journalists, authors, visual artists and actors as falling outside this relationship. The development of the welfare state after 1945 marked the culmination of this long-term trend as medical and educational professionals all effectively became public employees. And here we have, encapsulated, the central dynamic of British middle-class formation. The crucial weakness of cultural assets – that they do not in themselves form an axis of exploitation – has been offset in the British case by the way in which the state has underwritten the place of professional expertise in organisational hierarchies.

It is a different story, however, for managerial workers. It is not that they were materially badly off. As we have emphasised, organisation assets are axes of exploitation, and managers were, by the 1950s, a wealthy group of workers. Raynor (1969: Table 11) shows that in 1966 works managers earned more – in median terms – than most professional workers in industry (excluding the Head of Research and Design). But because organisation assets cannot be stored – they cannot be taken home or used elsewhere – they are insecure bases for class formation. As a result, managers were crucially dependent upon their employer, and hence have been unable to form as a distinct social class.

Two rather different classes relied upon property assets, however: first and foremost the dominant propertied class comprised large landowners, financiers and large industrialists. Set apart from this was the petite bourgeoisie, which, despite some mobility into and out of its ranks, came to occupy a distinctive niche by the Victorian period.

There is no evidence that the British patterns were in any way typical of other countries: indeed, it would appear that middle-class formation in Britain had little parallel with that in other capitalist countries. In France, as we have already stated in Chapter 2, a more cohesive 'service class' developed. Berlanstein (1988) shows that from as early as the mid-nineteenth century French management was firmly credentialled, and recruited from the Grandes Ecoles. By 1880 there were over 600 graduates of the Ecole Polytechnique in private enterprise. Using a detailed case study of one leading French firm, he showed that by the 1880s all senior management posts were filled from professional engineering ranks, and, as a result, 'the distinctive features of the French engineering profession deeply marked the nature of management' (Berlanstein 1988: 215–16). In France – unlike Britain, where professionals inhabited a separate occupational world from managers – management was constituted through professional groups. This was reflected in the creation, from the 1930s, of the idea of the 'cadre' class. This class of credentialled managers was regarded as a distinct élite class in French society (Boltanski 1985), in contrast to Britain, where managers continued to be a subordinate class.

In Germany Kocka (1990) also provides more evidence that there was a unified 'service class'. Kocka argues that in Germany – and other parts of central Europe – a more cohesive 'Burgertum' developed inhabiting the sphere of civil society in opposition to monarchical authority. While some tensions between professions and the business classes did open up during the nineteenth century, there was a reasonable degree of mobility between professional and business communities.

Much the same situation was found in the USA, where Chandler (1977) shows that credentialled managers played a much greater role. Professional engineers, in particular, were important forces behind the restructuring of American industry from the late nineteenth century (Noble 1977), and where graduate entry was also the norm in the large companies. As Urry (1986) has shown, this also led to the formation of a powerful service class, able to implement scientific management in a way that was not evident in Britain.

The key to these differing patterns – especially compared to the continent – appears to lie with the way in which the state intervenes in processes of economic growth.[5] In those countries where the state was of vital importance in developing industry, it could not but be involved in recruiting and training its managerial workforce. We have emphasised the long history of the British state, but its relative lack of direct involvement in manufacturing and the provision of basic infrastructures meant that it had little direct impact on developments in these areas. We now consider the way in which recent changes have affected these historical patterns.

# 4

# THE CONTEMPORARY
# RESTRUCTURING OF
# THE MIDDLE CLASSES

There are no shortage of accounts arguing for the recent development of new middle classes in the post-Second World War period. There has been a dramatic increase in the number of people in professional, administrative and managerial jobs since 1945 – in Britain the numbers have increased from around 12 per cent of the workforce in 1951 (Routh 1980) to around 27 per cent by 1983 (Heath *et al.* 1985), and sectors and occupations in which they work have proliferated. Until the 1980s debate centred around the issue to which these new, expanding occupations could really be regarded as middle class, and several writers endorsed the view that some of these professional and administrative jobs were in fact being down-graded – proletarianised – so that they formed a 'new working class' (Mallet 1975; Braverman 1974; see the discussion in Abercrombie and Urry 1983). But, in the more recent period it has been largely accepted that, by most measurable criteria, these jobs enjoy considerably better market and work situations than manual jobs (G. Marshall *et al.* 1988; Goldthorpe 1982; but see Crompton and Jones 1984) and that no simple proletarianisation process has taken place.[1]

In more recent years attention has instead focused on considering some of the ramifications of the increase in professional, administrative and managerial ranks. For some writers, as we have discussed above, these indicate the continued growth and maturity of a 'service' or 'professional-managerial class' (Goldthorpe 1982; Lash and Urry 1987). Other writers, however, emphasise the creation of a number of new classes. Poulantzas's (1975) and Bourdieu's (1984) 'new petite bourgeoisie', Gouldner's (1979) 'new class', Lash's (1990) 'post-industrial middle classes' are examples of this latter tendency.

The point to recognise here is that these latter interpretations are sociological glosses upon occupational change. For all these writers occupational change lies at the heart of changes to the middle classes more generally. Yet in this book we have argued that we need to begin by considering social class in terms of assets and the relations of exploitation in which they are embedded. Therefore, in order to address the contemporary formation of the middle class it is important for us to begin by considering the extent to which class assets have been fundamentally altered, if at all. Then we need to see how people draw upon different assets to actually form classes. While the analysis of occupational change is of major importance in this undertaking, it is not the centrepiece.

This chapter therefore proceeds by outlining the most significant changes to the nature of class assets. Here our main focus is upon the declining importance of organisation assets, and we suggest that this has posed a particularly acute crisis for managerial workers. Organisation assets have never been conducive to the storing of advantages, but in more recent times they are becoming less useful as axes of exploitation. Hence managers are increasingly attempting to trade in these assets for either cultural or (especially) property assets. We discuss the dramatic changes that have taken place to the managerial career in recent years. The class formation of the professional middle class, on the other hand, has been enhanced by recent changes, and the ability of those with cultural assets to pursue 'organisational projects' has been enhanced. We argue that property assets, which have hitherto been of relatively marginal importance in middle-class formation outside the ranks of the petite bourgeoisie, are becoming more integrally tied to processes of middle-class formation. We suggest that increasing numbers of the middle class can draw upon both property and cultural assets.

## THE EROSION OF ORGANISATION ASSETS

We have placed considerable theoretical emphasis upon the organisation as an axis of exploitation, as a vehicle that allows superordinates to exploit subordinates. Yet organisations vary in their structures, and it will be one of the major arguments of this chapter that the restructuring of organisations and organisational hierarchies has considerable import for understanding contemporary trends in middle-class formation.

Much of the current debate on the character of contemporary economic restructuring has been centred around the idea of a transition from Fordism to Post-Fordism, and related to this, between organised and disorganised capitalism (e.g. Lash and Urry 1987; Offe 1985; Harvey 1989; Aglietta 1979; Allen and Massey 1988). Fordism is a delightfully vague concept, however, stemming originally from Gramsci's observations on the practices of Henry Ford in Europe, and in Gramsci's usage there is a slippage from seeing it as based around changes in the production process alone – notably the significance of the assembly line – to seeing it as a wider social phenomenon, bearing on culture, family organisation and politics. Much of this slippage is perpetuated in recent accounts (see Sayer 1989), but the broader use is of greater sociological interest and will be considered here.[2]

There are three components to Fordism in the wider sense. Firstly, it refers to the economic centrality of mass production based around de-skilled tasks, involving standardisation of products, use of special-purpose equipment and the elimination of skilled by semi- and unskilled labour (Tolliday and Zeitlin 1986). Secondly, Fordism involves mass consumption in a homogeneous market which allows the standardised products to be sold profitably. Finally, Fordism was underwritten by Keynesian style state intervention to manage demand in the economy in order to ensure the buoyancy of the economy.

None of these concepts explicitly brings in the significance of organisation to Fordism. Nonetheless Aglietta (1979) who did much to bring the term into general use does refer to Chandler's work, as do Lash and Urry (1987) who develop the related concept of organised capitalism. The significance of Chandler's work here concerns his stress on the role of the 'visible hand' of corporate organisation for modern 'Fordist' companies. The crucial point is Chandler's emphasis on the way in which the link between mass production and mass consumption was dependent upon an organisational hierarchy in which a pyramidical managerial structure co-ordinated the production and distribution of commodities.

> Whereas the activities of single-unit traditional enterprises were monitored and co-ordinated by market mechanisms, the producing and distributing units within a modern business enterprise are monitored and controlled by middle management ... the existence of a managerial hierarchy is a defining characteristic of the modern business enterprise.
>
> (Chandler 1977: 7)

Drawing on Chandler's argument it seems that Fordism can best be conceptualised as characterised by a close, functional relationship between capitalism and bureaucratic organisational hierarchies, in which the mass production and consumption of goods rests upon the co-ordinating functions of a bureaucratic, pyramidical managerial hierarchy. The relations of super- and subordination within organisational hierarchies which provided an axis of exploitation could also be drawn upon – indeed, needed to be drawn upon – to ensure the profitability of capitalist enterprises. But, in this case, what is the significance of Post-Fordism for the salience of organisational hierarchies?

The concept of Post-Fordism (or Neo-Fordism: see Massey 1988b), like that of Fordism, covers a multiplicity of aspects of social life. It refers most clearly to the changing production methods used in industry, notably the shift from mass production to specialised production. This, in turn, is related to production for specialist market niches rather than a Fordist mass market, and takes place in a world market subject to intense international competition. And it also involves a changed relationship between the state and the economy, with corporatist forms of regulation being replaced by a more *laissez-faire* policy.

Many of the more radical changes suggested in this model have not in fact come to pass, especially in terms of state policy.[3] As Hardiman (1990) suggests, there are still strong tendencies towards corporatist politics, especially in countries such as Sweden and Austria who have strong traditions in this direction. Similarly, the economic significance of the large capitalist corporation does not appear to have declined in the way suggested by some writers who point to the growing role of small firms and flexible production (e.g. Lash and Urry 1987; Piore and Sabel 1984). Allen (1988a) shows that while average plant size in Britain has decreased the number of plants operated by large companies has increased and share of the largest 100 enterprises in manufacturing output has remained fairly constant. Much of the growth in small enterprises has occurred among service sector firms who mainly service the large companies. And, even in the private producer service sector, which in the 1980s saw a large increase in self-employment and small firms, there has more recently been greater rationalisation, with a considerable wave of mergers and acquisitions in recent years in accountancy, legal practices, estate agents and so forth, suggesting that large corporate ownership has come to predominate again (Leyshon and Thrift 1989).

Nor is there any evidence that the dominant propertied class – formed from the fusion of aristocratic, financier and industrial interests – has been undermined: indeed, if anything the reverse is true. John Scott's research (e.g. Scott 1989) has shown how most companies in Britain are dominated by what he terms a 'constellation of interests', in which relatively small groups of shareholders may combine to exert a dominating influence. Old capitalist families play a predominant role here. Similarly, analyses of the changing distribution of wealth have shown that in the 1980s the top 1 per cent of the population have increased their share of total income and wealth (Pond 1989).

The most significant change to which the concept of 'Post-Fordism' points concerns the changing relationship between organisations and capitalist accumulation. Whereas the Fordist firms benefited from drawing upon organisational hierarchies which allowed them to find a way of producing and distributing for a mass market, contemporary firms have found the institutional structures embodied by these organisational hierarchies a barrier to restructuring and to product innovation, and have developed a series of alternative ways of producing and distributing profitably.

The imperative of product innovation is particularly significant here. In the Fordist era the effectiveness of the large organisational hierarchies rested on their ability to distribute and market standardised products to mass markets rather than on their ability to develop new products. Large firms enjoyed a high degree of security offered by national tariff barriers. The renewed international economic competition caused by the erosion of such barriers has created a new economic climate where the development of new products able to compete internationally is central to economic success. And this leads to a new organisational shape, with the emphasis less upon co-ordination of diverse activities, and more upon creating frameworks which encourgage innovations.

The idea that the bureaucratic firm is in decline has been explored in three different bodies of work. Firstly, in Britain the interest in these issues has become focused on the idea of the 'flexible firm'. In Atkinson's (1984) well-known model, core workers, such as managers and professionals, become functionally flexible, moving between different strategic tasks quickly, while other workers become 'peripheral' and 'numerically flexible', so that they may be employed on temporary contracts and easily be dispensed with. The unfortunate problem with this interest has been that research has centred upon the question of numerical flexibility, or of functional flexibility among manual workers (Pollert 1988; Hakim 1987; Rubery 1988; Bagguley *et al*. 1990) and has not adequately discussed how these trends affect managerial jobs. The model seems to assume that all senior workers are functionally flexible and that companies increasingly rely on a key group of workers, who are insulated from the external labour market.

Secondly, American literature has developed the concept of the 'self-designing organisation' (Wieck and Berlinger 1989) that is more useful, though as in Atkinson's work it is as much prescription as description. These organisations are designed

> to take collective action in a continually changing environment that is evolving at a more rapid pace than in the past. The self-designing organisation seeks to match the variety in the changing environment with increased variety in the organisation.
>
> (Wieck and Berlinger 1989: 313)

And in such organisations managerial qualities are redefined. Loyalty and commitment, which as we have seen are central to the development of British managerial culture, are no longer so highly regarded. Indeed 'commitment can be a liability because it is a counterforce for change' (Wieck and Berlinger 1989: 313). In order that work is effectively performed, people's identities need to be 'de-coupled' from their jobs.

Finally, Stuart Clegg (1990) has argued that the Fordist organisation has given way to what he terms the 'post-modern organisation'. By this, he suggests that the centrality of hierarchical authority which defined the Fordist organisation – and which we have also argued is the basis for organisation assets – has given way to more plural types of organisational structure. He sees the rise of petty enterprise (as in French baking), and the influence of Japanese style organisations as being symptomatic of this general trend.

The crucial point that emerges from these accounts is that capitalist firms rely less on organisational hierarchies for many of their activities. Whereas the Fordist company had relied upon a pyramidical structure in which each manager was accountable to a superior manager – and hence all communication within the company flowed through the human agents at different places in the corporate hierarchy – this is no longer true. Market mechanisms, which Chandler argued were superseded by the 'visible hand' of managerial hierarchies, are reintroduced either explicitly (subcontracting, use of consultants), or implicitly (creation of internal cost centres). Capitalist organisations frequently prefer to employ specialists to carry out particular tasks. Sometimes these may be contractors, and at other times specialists employed within the organisation, but in both cases the point is the same: the specialists concerned do not owe their privileged position because of their place in the corporate hierarchy, but because they have specific competences and skills that can be used in a particular way. Coulson-Thomas (1988) argues that there are distinct trends in accountancy, and the business professions more generally, to move between specialisms.

> The expectation appeared to be that rather more of today's professionals would need to broaden their skills and become managers while the 'professional specialists' will increasingly work outside a traditional organisation on a consultancy or network basis.
>
> (Coulson-Thomas 1988: 7)

Much of this demand for new professional workers stems from corporate reorganisation consequent upon merger, privatisation, or restructuring. Hallet (1990) shows how the reorganisation of British Telecom into new divisional units, each operating as a separate cost and profit centre, created a considerable demand for the employment of accountants in order that the business activities of the respective units could be monitored.

Perhaps the most dramatic example of the way firms can restructure to dispense with a bureaucratic hierarchy comes from the use of franchises. In this situation a firm will devolve all managerial and organisational issues to people who run a particular outlet. While franchising is not an entirely new phenomenon – public houses are long-standing examples – its use has expanded dramatically since the mid-1970s, and many of the most dynamic firms in the 1980s adopted this format: outfits such as Benetton, Pizza Express, Pizza Hut, Kentucky Fried Chicken, McDonalds, the Body Shop, Swinton Insurance, Unigate, and so forth (Felstead 1990). Turnover in franchise businesses was expected to increase from £3.1 billion in 1988 to £7.7 billion by 1992, by which time employment in this sector is predicted to have reached 420,000.

Particular attention has also focused upon the structure of firms in the new 'hi-tech' and producer services sector, where high proportions of the workforce are professional. Kanter (1984), in a study of US 'hi-tech' companies, argues that this imperative leads to a greater use of teamwork. Rigid bureaucratic procedures get in the way of innovation, and as new procedures are developed the structure of the organisation changes. She argues that 'a more varied and less rigid internal labour market' develops in these firms (Kanter 1984: 124), that career patterns are more flexible, and that workers tend to move between functional specialisms, so allowing quicker promotion. She argues that the old pattern of the manager steadily being promoted to more and more responsible jobs within a functional specialism is no longer practised, but that workers are moved sideways, may work in teams, and in some cases firms use a greater number of specialists from outside.

In the British case Boddy *et al.* (1986) show that in Bristol there were a growing number of specialist workers, such as engineers, salespeople and professionals, employed by large firms. The same point is developed by Barlow and Savage (1986) and Savage *et al.* (1988) in their study of employment change in Berkshire, where much of the employment growth, in an area with a rapidly increasing private service sector, was for specialist workers with professional training.

These changes have had major implications on the career patterns and the spatial locations of many middle-class employees. Storper and Walker (1989) have argued that one of the effects of the decline of organisational hierarchies is the heightened importance of 'new industrial districts': areas where specialist types of production tend to congregate in order to reap the advantages of the agglomeration effects caused by their close proximity to other similar producers. Specialists with specific skills tend to settle in such places, facilitating the concentration of particular types of professional and specialist workers in these regions. This is likely to affect patterns of spatial mobility which impact on class formation: we pick up the implications of this in Chapter 8.

Career strategies also change. Organisational careers based on internal labour markets are undermined as the effectivity of organisation assets is reduced. Admittedly, research in this area is scanty. Gleave and Sellens (1984) argued that the use of internal labour markets was increasing, though they recognised the lack of research in this area, but recently Rubery (1988) has pointed to the weakly developed internal labour markets of many employing organisations. Nicholson and West (1988: Table 4.1) show that among managers 'self-directed career paths' are now as common as what they term 'conventional career patterns'.[4]

Whalley (1986) argues that there are major differences between old manufacturing and new 'hi-tech' firms in their reliance on internal labour markets. In a traditional Midlands manufacturing firm, most engineers hoped for internal promotion, while only a quarter had that expectation in a new London company. Rajan's (1987) work on banking is also revealing. He argues that in the rapidly growing financial services sector, the proportions of workers employed on career lines has been in rapid decline (see Table 4.1).

*Table 4.1* Percentage of workers in internal labour markets in financial services

|  | Banks | | Building Societies | | Insurance | |
|---|---|---|---|---|---|---|
|  | *1978* | *1985* | *1978* | *1985* | *1978* | *1985* |
| Career clerical | 61 | 41 | 45 | 30 | 62 | 56 |
| Non-career clerical | 30 | 40 | 49 | 55 | 25 | 26 |
| Specialists | 2 | 8 | 1 | 5 | 7 | 11 |
| Managers | 7 | 11 | 5 | 10 | 6 | 7 |

*Source*: Rajan (1987: Table 2.1).

Table 4.1 shows that the proportion of workers employed in internal labour markets has fallen from 68 per cent to 52 per cent in banks, from 50 per cent to 40 per cent in building societies, and from 68 per cent to 63 per cent in insurance companies. The proportion of specialists has increased considerably, testifying to the growing deployment of professionally trained workers within large organisations.

Our argument is also supported by the extensive evidence of the 'squeeze' on middle management (Scase and Goffee 1989). The role of middle management – which Chandler saw as central to the modern corporation – is undermined as the development of a series of social and technical innovations have also allowed firms to control their activities without using human intermediaries in the form of middle managers. Computerised technology may allow routine decisions to be made without recourse to middle or lower managers: Child (1986) shows that the growth of credit scoring in banks has led to a declining autonomy for branch bank managers. Appraisal and performance evaluation may allow the work of subordinates to be evaluated without being rigidly supervised on a regular day-to-day basis. Subcontracting allows activities previously carried out within the company to be provided on the market, and so forth.

We are now in a position to draw the threads together. Economic restructuring has involved a growing concern with product innovation, and capitalist firms which had previously relied upon organisational hierarchies increasingly look to either self-employed specialists or to professional specialists to carry out key tasks. As a result, the pyramidical organisational hierarchy is disrupted, and the power of organisation assets alone to convey reward is severely questioned. Firms increasingly look to those with specific skills to perform particular jobs, rather than rely automatically on bureaucratic procedures.

These developments are important in leading to a new role for formally educated and professionally qualifed workers. The division between the well-formed professional middle class, and the managerial middle class that characterised British middle-class formation for much of this century, is broken down as employers look to professionally educated workers to carry out specialist tasks. Professional workers, sometimes still employed by the state, may gain extra income through supplying specialist services to enterprises, and educationally qualified workers become prized commodities as employers recruit managerial staff. As we shall now discuss, these changes have severe ramifications on the strategies of managerial workers.

## THE DECLINE OF THE INTERNALLY PROMOTED MANAGER 1960–1989

The changes in organisational structures have reduced the extent to which organisation assets alone are viable axes for exploitation. As a result,

Table 4.2  Percentage of managers who have only worked in one company

| Researcher | Date of survey | Sample | % |
|---|---|---|---|
| Acton Society Trust | 1954 | 3,000 managers in large private firms | 44 |
| Clements | c. 1954 | 646 managers in 28 private firms in NW | 33 |
| Copeman | c. 1958 | 200 directors in British industry | 43 |
| Clark | 1964 | 818 managers in public/private firms in NW | 34 |
| Hall and Amado-Fischgrund | 1969 | 500 chief executives in GB | 46 |
| Birch and McMillan | 1970 | 964 BIM members | 17 |
| Deeks | 1970 | 229 managers in furniture industries | 14 |
| Lee | 1972 | 118 directors in private Coventry firms | 17 |
| Lee | 1972 | 48 managers in private Coventry firms | 23 |
| Guerrier and Philpott | c. 1975 | 1,304 BIM managers | 13 |
| Poole et al. | 1980 | 1,058 managers, BIM members | 14 |
| Alban-Metcalfe and Nicholson | 1983 | 1,364 BIM managers | 9 |
| Edwards | 1984 | 229 managers in large private industries | 24 |

Source: Studies listed in reference section.

managers increasingly attempt to convert their managerial position into more valuable assets. We discuss three ways in which this trend is visible. Firstly, there is the well-known propensity for managers to move between firms more regularly, which is a sign of increasing 'blockage' to internal promotions. Secondly, organisational careers offer less security to managers, so they are increasingly looking to convert their organisation assets into property assets by moving into self-employment. Finally, we shall examine the other trend, towards the professionalisation of management as managers attempt to convert organisation assets into cultural assets.

On the first point we can be brief. Numerous surveys of managers have indicated a growing propensity to move between firms. These do not need to be discussed here, since there are various summaries in Poole *et al.* (1981: Ch. 2), Edwards (1987: Ch. 3) and Lee (1981: 89ff). The basic findings have been tabulated in Table 4.2, and notwithstanding the variety of sampling procedures used, a clear trend appears.

Table 4.2 shows an apparently clear break between studies carried out before 1970 and those from 1970 onwards. All the studies carried out before 1970 reveal that a high proportion of managers – over a third – worked for one company all their lives. The proportion drops dramatically in those studies carried out after 1969, usually approaching 10 per cent.

Caution must be exercised in interpreting these figures. The surveys carried out by Birch and McMillan, Guerrier and Philpott, Poole *et al.* and Alban-Metcalfe and Nicholson are of members of the British Institute of Management. Since members of the BIM are more likely to see themselves as 'professional' managers they may be less likely to be loyal career managers, so biasing the sample. All the same, it is interesting that the most recent of the BIM studies, which the authors argue is comparable to previous ones, indicates a considerable decline for BIM members alone. Deeks' figures are from the, perhaps, unrepresentative furniture trades, characterised by small firms, while the samples from Lee and Edwards are rather small. Edwards' survey was of managers in large, 'blue chip' companies, perhaps accounting for the relatively high proportion of company loyalists.

The same picture is provided if we look at the proportion of managers who are highly mobile between firms: in 1958 only 13 per cent of Clements' sample had worked for four or more companies, but by 1983, according to Alban-Metcalfe and Nicholson, the proportion had risen to 43 per cent (see Nicholson and West 1988: 46ff).

The overall pattern of declining loyalty seems apparent. But it is also important to clarify how this is related to position in the organisation. In the 1950s and 1960s senior managers were more loyal: the figures given by Copeman and by Hall and Amado-Fischgrund – both for senior managers – are the highest apart from the Acton Society Trust's early study. This seems to be evidence that organisational loyalty brought its rewards in terms of promotion to senior jobs. The picture for the 1970s seems rather different. Lee's figures indicate that directors in Coventry exhibited less loyalty than more junior managers. It would appear that whereas loyalty tended to be rewarded by the company in the past, today it does not appear to lead to greater chances of becoming a director. These tend to be appointed from outside, and are hence testimony to the declining salience of the internal labour market that we have discussed above.

By the mid-1970s figures suggest that the differences between the loyalty of managers and professional workers were becoming narrower. Table 4.3 indicates the length of time spent by differing groups of middle-class employees with their current employer in 1979 (these figures have not been published in more recent *New Earnings Surveys*). It shows that managers were slightly more likely to be loyal than were professionals – which is especially true for women. However – except for senior managers – the differences are not marked, and professionals in services also exhibit high rates of loyalty to one firm. Only among welfare professionals and salespersons are there especially low rates of loyalty: in the former only

*Table 4.3* Percentage of occupational groups with differing lengths of service, 1979

| Occupational group | Less than 5 years (%) | 5–9 years (%) | Over 10 years (%) |
|---|---|---|---|
| | | Men | |
| 1 Senior Management | 21 | 20 | 60 |
| 2 Professional | 40 | 21 | 39 |
| 3 Professional: health, etc. | 40 | 29 | 31 |
| 4 Literary | 44 | 20 | 36 |
| 5 Professional: services | 28 | 22 | 50 |
| 6 Managerial | 30 | 20 | 50 |
| 7 Clerical | 32 | 25 | 43 |
| 8 Selling | 48 | 22 | 29 |
| 9 Security | 38 | 26 | 37 |
| All non-manual occupations | 35 | 24 | 42 |
| All occupations | 38 | 23 | 39 |
| | | Women | |
| 2 Professional | 48 | 24 | 28 |
| 3 Professional: health, etc. | 55 | 27 | 17 |
| 5 Professional: services | 55 | 27 | 18 |
| 6 Managerial | 42 | 25 | 34 |
| 7 Clerical | 56 | 25 | 19 |
| 8 Selling | 61 | 23 | 14 |
| All non-manual occupations | 56 | 25 | 19 |
| All occupations | 54 | 25 | 20 |

*Source: New Earnings Survey.*

31 per cent of men and 17 per cent of women have worked for their current employer more than ten years, in the latter 29 per cent of men and 14 per cent of women.

The trend towards greater managerial mobility could be explained in terms of push or pull factors. Managers might be frustrated by lack of promotion prospects in their company, or be attracted by opportunities elsewhere. It is extremely difficult to probe the importance of these by using conventional attitudinal surveys (as, for instance, in Nicholson and West 1988), since these will elicit self-justifications and excuses. Indirect questioning is of more value in probing this issue, and this suggests that considerably more managers think it very likely that they will move to a different employer or be made redundant in the next year than will be promoted (Nicholson and West 1988: 89). Indeed, only 6 per cent expected promotion![5] This tends to support the first idea, which is also consistent with our argument that as internal labour markets decline promotion prospects worsen.

The declining salience of organisation assets tends to force managers to convert their organisational position into cultural or property assets in order to provide a more secure base. The growing reliance on property assets is of particular interest here, and is manifested in a number of ways. Managers increasingly use their managerial experience as a springboard for an entrepreneurial career in which they attempt to maximise property assets.

In recent years the most notable examples of this have been as managers' 'buy-outs' of existing companies. Management buy-outs allow the managers of firms to become its owners. In over three-quarters of the companies bought out by managers, surveys by Bruce *et al*. (1990) show that managers held over half the shares of the reconstituted firm. The value of companies bought out by management rose from £50 million in 1980 to £1,176 million in 1985 before falling slightly in 1986 (Wright *et al*. 1987).

Buy-outs are, however, simply the most complete of a number of strategies by which managers are incorporated into a firm's owning interests. Executive Share Options (ESO) allow senior managers to gain direct ownership stakes in their firm, and by the later 1980s, encouraged by tax regulations, virtually all large firms in Britain had their own ESO scheme (Bruce *et al*. 1990).

Another dimension of the conversion of organisation into property assets is the movement of managers into self-employment. This is by no means an established empirical fact, but there is an increasing amount of evidence suggesting that it is of growing significance. Curran and Blackburn (1990) show that the numbers of registered self-employed rose from 2.0 million to 3.2 million between 1980 and 1988, while the number of companies registered for VAT rose from 1.3 million to 1.5 million between

1980 and 1987. This increase in self-employment has occurred in other advanced capitalist societies (Wright and Steinmatz 1989).

There is also clear evidence that much of the rise in self-employment is in sectors of the economy where large- scale enterprises have, until recently, been predominant. Curran and Blackburn show that the fastest rates of increase in self-employment between 1984 and 1987 were in 'metal goods, engineering, vehicles' (+47 per cent), the financial services (+34 per cent) and 'other production industries' (+32 per cent). And, throughout the whole range of manufacturing industry, the decline in the average size of firms is well known. In manufacturing the average firm employed 104 in 1972 but only 63 by 1982. These changes do appear to be related to changing managerial aspirations.

It is frequently argued that the rise in self-employment is caused by marginalised workers trying to make a living any way they can. It is clear that the idea that the self-employed are overwhelmingly recruited from marginal manual work, does not account for the increase in self-employment in its entirety. It is true that the rise in self-employment among ethnic minorities has been marked (Waldinger *et al.* 1985; Ward 1985), and can be attributed to the racist exclusion they experience in getting ahead in other ways (see the discussion in Sarre 1989). Rubery (1988) also argues that much of the increase in self-employment may simply be a response to unemployment, but Hakim (1989), and others, have shown that only a quarter of entrants to self-employment do so as a response to unemployment. Mason *et al.* (1989) found that 27 per cent of new starts in Hampshire since 1979 did so because of redundancy. Similarly, they show that those areas with the highest proportion of self- employed – especially in the south of England – tend to be the most prosperous.

As for more positive evidence, it would appear that the closest correlates of self-employment are coming from an employing or managerial background (Burrows 1990). It may hence be that a significant number of the self-employed will be marginalised workers whose reliance on organisation assets has proved insecure. It is certainly true that greater numbers of managers appear to be looking towards a future in self-employment, rather than to internal career progress. Peppercorn and Skoulding (1987) show that many managers now wish to work in small firms rather than large ones. According to their survey of over 2,000 managers, 23 per cent want to move into self-employment, almost as many as the 24 per cent who wish to work for large firms employing over 2,000 workers. Another survey found that one-third of managers in a manufacturing firm had a business on the side (*Management Today*, Feb. 1985). Nicholson and West (1988: 61) show that it is considerably more common for managers to move from large to small firms than vice versa. The route by which managerial workers move into self-employment is particularly well known in private services or 'hi-tech' employment, where it is known as the 'Fairchild' phenomenon (Dickens and Savage 1988).

It would appear that this route is favoured by those managers who are short of credentials – as an alternative, perhaps, to choosing the professional route. Highly educated workers seem relatively unlikely to enter self-employment. Outside the special sphere of professional self-employment, 'there is a strong inverse relationship between educational attainment and the propensity to self-employment' (Curran and Blackburn 1990: 11; Burrows 1990).

We have so far concentrated on the way in which managers may seek to convert organisation assets into property assets. The other route, towards the acquisition of cultural assets, appears to be of less significance. We are not convinced of the idea that managers are becoming professionalised, if this is taken to mean that managerial workers are becoming more likely to have an independent cognitive base allowing them a degree of independence from their employer.

Table 4.4 indicates that there has been only a slow and unspectacular rise in the proportion of managers with degrees – from around 19 per cent in older surveys to around 33 per cent more recently. This means that, given the considerable rise in the number of degrees awarded in Britain since the 1950s, managers are actually proportionately less well qualified than previously. The figures of Crockett and Elias are remarkable, indicating an exceptionally low level of educational attainment. Their figures, furthermore, are derived from the National Training Survey, which is probably more representative than the BIM surveys, which are more likely to represent qualified managers.

*Table 4.4* Educational qualifications of managers

| Survey | Date of survey | Graduates (%) | Oxbridge* (%) |
|---|---|---|---|
| Acton Society Trust | 1954 | 19 | 28 |
| Clements | 1954–55 | 25 | 38 |
| Clark | 1964 | 35 | 24 |
| Leggatt | 1970 | 21 | 14 |
| Melrose-Woodman | 1976 | 28 | 14 |
| Poole *et al.* | 1980 | 33 | 14 |
| Crockett and Elias | 1985 | 3 | ? |
| Gill and Lockyer (nd) | (*c.* 1980) | 33 | ? |

\* Oxbridge (%) means the proportion of graduates from Oxford or Cambridge.
*Source*: Studies listed in reference section.

It seems unlikely then that existing managers can upgrade their qualifications very easily. Although there has been a considerable increase in managerial education, much of this takes the form of short courses on specific, context bound topics and does not help to provide an independent cognitive base. Because this limits the extent to which they can pursue professional projects, managers tend to pursue entrepreneurial careers.

The weakness of time-served managers is further exacerbated by the growing use of management trainees who are groomed for senior managerial jobs, so reducing the opportunities of the non-credentialled managers. The proportion of graduate trainees who are given positions in large firms has increased very suddenly in the recent past. Until the early 1970s it was very rare for manufacturing firms to employ graduates (Bury 1973) and those firms that did accept them were sceptical of their value (Greenway 1973). By the early 1970s graduate unemployment reached a high level of 7.8 per cent (compared with 3.8 per cent nationally), and the relative cheapness of graduate labour encouraged a sudden increase in demand. Parsons and Hutt (1981) found a 16 per cent increase in graduate recruitment between 1974 and 1979 – a trend that continued into the 1980s.

This trend is part and parcel of the decline of the internal labour market. As top management becomes a specialism, graduate trainees are recruited as workers who can be rushed through the early stages of employment so that they are potential senior managers at a relatively young age.

The general implications of these trends can be summarised quickly. Junior managers, recruited from within the company, who previously had the possibility of slow progress to senior positions through internal labour markets now frequently find their way blocked, partly by the erosion of middle management, and partly by the growing use of specialists at the top. Insofar as they have many clear options, the most viable appears to be the attempt to convert their organisation assets into property assets. Professional workers, who relied overwhelmingly on either state employment or private practice, have, however, found a new series of openings as firms restructure, so increasing the advantages associated with cultural assets. The self-employed petite bourgeoisie, however – marginal throughout the century – takes on a new role as providers of specialist services to large companies, and from an infusion of managerial workers.

## RESTRUCTURING THE PROFESSIONAL MIDDLE CLASSES

If we have argued that there have been profound changes in managerial work, then what developments have occurred in the heartland of the professional middle class, in public sector employment and private practice? There is currently a considerable discussion concerning the applicability of the 'restructuring' thesis, developed by Massey (1984) and others to analyse change in capitalist manufacturing industry to areas outside manufacturing. Urry (1987), Mohan (1988), Pinch (1989) and Bagguley *et al.* (1990) have all argued that many of practices Massey identifies – such as subcontracting, rationalisation, investment and technical change – can be found, in various forms, in the public services.

While restructuring has undoubtedly taken place in many forms of public sector employment, it has also not been able to seriously dislodge the position of professional workers. Changes can only be implemented from inside the organisations concerned, in response to political pressure. The result has been that key groups of professionals well established in the public services have largely been able to deflect the adverse effects of restructuring onto other social groups within the organisation. Furthermore, they are also often well placed to take advantage of shifts towards the commodification of services by also engaging in private practice. The result, we suggest, is that the already strong presence of professional workers within British society has been enhanced, rather than undermined.

The initial starting point for this argument must be that despite political rhetoric to the contrary, public services have continued to expand, in various guises, even under a Conservative government apparently committed to reducing the role of the state. As Gamble (1988: 235) suggests,

> the institutional and cultural transformation required to make the free economy a reality, and a plausible accumulation strategy for the 1990s, has faltered because the Thatcher Government has so far rejected the need, except in a piecemeal fashion, to create the kind of machinery to carry through such a programme.

The course of public spending illustrates this most clearly. Not only has it not fallen in aggregate terms, but its degree of support for the middle classes might have actually increased.

As Dickens (1988: 1979) points out, public expenditure has actually risen slightly: in 1980 prices, central government spending rose from £30.5 million in 1975 to £34.7 million in 1985. Local authority spending fell only slightly, from £25.4 million to £24 million in the same period. And, the weight of public spending cuts have been unequal, falling primarily in areas of capital expenditure – notably the construction of council housing – which traditionally employ large numbers of manual workers. Le Grand and Goodwin (1987) show quite clearly that the area of expenditure most heavily restricted in the early 1980s was in public housing (where expenditure fell by over 60 per cent). This service was distinctive in that it was primarily directed to working-class consumers and provided by working-class suppliers, whereas most other services have either middle-class suppliers or consumers, or both. Dickens (1988) shows that staffing within local authorities has fallen in areas employing manual workers (notably in building and in refuse collection) but has been static or risen in those sectors

73

employing professional labour (teaching and social services). Pickvance (1987) demonstrates a similar point in examining the impact of 'contracting out' in local authorities. Senior workers within local authorities have been far less likely to lose their jobs through contracting out than manual workers.

In other areas the changing direction, rather than the amount, of public expenditure indicates the continued closeness of the relationship between professions and the state. A good example of this concerns changes in legal practice. On the one hand, the 1980s saw a series of government legislation which apparently undermined legal monopolies. The solicitors' monopoly on conveyancing was ended, as was the privileged position of barristers in having sole rights to represent clients in the courts. However, as Abel (1989) shows, these changes do not amount to much: the monopoly on conveyancing was not lifted but simply extended slightly and, generally, former solicitors have become the licensed conveyancers. Changes to the privileges of barristers will affect relations with solicitors and may well reduce the differentiation between them, but are unlikely to change the relationship between the legal profession as a whole and their clients.

As Abel (1989) also shows, there are contradictory tendencies at work in terms of the reliance of solicitors on the state for employment. On the one hand, it is clear that the proportion of lawyers directly employed in the public sector has fallen substantially, largely because of the inability of public sector salaries to compete with those offered in the private sector: 'between 1975/6 and 1985/6 the number of government solicitors with practising certificates grew at considerably less than half the rate of those in private practice and at only one fifth the rate of those in private employment' (Abel 1989: 315). But, to be set against this trend, is the fact that state-dependent Legal Aid Work has increased dramatically: between 1975/6 and 1984/5 legal aid payments to solicitors increased from £40 million to £281 million, and the rate grew even faster for Legal Aid Payments to barristers. While the state's role as a direct employer might be decreasing, it still underpins the privileged position of professional employees, while allowing them also to gain custom on the free market.

The situation in the health services is more complex. Here there is no doubt that overall state funding has actually increased, and employment in the National Health Services (NHS) rose by 11 per cent between 1976 and 1984 (Mohan 1988). Much has been written about the way in which restructuring has been directed at manual and ancillary workers (e.g. Bagguley *et al.* 1990: 70ff). Mohan shows that while the number of medical staff rose by 18 per cent between 1976 and 1984, and the proportion of nurses by 17 per cent, the number of ancillary workers fell by 10 per cent. This largely reflected the way in which ancillary services were contracted out, but professional services left secure. Child (1986) has also shown how hospital consultants, in contrast to bank managers, have been able to use new technology to augment their authority by controlling the interpretation of its results.

The growing public financial support for medical services is not in doubt. But there is more uncertainty concerning the significance of changes to managerial structures within the NHS. Some writers (Klein 1984) doubt the extent to which Conservative policy (at least until 1983) seriously attempted to erode professional powers. Other writers have emphasised the significance of tendencies apparent in the creation of General Management in 1985, as leading to the subordination of professional to managerial hierarchies (Flynn 1990). However, it needs to be recognised that this tension is long standing, and should not be seen as a new development (Heller 1978; Levitt 1976; Ham 1985). The real impact of the introduction of General Management is difficult to gauge. It has certainly eroded the position of nurses who previously shared management of the NHS, but who now need to enter General Management in order to have any managerial voice (Pinch 1989: 922). The male medical profession, however, seems less affected. Harrison (1988) argues that general managers accept the general professional culture, and more recent initiatives, especially the 'Resource Management Initiative' (which allows clinical budgeting to be introduced within the NHS), give greater power to consultants who are to take on executive responsibility for clinical performance (Dent 1990). Pinch (1989: 921) reports how in some Southampton hospitals it is assumed that 'since medical costs are expensive, the only persons who can effectively control them are doctors', but he also notes considerable variety in arrangements at other hospitals. Dent sees these changes of the 1980s as attempting not to subordinate hospital doctors to a new managerial hierarchy, but to police themselves through new managerial apparatuses, a development similar to that taking place in some areas of higher education, where new managerial grades are being created (principal lecturers within the polytechnics, for example) but are being recruited from existing professional workers. And here it is important to recognise that although NHS General Managers are sometimes appointed externally, the vast majority are internal appointees.

There is a crucial point to make here. Many accounts of changes in the professions in the 1980s continue to draw upon an outdated 'trait theory' whereby the loss of 'professional autonomy' is seen as a serious attack on professionalism. Starkey (1989: 391), for instance, talking of the introduction of contracts for professional workers, declares that 'we are witnessing a shift in power from professions to the state', when in fact, as we have seen, no such antinomy can be sustained: professional autonomy is based upon state intervention. The crucial thing is not the formal character of professional autonomy, but to consider how cultural assets are applied in particular contexts to achieve privileged rewards. In this respect the development of managerial structures, if they are to be filled by professional workers, may be of little real significance. One way of considering whether this is the case is to see if the market and work situation of these groups is actually changing in the light of recent initiatives. And, in this context, the evidence seems to suggest that many of the changes have had little real impact. Examination of the growing use of contracts in professional work shows that they do not, in themselves, indicate any substantial change in the position of professional employees. Beginning with Lecturers in Further Education in 1975, contracts have now been introduced in a variety of fields – most recently in general practice – and Starkey (1989) argues that they are testimony to the development of 'low-trust' relationships. However, Starkey's account (1989) shows that in some cases – notably among hospital consultants in the late 1970s – it was the professional groups themselves who began to agitate for contracts, since they felt that they would be able to use clauses specifying the length of the working week to claim extra, out of hours, payments. In other cases, workers themselves seem quite prepared to be governed by contract: Lecturers in Further Education saw their contract as a gain since it allowed their working time to be properly specified for the first time.

The changing professional division of labour is also witnessed by the changing pattern of gendered employment. As we have seen, the formation of the modern professional middle class has relied upon a gendered division of labour in organisational hierarchies, with 'ancillary' work being hived off to female workers. In the past two decades a far higher proportion of women have entered professional employment (Crompton and Sanderson 1990). Research suggests, however, that they are largely moving into newly emerging subordinate jobs within an expanded professional division of labour. Walby (1990: 26f) shows that while women are moving into higher status jobs, they are also concentrating more in specific types of employment there. Crompton and Sanderson (1990) discuss the rise of 'niche' jobs for professional women, where professional qualifications may be used to secure employment in permanent, relatively well-paid jobs, but where there is limited prospects of career development. Crompton and Sanderson also show the development of these niches in hospital pharmacies. Podmore and Spencer (1986) and Abel (1989) show that women solicitors are concentrated in certain types of legal work (conveyancing, family law and probate), tend to be less well paid, are more likely to be public employees, and are less likely to be partners in firms than their male equivalents. In accountancy young women are less likely to be partners than equivalent younger men (Crompton and Sanderson 1990). The developments in nursing, discussed above, also fit into the pattern whereby the restructuring of management usually has the most adverse effects on women workers. Although it is too early to demonstrate the point, it may well be that the expanded professional division of labour is related to new processes of demarcation as new professional specialisms emerge, and that women tend to be employed in the subordinate specialisms. Women can gain access to cultural assets, and gain qualifications, but these cannot be as easily applied in organisational or propertied contexts as they can for men. We return to this point in Chapter 7.

This discussion has indicated that the position of the professional middle classes has changed, but in an uneven and contradictory way. Apparent attacks on the position of professions – embodied in the use of contracts, or the undermining of legal monopolies – have not always had important effects in changing the market and work situation of these workers. This is particularly so since attempts to create managerial hierarchies within professional employment usually involve staffing these new hierarchies with professional workers. In this case the professional division of labour may be changing, but only if one holds to a 'trait theory of professionalism' can it be taken as direct evidence of decline.

*Table 4.5* Middle-class earnings, broken down by occupational group, 1973–89

| Occupational group | 1973 weekly earnings (£) | Increase 1973–79 (%) | Increase 1979–89 (%) | 1989 weekly earnings (£) |
|---|---|---|---|---|
| *Men employed full-time* | | | | |
| 1  Top managerial | 91.8 | +87 | – | – |
| 2  Professional | 58.3 | +121 | +213 | 404.2 |
| 3  Professional: welfare | 50.9 | +122 | +181 | 317.8 |
| 4  Literary | 50.3 | +128 | +190 | 331.8 |
| 5  Professional: services | 50.6 | +136 | +172 | 324.3 |
| 6  Managerial | 49.7 | +130 | +177 | 317.0 |
| 7  Clerical | 35.1 | +138 | +153 | 211.9 |
| 8  Selling | 38.2 | +147 | +156 | 241.5 |
| 9  Security | 45.2 | +131 | +164 | 275.5 |
| All non-manual | 48.1 | +135 | +186 | 323.6 |
| All occupations | 41.9 | +142 | +166 | 269.5 |
| *Women employed full-time* | | | | |
| 2  Professional | – | – | +220 | 302.8 |
| 3  Professional: welfare | 31.4 | +155 | +195 | 236.2 |
| 4  Literary | 27.3 | +197 | +202 | 244.9 |
| 5  Professional: services | – | – | +193 | 220.4 |
| 6  Managerial | – | – | +210 | 218.9 |
| 7  Clerical | 22.4 | +167 | +174 | 164.6 |
| 8  Selling | – | – | +201 | 142.3 |
| 9  Security | – | – | +201 | 246.9 |
| All non-manual | 34.7 | +167 | +195 | 195.0 |
| All occupations | 23.1 | +167 | +189 | 182.3 |

*Note*: Earnings are gross weekly earnings for full-time workers whose pay was not affected by absence. Dash (–) indicates no information because insufficient numbers.
*Source: New Earnings Survey.*

The key issue, we would maintain, is to determine whether legal and occupational changes have actually led to an erosion of the market and work situation of these employees. One way of surveying this issue is to consider evidence on changing patterns of earnings between different middle-class groups, to consider how they have changed over time. We can examine the changing character of pay differentials between middle-class groups by using the evidence of the *New Earnings Survey*, which has evidence on salary rates for middle-class occupations from 1973.

Table 4.5 shows that the dominant trend in middle-class pay between 1973 and 1979 was towards homogenisation: after 1979 towards diversification. In 1973 the small number of (male) top managers earned considerably more than the rest of the middle class: 57 per cent more than the next highest grouping (professionals), and 90 per cent more than male non-manual workers as a whole. The rest of the male middle class earned broadly similar amounts. Between 1973 and 1979 non-manual workers as a whole saw their earnings rise less quickly than manual workers, and those non-manual workers who had the largest proportionate rise were from the lowest-paid non-manual sectors (particularly selling and clerical). The differentials of top managers were particularly eroded in this period. Comparison with Raynor's (1969) figures show that the 1970s therefore marked the end of a long period during which managerial incomes had marched well ahead of those of other groups.

The figures on female pay are less useful, since there are data on only three female occupational groups. It was also clear that, at least for women employed full-time, their pay was rising faster than their male equivalents. So, it does appear to make sense to talk about growing middle-class homogeneity in this period. The effect of pay policy introduced by the Labour Government, the revelations of the Plowden Commission on Income and Wealth (which documented the extent and degree of salary differentials) and an economic recession produced, in this period, a more unified middle class.

Yet the figures for the period 1979–89 show a different story. They reveal that in contrast to the earlier period non-manual workers' earnings outflanked those of manual workers – indeed to a considerable degree. And, within non-manual work it was the lowest-paid sectors whose earnings began to fall back relative to those better paid. For men, the largest proportional increase in income has been among professionals (+213 per cent). These are primarily established professions, usually based in the private sector. Managers, on the other hand, continued to fall behind relative to other occupational groups (though there are no figures for top managers). The primarily public sector professionals in health, welfare and education have – despite frequent rhetoric to the contrary – not performed badly. Their rate of pay increase (+181 per cent) is only slightly below the average for all non-manual workers. The picture for women workers is also striking. In all cases the rate of increase for women employees is greater than for their male equivalents: a fact which suggests that women's access to middle-class employment is having significant impact on their earnings.

The rhetoric of the public sector under siege needs therefore to be treated with care. The professional middle class seems to have been able to insulate itself from the direct effects of public spending cuts. There have been changes in the structure of management in some fields, but we have argued that professional expertise always has to be applied to specific contexts through 'organisational projects'. We may simply be seeing a changing type of 'organisational project' rather than a fundamental under-mining of professional power as such. Since many professional workers are employed in managerial posts it remains to be demonstrated that these changes mark any serious erosion of the powers of cultural assets: indeed, it might be true that they reflect the growing 'currency' and marketability of professionally trained workers who have managerial experience.

## CONCLUSION

Economic restructuring, we contend, is having a major impact on the salience of the varying-class assets affecting middle-class formation. It would seem that the declining value of organisation assets has severe repercussions on the career strategies of middle-class employees. The currency of cultural assets has, however, been expanded, and the petite bourgeoisie's marginality has been offset to some extent by the increasing turn of managers to it. Some of the implications for processes of class formation – such as the declining importance of the managerial middle class – are already apparent from these observations. However, we have emphasised previously that classes are not, in our view, occupational groupings and can be affected by forms of exploitation which originate in other fields (to use Bourdieu's terms). We therefore postpone our examination of how the middle-class formation is actually changing until we have considered the significance of changes in the housing markets and in cultural processes, which are the subjects of the next two chapters.

# 5

# THE HOUSING
# MARKET AND THE
# MIDDLE CLASSES

## Class, tenure and capital
## accumulation

One of the most dramatic social changes in post-war Britain has been the expansion of owner-occupied housing. The proportion of households owning (or, at least, purchasing) their homes has increased from around 30 per cent in 1945 to around 70 per cent by 1990. There is currently a lively debate about the significance of this shift in hosuing tenures for social and political cleavages (see Saunders 1990; Barlow and Duncan 1989; Forrest *et al.*1990; Hamnett 1989). In this chapter we explore the idea that the restructuring of the housing market is of major significance in affecting the salience of petty property assets, and hence by implication the contours of middle-class formation.

Our argument is that owner-occupied housing is indeed playing an increasing role in structuring middle-class formation. We first show the historical processes by which middle-class people have moved into owner-occupation in order to show that the association between petty property ownership and the middle classes is relatively recent. Then we probe the relationship between the middle classes and owner-occupation in the contemporary period. Four issues command our attention. Firstly, we consider whether owner-occupation can be regarded as a 'middle-class' tenure by examining the types of people gaining access to it. Secondly, we consider whether capital gains can be accrued by purchasers of housing as a result of house price inflation, with implications for the social distribution of wealth and, hence, class formation. Thirdly, we consider the role of inheritance in providing windfall gains to middle-class households. Finally, owner-occupation may allow the possibility of 'entrepreneurial' activity, both in terms of housing 'strategies' for 'trading up' the market and also in the sense that it allows the release of equity for consumption or investment purposes. In the last part of the chapter we consider how these changes in the housing market are likely to affect processes of middle-class formation.

# THE MIDDLE CLASSES IN THE HOUSING MARKET 1890–1990

The association between the middle classes and owner-occupation is relatively recent. For much of the nineteenth century, and into the twentieth, only the petite bourgeoisie were heavily involved in the purchase of housing. The way in which small-scale landlordism represented a means of stabilising an essentially insecure economic position – and hence appealed to the marginal petite bourgeoisie – has been discussed in detail elsewhere (Ball 1981; Gauldie 1974; Kemp 1982, 1987; Rose 1981). Before 1919 nearly all housebuilding in Britain was for the private rented sector. Until the 1920s and 1930s, owner-occupation formed only a fraction of the total stock: around 10 per cent of householders owned their dwellings before 1914 and by the beginning of the Second World War the number of owner-occupiers had risen to almost 33 per cent (Merrett and Gray 1982; Ball 1983).

The first signs of a more general middle-class interest in owner-occupation can only be found at the end of the Victorian period. The late Victorian housing market was dominated by private renting, with new construction subject to broad boom and slump cycles (Weber 1955; Saul 1962; Habbakuk 1962; Parry-Lewis 1965; Gauldie 1974). This distinct boom–slump cycle was partly caused by the relationship between building and land costs and rent levels, but the changing nature of housing demand during the late nineteenth century was also significant. In particular, while the second housebuilding boom at the turn of the century may have initially been triggered by foreign investment flows (Habbakuk 1962; Pollard 1985), rising domestic demand, mostly from the middle classes, was probably a more important underlying factor. Particularly significant was the growth of new manufacturing industries outside the 'traditional' urban areas, which boosted the development of middle-class housing around London (Saul 1962; Gauldie 1974). It certainly was not due to working-class demand: average real wages declined between 1896 and 1910 and the salary necessary for a three-bedroomed suburban house (£150) was beyond the reach of the average skilled worker who might earn £110–£120. The expanding managerial and professional groups had greater choice in the housing market, however (see Jackson 1973), and they therefore fuelled the demand for this type of housing. Once the speculative boom had begun, investment capital poured into housing development. By 1900, though, problems of overproduction had emerged and investors – of whom there may have been as many as 300,000 (Pollard 1985) – sold their housing assets. Building societies began to accumulate surplus funds, but when the general trade cycle improved after 1906 there was a swing towards manufacturing investment, away from housing. In this way, therefore, the middle classes played an important and early part in boosting housing demand, but towards 1914 it appeared as if the shift towards owner-occupation might be reversed.

After 1918, however, the trend towards owner-occupation accelerated. During the 1920s and 1930s, the British housing provision system changed radically. Not only was there a fundamental shift in tenure, but for much of the inter-war period there was a massive building boom. Broadly, the inter-war era saw the replacement of a housing provision system dominated by private renting with one where two dominant forms of tenure emerged – public renting and owner-occupation. The state played a greatly enhanced role via the provision of local authority housing and speculative developers expanded the production of owner-occupier housing. In the 20 years from 1920 to 1940 over 4.6 million dwellings were completed, more than in the entire period from 1875 to 1919 (figures from Feinstein 1965). Annual housing completions grew rapidly from about 26,000 in 1920–21 to 350,000 in the mid-1930s (Merrett 1979; Merrett and Gray 1982; Ball 1983), with the highest annual output in 1927 and 1937. This represents a per capita housebuilding rate unmatched at any time before and after.

While the inter-war years represented something of a formative period for local authority housing provision in Britain, the overwhelming bulk of housing was provided by speculative developers, building largely for owner-occupation. Of the 4.6 million completions during the 1920s and 1930s, about 26 per cent, or 1.2 million, were built by local authorities. Owner-occupation as a housing tenure expanded from 10 per cent of the housing stock in 1914 (with the balance comprising private renting) to 32 per cent in 1938 (with private renting forming 58 per cent and local authority housing forming 10 per cent) (Merrett and Gray 1982).

The reasons for this boom in homeownership were related to both production and consumption factors. For much of the inter-war period building costs fell, from a post-First World War peak in 1920 to around half that level in 1933 (Feinstein 1965; Maywald 1954; Fleming 1966). During this period the housebuilding industry also saw a gradual improvement in productivity, as innovations in building materials filtered through (Bowley 1966; Ball 1978). Land prices also fell until the late 1920s – and even by the late 1930s, land prices were below their previous peak at the turn of the century. While the conditions for speculative housebuilding were right during the inter-war years – cheap land, a lack of planning, stable or falling building costs – levels of demand were also high, based on the expansion of middle-class groups, as discussed in Chapter 3. These new middle-class groups – especially those whose status within the middle classes was marginal – saw suburban owner-occupation as a reinforcement of their class position. Burnett (1986: 251) argues that these new middle classes were 'keenly anxious to demonstrate their arrival by the adoption of a lifestyle which separated them from the respectable poverty from which they had risen'. In addition, the squeezing of the traditional middle classes through increased tax rates, stagnating incomes and the rising cost of private education and domestic labour meant that the family size was decreasing and there was a demand for smaller houses. As Burnett (1986: 251) argues, there was 'a growing convergence of standards between the established members and new entrants to the class, reflected, among other things, by an increasing standardized type of house appropriate for a small family with little domestic help'.

Initially owner-occupation was more or less explicitly restricted to the middle classes (and above) because of the need for mortgagees to have a high and secure income. In practice, the minimum income needed was around £4 10s to £5 10s, the level of wage earned by skilled technicians, foremen, supervisors and inspectors, and clerical officers. Higher paid income groups such as teachers, bank officials, executive class civil servants and lower-paid professionals, with weekly earnings of £6 to £10, could afford to buy houses costing £1,000 or more (Jackson 1973). During the early part of the inter-war housing boom, therefore, the house-buying population was predominantly drawn from the higher income groups and salaried classes. By the early 1930s, though, this market had been saturated (Merrett and Gray 1982) and builders were seeking new markets among the lower paid. The expansion of the building society movement at this time was instrumental in this process, lending down market by lengthening the mortgage repayment period and reducing the size of the initial deposit (Boddy 1980; Craig 1986). In Greater London, though, the process of drawing in a wider group of owner-occupiers was retarded through a rise in average house prices at that time. According to Jackson's estimates, the average range in the late 1920s was £600–850, with a standard semi-detached house costing over £700. Between 1930 and 1935, the range was £550–1,000, with a standard semi-detached house costing upwards from £850 (Jackson 1973). *By end of the 1930s salaried professional and managerial workers were predominantly owner-occupiers*. One survey in 1938–39 showed that 65 per cent of civil servants, local government officials and teachers were homeowners. The working class were, however, unlikely to own: another survey, the previous year, showed that only 18 per cent of manual workers and non-manual workers with incomes below £250 per year owned their own homes (Merrett and Gray 1982).

Since 1945 the extent of owner-occupation has increased yet further, from around 30 per cent of the housing stock to around 67 per cent by the late 1980s. This growth has been especially dramatic since the election of a Conservative government in 1979 committed to expanding the 'property owning democracy'. To some extent this has reduced the association between the middle classes and owner-occupation: as the numbers of owner-occupiers grew, so increasing numbers were drawn from outside the middle classes. Yet, as Hamnett (1984, 1989) shows, there has also been a process of 'socio-tenurial polarisation', whereby council tenure is increasingly associated with the semi-skilled and unskilled working class, while virtually all the middle classes have owner-occupied dwellings. And, while Saunders (1990: 319) is right to point out that many owner-occupiers are not middle class – and indeed by the 1980s the majority of skilled manual workers were also owner-occupiers – there is little sign that the class differential in tenure is declining. Hamnett (1989) shows that although between 1961 and 1981 the proportion of the intermediate classes in owner-occupation increased, so did that of the professional and managerial groups, and their relative lead over other groups was little changed.

Furthermore, it is clear that while owner-occupation cannot be regarded in any simple way as a middle-class tenure, access to owner-occupation, which depends primarily on income, is still easier for those in managerial and professional work. Surveys continue to show that those in middle-class employment have the highest likelihood of moving into owner-occupation from other tenures. Savage *et al.* (1991) show that while 87 per cent of the children of existing council tenants in Guildford had moved into owner-occupation if they were in professional and managerial work, only 57 per cent of children in skilled manual employment, and 24 per cent of those in unskilled manual work, had done so. This finding is particularly striking since, as they are the children of council tenants, they are unlikely to have windfall money from inheritance to aid their move into owner-occupation.

## CLASS, TENURE AND CAPITAL GAINS

While owner-occupation is not necessarily a middle-class tenure, it has, as we have seen, developed initially due to middle-class demand, and the middle classes are strongly associated with it. The issue we now discuss is the extent to which the ownership of petty property is likely to convey material advantages. Might it be an indication of the growing importance of petty property assets for middle-class households?

There is certainly no doubting the economic significance of owner-occupation. Housing represents the major item of expenditure for most people, whether they are renting or, as is most likely to be the case today, buying. Historically vast amounts of capital have been tied up in the British domestic property market. In 1898, for example, the total of sales, leases and mortgages amounted to £393 million, compared to domestic exports of £233 million (Offer 1981). Today, around two-thirds of all dwellings are owner-occupied and at the height of the house price boom in 1988 some 1.7 million dwellings were bought and sold at an average price of £49,355 (Holmans 1990). In macro-economic terms the housing market is therefore extremely large, and there seems no intrinsic reason why it should not have a major impact on class formation, since a great deal of wealth is tied up in the owner-occupier housing system.

Debate centres around two issues. Firstly, to what extent can the money tied up in the housing market be extracted by households for their own benefit? Secondly, assuming that some gains can be made, are all owner-occupiers able to benefit or are its rewards selective? Opinion divides between Peter Saunders, who in a number of publications has celebrated the virtues of owner-occupation, and a more sceptical group of writers, such as Alan Murie, Ray Forrest and Simon Duncan, who question the general significance of owner-occupation as a vehicle for the acquisition of wealth.

On the first issue, Saunders is unequivocal. He believes that 'compared with non-owners ... owners gain irrespective of whether or not they can turn their assets into cash ... increasingly these capital gains are realizable and are being realized' (Saunders 1990: 155). On the second point Saunders is equally definite. He sees the argument that it is primarily better-off homeowners who make capital gains as fallacious and 'yet another example of left-wing sociological mythology' (op. cit.: 170). Let us consider these issues in turn.

The idea that owner-occupiers make money from owning housing is a popular one. It was recognised by the Conservative Party in 1979, and formed an explicit element in their housing policy. In the debate on the Queen's Speech following the May general election, Michael Heseltine stated:

> I believe that, in a way that was quite unpredictable, ownership of property has brought financial gains of immense value to millions of our citizens. As house prices rose, the longer one had owned, the larger the gain became ... It is not my purpose to argue whether the rate of gain has exceeded the rate of inflation or whether people have simply preserved their original asset in real terms. What it is my purpose to argue is that this dramatic change in property values has opened up a division in the nation between those who own their home and those who do not. The further prices advanced the further the tenant fell behind and no tenant fell further than the local authority tenant.
>
> (*Hansard*, Vol. 967, Cols 408–9)

It is certainly true that house price inflation in Britain has been endemic during the years after the Second World War. Since the end of the 1950s house prices have risen rapidly in real terms: over the entire period since 1943 real house prices have risen five-fold. During the 1970s and 1980s, however, the pattern has become increasingly cyclical, with price booms followed by sharp slumps (Ball 1983; Holmans 1990). This is largely because the housing system has become dominated by owner-occupiers, meaning that the matching of supply and demand has become more complex as chains of purchasers have grown longer, as well as changes in the supply of loan credit (Ball 1983).

No one seriously doubts the rise in house prices in real terms, and the potential this gives for capital gains, as owners are able to sell their houses for prices higher than the prices they bought them for. But the crucial question is whether these capital gains are actually achieved in practice. Duncan (1990), for instance, argues that transaction costs (costs to lawyers, estate agents and so forth), and routine maintenance and repair costs, will eat into any potential capital gain that might be made.

Saunders, using data from a 1986 household survey of Slough, Burnley and Derby, attempted to measure the capital gains for his sample of 450 households by comparing purchase and sale price of owner-occupied housing. He concludes that all groups of owner-occupiers make capital gains. The 'service class' made a mean gain of £3,024 for every year they had been owner-occupiers, while the intermediate class had managed to make £2,361 and the working class had made £2,277 (Saunders 1990: 171). Saunders argues that on a year-to-year basis, and controlling for the type of house purchased, the advantages of middle-class owner-occupiers over working-class owner-occupiers is quite small. The median real annual gain for the working class is 67 per cent of that of the service class. Saunders' data also show that the date of purchase in relation to the house price inflationary cycle plays an important part in determining the level of capital gain – the earlier the better – as does the value of the dwelling purchased – the more expensive the house, the greater the gains.

Saunders' research has severe problems, however. He excludes from his calculations the costs of maintenance and repair, etc., that Duncan argues might eat into any capital gain. More importantly, it is questionable that the annualised figures are as meaningful as those which indicate the total gain made by households over their entire lifetimes. Annualised gains are statistical artefacts, while total gains indicate the actual amount of money that differing types of households have made from their careers in owner-occupied housing.[1] Here, despite Saunders' equivocations, it is clear that the service class has made much more money from owner-occupied housing than the working class. According to Saunders' figures, the mean real net capital gain is £30,523 for the service class compared to a figure of £6,734 for the working-class owner-occupier, a massive discrepancy (see Saunders 1990: Table 3.3). The longer history of the middle classes in owner-occupation has allowed them to accrue much more money from it than is the case for the working class, who tend to have entered owner-occupation more recently.

It would appear then that the material benefits of owner-occupation have primarily gone to middle-class households. This is also the argument of Forrest and Murie (1990), who have also examined this issue. They argue that there are major divisions within owner-occupation, and that middle-class owner-occupiers have made far more gains from it than have working-class households. Forrest and Murie compared the housing and work histories of a sample of middle-class and working-class owner-occupiers in Bristol, and found fundamental differences in the capital gains achieved among the two groups. Among 25 working-class households the largest capital gain (measured here as the difference between the current, 1987,value of the house and the price of the first property purchased) was £22,750. Among the middle-class owner-occupiers the highest capital gain was £135,850, and *no households at all had made a gain of anything less than £65,000* (Forrest and Murie 1990).

One final point can be added here. Many of those who argue that owner-occupiers are a fragmented group and that the middle classes tend to gain more from ownership make much of the spatial differentiation in housing types, and particularly in house price inflation. Houses in 'middle-class' areas tend to increase in value faster than those in 'working-class' areas. This observation has been confirmed by subsequent research at all relevant spatial scales. At the regional level, the South East of England tends to have the highest rate of house price inflation. Although Hamnett (1984, 1988) has argued that regional house prices tend to even out, so that booms in the South East filter through to other regions after a few years, thereby maintaining a rough comparability of regional house prices, in the 1980s southern England appears to have moved further ahead of the rest of the country, although the property slump of the early 1990s will have eroded its growing lead.

Figure 5.1 shows average house prices in relation to the national average. It shows that the gap between London and the 'Rest of the South East' (ROSE) and the other regions opened up during the early 1970s and late 1970s bouts of inflation, with a period of convergence during the 'inter-inflationary' years. Since about 1980, however, there does seem to have been a steadier divergence between the South East (and East Anglia and the South West) and other regions during the house price boom of the 1980s. Northern regions, Scotland and Wales have seen a steady divergence from the national average, such that in 1987/88 the 'spread' between the regions was much greater than in 1973. It is also the case that the total percentage rise in house prices since 1969 is noticeably greater in London, ROSE, East Anglia and the South West when compared to the rest of Britain (see Hamnett 1988: Table 2; Evans 1990: Table 4). This implies that southern England has seen a much faster inflation in house prices during the last two decades or so, and that this will still remain despite the house price falls of the later 1980s.

This growing 'gap' between the South and other parts of the United Kingdom is even more evident when we look at the absolute price differences between the most expensive and the cheapest regions. In the first

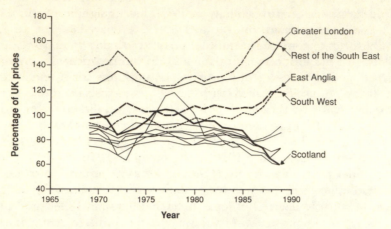

*Figure 5.1* Regional house prices in relation to UK house prices
*Source*: Housing and Construction Statistics

quarter of 1990, the 'average' dwelling in Greater London cost £87,266, according to the Nationwide Anglia Building Society. In the Outer Metropolitan Area the average dwelling was slightly more expensive, at £87,631, and slightly cheaper in the Outer South East (£74,547). In the Northern region the equivalent cost was £43,991, while in Northern Ireland the average dwelling was only £28,997. For over fifteen years the gap between the cheapest and most expensive region for house prices has been growing: in 1975 the average price in the cheapest region was 64 per cent of the average in the most expensive; in 1980 it was 60 per cent, in 1985 it was 54 per cent, and 33 per cent in 1990.

The same point is also evident at smaller spatial scales. Coombes *et al.* (1990) show that in the 1980s the considerable variation in local house prices can best be accounted for by the proportions of professionals and managers living in different local labour market areas. In other words, those areas with the highest proportion of professionals and managers tended to have the highest house prices in 1985. This indicates that professionals and managers appeared to be best placed to buy the most expensive forms of housing, and also that they stand to gain most in absolute terms from further house price inflation.

In short, rather than being an example of 'left wing sociological mythology' as Saunders suggests, the evidence firmly points towards the conclusion that middle-class households have been able to accumulate far more money in the course of their housing careers than have working-class households. The amount of capital gains made by middle-class households in the course of their housing careers appears to be considerable, in absolute terms, and this suggests that the ownership of petty property in the form of owner-occupation may well be of major significance in structuring middle-class formation.

The advantages enjoyed by middle-class households do not stop here, however. As well as appearing to gain most from house price inflation there is also some evidence that the middle class pay less for it, since some employees gain significant help with their housing costs from employers. Although admittedly there is little firm evidence on the question of employer-related housing subsidies, these subsidies seem to take a variety of forms, ranging from grants for fixtures or fittings to complex mortgage enhancement schemes. Salt (1990) and Forrest and Murie (1989a) have suggested that these subsidies may be of considerable importance to certain households in specific sectors of the labour market. A Confederation of British Industry survey of 208 firms in the South East in 1988 (CBI 1988) indicated that 80 per cent offered specific measures to employees to encourage them to move into the area. However, there were distinct differences in the type and amount of subsidy and help depending on occupation. For staff transferred into the area at the company's request, almost half (46 per cent) of professional and managerial employees were offered financial assistance towards housing costs compared to 31 per cent of manual, technical or clerical staff. Over half the professional and managerial staff were given increased pay on the move, compared to 44 per cent of manual, technical and clerical staff. In the case of new recruits moving to take up a job, only 27 per cent of professional/managerial staff, and 14 per cent of manual, technical and clerical staff, were offered financial assistance towards housing costs.

In a survey of purchasers of converted flats in London it was found that a relatively high proportion (29 per cent) of the respondents were in receipt of some form of employer-related support towards their housing costs. This mainly took the form of mortgage subsidies or reduced interest loans (61 per cent of those receiving support) and housing allowances (22 per cent) (Barlow and Hamnett 1987).

The importance of employer-related housing subsidies is that these households are, as Forrest and Murie (1989a: 353) point out, 'effectively cushioned from the vagaries of the (housing) market. For this group, movements in interest rates and the retention of mortgage interest tax relief may be of little significance'.

There are also important implications here for the transmission of class assets between generations, in the form of property. The growing significance of housing inheritance is also a much debated topic within housing research (Saunders 1990; Forrest and Murie 1989b). The growth of owner-occupation since 1945 suggests a growing number of houses being inherited as existing owners die. As a result, while residential property was only 24 per cent of the total value of capital estates in 1968–69, this rose to

42 per cent by 1982–83 (Saunders 1990: 158). In one respect this may be seen as being likely to 'democratise' inheritance, as more and more people stand to gain something by inheriting the houses of relatives: as Saunders (1990: 160) suggests, 'we may expect that many households across different classes and regions will inherit significant amounts'.

In fact, the extent of inheritance is still quite restricted. The most recent survey, in 1988, found that only 9 per cent of households had inherited property (Harmer and Hamnett 1990). And inheritance is class specific. Of crucial importance in affecting the chances of inheriting at least in the next decade or so is the length of time a household has spent in owner-occupation. Houses are normally purchased when a household is relatively newly formed, and it will take several decades before it is likely that they will die and pass on their property: thus 95 per cent of inherited property is owned outright, suggesting that it has been bought at least 25 years before. Hence, those groups with long histories in owner-occupation are more likely to be the immediate recipients of the benefits of inheritance. As we have seen above, these tend to be middle-class, rather than working-class owner-occupiers.

Most of the inheritors – usually children of the deceased – will already be owner-occupiers, since they will probably be well into middle age. It is therefore likely that they will use the windfall for investment purposes, so becoming increasingly reliant on the returns made possible by investment. In one survey, 11 per cent of respondents declared they would use the money to start themselves in business (Saunders 1900: 160).

The answer to the capital gains question therefore seems to be that not everyone makes equal amounts of money out of homeownership. It all depends on geographical location, length of time in owner-occupation, the value of dwellings purchased and dates of purchase and sale. But – and this is the crucial point – the middle classes are generally more likely to be in situations where returns can be achieved. Their greater length of time in owner-occupation is likely to increase the amount of absolute gains accumulated and to increase the chances of inheritance taking place. Their greater income and longer history in owner-occupation also allow them to occupy more expensive housing which tends to inflate in price more. They tend to live in those areas – in the South and the suburbs – which see greater house price rises. In short, the evidence – including that provided by Saunders – shows that the middle classes have benefited more from homeownership than the working classes, and that most of them have derived considerable financial gains from owner-occupation.

## HOUSING 'CAREERS' AND 'ENTREPRENEURSHIP'

It appears to be true that homeownership is a source of considerable wealth for many middle-class households. But can we take the argument a stage further and argue that they are pursuing 'entrepreneurial careers' through homeownership? In a study of affluent homeowners in Bristol – all professional and managerial 'executives' – Ray Forrest and Alan Murie sought to shed light on the extent to which certain households 'actively manipulate the housing market to climb a housing ladder ... (making) decisions about when to move and what to buy related to obtaining the best return through housing transactions' (Forrest and Murie 1989a: 336). A further objective of this research was to test the Farmer and Barrell (1981) hypothesis that there is a social group from which small business proprietors are traditionally drawn which channels its entrepreneurial energies into housing speculation rather than business activity.

From the research it is clear that the evidence for such a group is, to say the least, confused. As Forrest *et al.* (1990: 155) put it, 'Farmer and Barrell's representation of this group suggests that it is an exotic group with secure jobs rather than a large sector of homeowners. Attempts to identify the group in practice suggest they are a minor protected species.' Again, there are a number of contradictory research findings. Forrest and Murie (1989a) argue that this type of 'entrepreneurial' homeowner is more likely to be one for whom mobility and occupational careers are not of paramount importance, in highly paid jobs which do not involve regular relocation. 'But', they argue, 'the case is not proven' (Forrest *et al.* 1990: 156). Saunders (1990), however, takes a different view. He argues that almost a fifth of households in his survey expresses an investment view of the benefits of owner-occupation (although an investment view is not always commensurate with investment behaviour). Saunders also brings forward other evidence – notably the various surveys of the reasons for housing moves – to support his claim that the bulk of households move for investment reasons:

> The fact that so many owner-occupiers now move so frequently, and yet move across such small distances and without any employment-related motivation, can only be explained by the fact that many of them are following a deliberate and coherent investment strategy through the housing market.
>
> (Saunders 1990: 200)

While it is true that the frequency of moves has grown in recent years, and the average distance moved tends to be relatively low, this does not inevitably mean that owners are behaving 'entrepreneurially'. Demographic shifts, such as a growth in the number of young and elderly households, rising levels of divorce, as well as the changing structure of the labour and housing market, the location of schools and transport facilities, are all likely to influence the rate and pattern of household mobility.

Entrepreneurial housing strategies might not be so much investment directed as use-value directed.

There is some more evidence on this issue. It is noteworthy that in a survey of purchasers of converted flats in central London during the height of the house price boom in 1987 (Barlow and Hamnett 1987), it was found that few households had moved from their previous residence expressly for investment reasons. The reasons for moving were heavily conditioned by the type and tenure of their previous residence. For example, around two-thirds of households previously living in flats moved in order to obtain a larger dwelling, while 29 per cent of previous houseowners moved because of a change in family circumstances (usually divorce or separation). Not surprisingly, over two-thirds of ex-private tenants said they had moved in order to buy a dwelling. When the relationship between the purchase price of the current residence and sale price of the previous residence was examined, it was found that there was no clear pattern of 'trading-up' moves (where people move to more expensive housing, using capital gains on the sale of their existing property to pay a larger deposit). Previous houseowners were balanced fairly evenly between movers up and movers down the market, while previous conversion-owners tended to have traded down. Only respondents previously living in purpose-built flats had moved up-market to any extent. Given the buoyancy of the housing market at that time and the fact that most households were in relatively well-paid professional or intermediate occupations, we might therefore have expected more housing 'careerists' than was actually the case. We must therefore conclude, along with Forrest *et al*. (1990: 157), that there is 'little evidence that people pursue housing careers in the sense of planned, long-term trajectories related to maximising financial gains'.

However, although it appears that relatively few households behave in an overtly entrepreneurial way in housing career terms, a number of households are certainly able to use the housing system to release equity for non-housing-related activities. Considerable attention has been paid in recent years to the amount of 'equity release' from the housing market, whether through remortgaging, overmortgaging, specific old-age equity release schemes, or inheritance or trading down. Estimates of the amount of capital released in this way vary from about £6 billion per annum in the mid-1980s to £12 billion (see Saunders 1990: 155–63 for details). Remortgaging, overmortgaging and trading-down are estimated to have generated some £4 billion a year in the mid-1980s (Holmans 1986). Each year during the early 1980s the General Household Survey indicated that 4–5 per cent of owners had raised loans on the security of their homes and used the proceeds for purposes other than the purchase of their current accommodation (see Forrest *et al*. 1990). While most (60 per cent) were using the money to improve or repair their homes, almost a fifth (19 per cent) were using the loan to finance business ventures. Saunders' survey showed that a much larger proportion had taken out money through remortgaging or overmortgaging (a third) (Saunders 1990). This procedure was more common for middle-class households and owners of higher value housing: 40 per cent of the service class had extracted money this way. Not surprisingly, most households (87 per cent) had used this money for repairs and improvements. In addition to this group of households a further 9 per cent had raised loans on their dwelling, with over half spending this money on things unconnected with the house. Eleven per cent of households had traded down at some stage. Clearly, then, equity withdrawal from the housing market for non-house-related expenditure is not negligible in Britain, although it is likely to follow a cyclical path depending on the prevailing real rate of interest.

The identity of these households is not possible to determine. Neither Saunders (1990) nor the General Household Survey breaks down the group withdrawing equity from the housing market in any detail. However, we can derive some clues from the work of Geraldine Pratt on Vancouver owner-occupiers (Pratt 1989). She argues that self-employed workers (at least in Vancouver) display a more pragmatic and rational approach to the housing market, often preferring to rent. This is said to be partly because of the greater variability in personal incomes of this group, but also because of a 'concern that mortgage debt traps one in a job or saps one's entrepreneurial initiative' (p. 306). However, it was also clear in this survey that a number of households had used the inflationary housing market to amass capital and start business ventures. She concludes that for this group 'work was a central concern and homeownership was put to work in the service of the business' (p. 306). If her arguments are applicable to Britain, it suggests we have come full circle since the 1890s. In that period the petite bourgeoisie were heavily involved in owner-occupation: today it would appear to be the salaried middle classes who are more active.

## OWNER-OCCUPATION AND CLASS FORMATION

We have established the case that petty property ownership is of increasing significance for large numbers of middle-class households. We now begin to draw out some of the implications of this argument in order to show how it may have wider significance in affecting processes of middle-class formation. Two issues command our particular attention. Firstly, we consider how the growing importance of petty property assets relates to that of cultural assets, whose growing significance we pointed out in Chapter 4. Secondly, we consider the significance of petty property on household relations, and suggest that it may well lead to the increasing significance of household type in affecting middle-class formation.

In Chapter 4 we emphasised that cultural assets have become greater currency in middle-class employment as the security offered by organisation assets has been reduced. The emergence of owner-occupation encourages a situation where the middle classes can also draw upon petty property assets. One consequence of this pattern is the trend towards the investment of cultural capital in housing. Cultural assets, rather than being confined to 'pure' artistic or leisure fields, are increasingly invested in housing, so that the aesthetics of the middle-class residence plays a major part in the exhibition of specific cultural tastes and values.

This is a recent development. Oliver *et al.* (1981) argue that in the 1920s and 1930s owner-occupiers rarely took a great interest in the aesthetic character of their houses. Prospective purchasers in a given area were faced by a relatively limited choice of semi-detached housing. Nevertheless,

> the success of housing of this type suggests that by a subtle alchemy the combination of Arts and Crafts domestic design, speculative development and house purchasers' needs and desires, produced a model which had wide appeal to the newly suburbanised class.
>
> (Oliver *et al.* 1981: 203–4)

Oliver *et al.* see the design of inter-war suburban housing as reflecting and reinforcing an individualistic philosophy; one placing emphasis on private ownership, self-determination and social mobility as the keys to personal development. One result of catering on a mass scale for such individualism was that estates were 'rarely designed positively as significant places in their own right' (Oliver *et al.* 1981: 114). Minor design variations were used in the inter-war estates to emphasise individuality. Thus two adjoining semi-detached houses would be provided with relatively superficial additions. Housing estates nevertheless contained a very limited number of housing types. Developers were aiming to reduce their risks as much as possible and they therefore targeted what they saw as a mass market. At this stage architects promoting the modern movement in architecture were relatively unsuccessful in influencing the design of new housing. According to Oliver *et al.* this was because the imagery of the new style was too close to that of the factories in which much of the population worked. This factor, together with the reaction against the Victorian terrace from which many of the lower middle-class purchasers had come, mitigated against the development of the 'Sunspan' house or other 'modern' designs.

In the present period, however, the situation has changed. The growth of owner-occupation and the salience of cultural assets has led to a growing concern to invest cultural assets in order to provide the kinds of housing that enhance cultural distinctiveness. As a result, developers have begun to produce certain types of housing targeted at key social groups. The geographical location of housing demand (and price) have long been the principal preoccupations of private developers but there is today a far greater concern with the precise nature of effective demand than was the case in the inter-war years. Although there is as yet little detailed empirical research on this topic, it seems that this aspect has become increasingly important during the 1980s as the market for first-time buyer housing – the 'starter homes' of the 1970s – started to decline.

For developers housing demand has become increasingly fragmented into 'niche markets': 'active retired', 'empty nesters', 'first-time buyers', 'lifestyle units' and so on. In a survey of developers in Berkshire in 1988 a number of firms voiced their concern that consumers were becoming increasingly discerning (Barlow 1990). As a result, these firms were increasing their expenditure on marketing and paying more attention to 'kerbside appeal', or the immediately attractive features of their housing. Advertising material for new housing increasingly focuses on imagery and lifestyle for certain targeted groups. This might involve proximity to particular forms of cultural consumption such as marinas or sporting facilities, or an emphasis on the historic associations of the locality in question (see Thrift 1987). One builder advertised an estate (in nine languages) in the following way:

> Master Builder provides the ultimate living experience in Wiltshire. In the Roman Village of Shaw, nr. Swindon, Roger Malcolm, the master builder, is building the finest home setting in Britain. Only when you view our home quality will you know the claim to be justified. Share in the highlife-style of a small exclusive community with Residents Club House, Swimming Pool, Tennis Courts at your disposal ... Choice of Five Superb Designs, 3 or 4 bedrooms; 2 or 3 bathrooms, Finest Kitchens in Europe ... Eight only to be built per year.
>
> (In *Financial Times* 1/8/84)

Developers have therefore become increasingly concerned with the fragmentation of the market. They now cater for and actively support the attempts of different groups to assert their social-cum-personal identities. Especially important are distinctions resulting from different stages of the life cycle (with resulting changes in the household sizes) and the acquisition of cultural or symbolic capital by those with high levels of economic assets. And, as Evans points out:

> advertising and marketing has become an increasingly important part of the selling process. The portrayal of lifestyles and other forms of imagery associated with the house are relied upon heavily. Brochures advertising housing will put a lot of emphasis on the lifestyles the future occupant might enjoy.
>
> (Evans 1990: 13)

The best documented contemporary example of this general trend is in gentrification – the conversion of old, urban housing into that geared to the relatively affluent middle classes (Zukin 1985; Smith and Williams 1987; Smith 1987b; Mills 1988; Jackson 1991). Jager (1987), borrowing from Bourdieu, argues that a new middle class defines itself as a distinct social group precisely through such residential conversions. On the one hand, the process of gentrification gives it status. It indicates that they are in possession of a particular kind of culture, one which entails some knowledge of 'history' or 'tradition'. And such knowledge provides them with a certain kind of distinction, it 'expresses their candidature for the dominant classes' (p. 80). On the other hand, this newly emerging social group is anxious to distinguish itself from the working class. While these people may own old working-class housing, they remain anxious to engage in various forms of restoration which make their homes distinct from those of the genuine working class. So although, for example, old materials are used in the construction of these houses, they are used in a cleaned-up, sanitised, form. History is incorporated (including, in the Australian case, genuine bricks with the thumbprints of nineteenth-century convicts!) but in a sandblasted or whitewashed form which allows the resulting product to remain distant from origins as a working-class slum. Yet in the very same process they also protect the economic potential of their housing.

Gentrification is of particular interest for a number of reasons. It appears to testify to the growing prominence of professional workers in the housing market. Damaris Rose (1988) argues that – at least in Montreal – gentrifiers tended to work in professional rather than managerial employment. In particular, it appears to be the less affluent professionals, confined to the less responsible field of employment, who play a particularly important role (see also Marcuse 1990). In part this reflects their need to minimise costs in transportation and service provision, but it may also be related to efforts to maintain cultural distinctiveness in the home when it proves particularly difficult to do this at work. Gentrification is hence indicative not only of the growing prominence of professional workers in the housing market, but also of differentiation between groups of professionals.

The really important point, however, which arises out of a consideration of gentrification, is the importance of the household. Randolph (1990), when discussing the relationship between labour and housing market, makes the vital point that while individuals enter the labour market, the housing market is populated by households. Hence, for this reason, the growing salience of petty property assets has the effect of heightening the specific importance of differing types of household structure on middle-class formation. In the case of gentrification feminist writers such as Rose (1988) have shown that it is the household characteristics of gentrifying groups that give them their most distinctive character. She shows that many gentrifiers are single women, and most of these households have no children. The location of groups of gay men in specific urban locations is testimony to the same point (in the case of San Francisco, see Castells 1983).

The evidence is clear that specific housing areas are taking on particular roles, geared to differing household types. Within the South East very specific subregional housing markets have developed, allowing particular types of middle-class households to concentrate in particular areas. According to Barlow (1989) there have been distinct differences in house price inflation in the South East, according to the type of housing and the subregion. Barlow suggests that these trends are related to the way housing demand has shifted around the region, with local housing markets playing specific roles within the broader regional structure. London stands out in its high proportion of young first-time buyers, followed by Kent, Bedfordshire and East Sussex. Surrey has by far the lowest proportion of first-time buyers. There are also distinct variations in the average age of purchasers: the youngest buyers are in Bedfordshire and the oldest are in East and West Sussex. This is related to the numbers of retired purchasers on the south coast. In terms of employment status and income it appears that the typical buyer in Surrey and Berkshire is the relatively well-paid professional and managerial employee, whereas in London he or she may be well paid but is more likely to be in a junior managerial or clerical position. Skilled manual employees form a proportionately larger share of the market in Kent, Bedfordshire and Essex, and have a lower than average household income. Both London and Surrey stand out, albeit for different reasons. London purchasers are commonly first-time buyers in higher-earning junior managerial or clerical jobs. These owner-occupiers also tend to be slightly older than average. In Surrey, however, buyers are most likely to be highly paid professionals or managers, who were also previous owner-occupiers. This information therefore confirms that the owner-occupier housing market in the South East is segmented according to very specific types of socio-economic status and household structure.

In Chapter 2 we drew attention to the way in which a common set of patriarchal gender relations may serve to unify the middle classes into a possible 'service class'. The rise of petty property ownership, we contend, is likely to fragment the middle classes since it tends to emphasise the significance of household types (single person, dual earner, with or without children, and so on) as determinants of particular types of property ownership. The various types of middle-class household are increasingly becoming categorised by household type into different housing areas: gentrified areas of single people; suburban areas of nuclear families; retirement areas, and so on. We pick up the full implications of this in Chapter 8.

We have now investigated the changing salience of organisation assets and property assets in contemporary Britain. We have also touched upon the growing presence of cultural assets, and their increasing currency outside the specfic spheres of employment with which they have been historically associated. We now complete our analysis of the changing effectivity of the assets affecting middle-class formation by considering the nature of cultural assets in contemporary Britain in more detail.

# 6

# CULTURE, CONSUMPTION AND LIFESTYLE

There are many cultural images of the middle classes, but two distinct views prevail. On the one hand, the middle classes are respectable, traditional and deeply conformist, like the middle classes of George Orwell's *Keep the Aspidistra Flying*; on the other is the modernist inspired idea that the middle classes are 'cultural standard bearers', avant garde, radical and innovators of new cultural styles and forms.

Until the 1960s it was usually felt that the former cultural pattern was becoming more common. The 1950s in particular saw a series of laments about the conformist character and weak cultural calibre of the middle classes, from C. Wright Mills' *White Collar* and W.F. Whyte's *Organisation Man* to the 'Angry Young Men' depicted by John Osborne and Colin Wilson. But since this period the tide has turned, and from the 1960s the middle classes have increasingly been hailed as the cultural dynamos of modern (or post-modern) times. For Gouldner (1979) they are the 'new class', able to generate progressive cultural and political projects. For Ingleheart (1971) they are the repositories of 'post materialist values'. For Pfeil (1988) and Lash and Urry (1987) they are the social bases of post-modern culture.

To what extent is this apparent cultural shift linked to a wider change in the nature of cultural assets? To what extent is the form of cultural capital we alluded to in Chapter 3 – based around an aristocratic derived appreciation of 'high cultural' aesthetic practices – still of major importance? In what ways have cultural assets themselves been democratised or restructured?

Our argument inevitably takes its starting point from Bourdieu's pioneering account, but we shall suggest that it has some theoretical weaknesses, which means that it cannot be applied wholesale to the British situation. In order to remedy this we shall then draw upon a hitherto relatively unused survey of spending patterns among the British middle classes to refine and develop his approach.

## LESSONS FROM BOURDIEU

As we saw in Chapter 1, Bourdieu's focus is on the interplay between cultural and economic capital. His key point is that people actively invest cultural capital to realise economic capital – and vice versa. The complex interplay between these two forms of capital gives rise to the emergence of a number of different social groups. He varies in his analysis of these, but tends to focus upon three. Firstly, there is a dominant class – the 'industrialists' and managers of large-scale capitalist enterprises. These have large amounts of economic capital, but less cultural capital. Secondly, he identifies what he calls 'the new petite bourgeoisie', a group of people in the fast-developing service sectors such as marketing, advertising, public relations, the media and the helping professions. These he sees as well endowed with cultural capital. Indeed, they tend to be standard-bearers and taste-setters for other groups, including the 'industrialists' and senior managers. Finally, there is a group that is typically low in economic capital and high in cultural capital: the teachers, the artistic producers and the intellectuals. The 'new petite bourgeoisie' has some similarities with this group, although their levels of economic capital are higher and their lifestyles remain quite distinct from those of the intellectuals and artistic producers. (For a discussion see Honneth 1986).

It is important to recognise that Bourdieu is not providing a new classification to set alongside more orthodox ones here. As he states, 'as far as classes are concerned I wanted to break away from the realist view ... which leads to questions of the type, 'are intellectuals bourgeois or petit bourgeois?' – questions ... about limits and frontiers' (Bourdieu 1990: 49–50). He is more concerned with drawing attention to the dynamic process of class formation as it arises out of the interplay of the two assets.

Thus the greater part of *Distinction* is a detailed analysis of relations and struggles between these groups in France in the 1960s. He argues that they all have common interests in the status quo. All are broadly concerned with legitimising and reproducing the division between capital and wage labour. Even the subordinate groups within the middle classes have an interest in preserving the established order. Intellectuals, for example, will normally go to considerable lengths to ensure that cultural, economic and political democracy are not extended to the working class.

But Bourdieu's main contribution is to show that the dominant and subordinate groups within the middle classes are engaging in endless though reasonably genteel battles to assert their own identities, social positions and worth. The upwardly mobile 'new petite bourgeoisie', for example, are constantly finding that the social field they are entering is already occupied by previous well-established generations. And those who manage and control the means of production still exercise considerable influence over whether, and if so how, their cultural tastes are adopted.

Nevertheless, those with high levels of economic capital are the socially dominant group. It is still they who establish whether or not the 'new' ways of life being established by the more subordinate middle classes are widely endorsed and adopted. In contrast to the dominant group, the investments and achievements of the more subordinate social classes are mainly in the cultural sphere. They are obliged to realise these cultural investments if they, and their children, are to succeed in a society which largely depends on the possession of money. They will, as part of their struggle, attempt to ensure that 'culture' maintains some degree of autonomy from the dominant classes. Such autonomy means that culture, as they define it, remains relatively exclusive. And such scarcity is a means by which the cultural producers or intellectuals can hopefully ensure that their specialised knowledge remains valuable.

The result is a series of cultural battles. Bourdieu sees the 'industrialists' and senior managers as typically indulging in business meals, foreign car riding, auctions, second homes, tennis, water skiing and Parisian Right-Bank art galleries. The trend-setting and rapidly emerging new petite bourgeoisie are typically 'uneasy with their bodies'. They engage in the new 'Californian sports', indulging not only in extensive exercise but in health foods and other forms of apparently healthy living such as non-alcoholic drink. They share some of the same values of the intellectuals and artistic producers, but they also tend to be individualistic and hedonistic, the healthy body being used as a form of display. Their individualism leaves them socially detached. Their leisure patterns are, in Bourdieu's words, 'an inventory of thinly disguised expressions of a sort of dream of social flying, a desperate effort to defy the gravity of the social field' (Bourdieu 1984: 370). The artistic producers – intellectuals – by contrast, engage in other, quite distinct, lifestyles. These are characterised by 'Left Bank galleries, avant garde festivals, *Les Temps Modernes*, foreign languages, chess, flea markets, Bach and mountains' (Bourdieu 1984: 128–9, Fig. 5).

Some writers have argued that Bourdieu's account is of general relevance and can be applied outside France. Lash and Urry (1987) and Featherstone (1982) have used it to throw light on the social bases of post-modern culture throughout the developed capitalist world, and Urry (1990) and Bagguley *et al.* (1990) have used it to analyse divisions within the 'service class' in Britain. It is very doubtful, however, if Bourdieu's account can be generalised in this way. Bourdieu assumes a two-way interplay between those with cultural and economic capital: he has no place for a consideration of those relying on organisation assets. In *Distinction* he does not distingish managers from industrialists. In the French case this is no doubt understandable since, as we discussed in Chapter 3, managerial workers are not as distinct from professionals and the propertied workers as they are in Britain. But there is a further point here. Given the significance of educational qualifications in France, not just in professional employment but throughout the ranks of managerial 'cadres', his analysis of the translation of cultural capital into economic capital is clearly of major importance, since all forms of career development depend upon credentials. In the British case, where managers are not, by and large, credentialled, the picture is bound to be rather different. As a result, we would argue that Bourdieu's portrait of patterns of cultural distinction cannot be imported wholesale.

A major indication of this is the fact that there is no *conceptual* (or empirical) space in Bourdieu's framework for the 'organisation man'. This is the term coined by Whyte (1957) to describe the senior white-collar worker living under the close protection of a large private or public corporation. *His* whole way of life and security was, according to Whyte, dependent on the corporation. Not only was he selected and trained for work by the corporation, he was wholly dependent on the large institution for career-advancement. Still more important from the viewpoint of our concerns here, his life outside work was also closely linked to his position as 'organisation man'.

Whyte argued that the suburban communities constructed in America during the 1940s and 1950s were being made in the image of the organisation man. Rapid recruitment of this group meant that most of them had left behind their family roots in small town America. The new suburbs were where organisation man and his family achieved, or attempted to achieve, a new kind of respectability. This Whyte saw as mirroring the respectability of their childhood communities while at the same time reflecting their new-found status. According to Whyte, however, there was an important contradiction here. Organisation man was directly tied into the demands and dictates of the company for which he worked, accepting the need for spatial mobility and relocation, for instance.

Whyte's view of the suburban way of life led by these organisation-led senior managers and professionals has also become something of a stereotype for the present post-war period. Not only are they seen as highly mobile, they supposedly lead a highly regularised way of life. They indulge in what Whyte calls 'inconspicuous consumption', the priority being not to break ranks with the group norms and cultural practices of the area in question. Furthermore, the individual lives of each household is, according to Whyte, highly standardised. Their consumption patterns are supposedly organised around 'budgeting'. This leads to what Whyte terms 'little sense of capital'.

The benevolent economy has insulated the organisation man from having to manipulate large personal sums; indeed, it has relieved him from even having to *think* about it. Tax withholding, that great agent of social revolution, has almost removed from his consideration one of the largest single items in his finances, and package mortgages have

102

done the same for real-estate taxes. So with all the other major items. No longer does he have to think about setting aside large sums; the government and the corporation have assumed the prerogative. It is not merely that you don't have to worry about big sums, a young couple can explain; you don't even have the choice.

(Whyte 1957: 298; his emphasis)

No one claims that Whyte's account is a scholarly, detached work of social science. The important point here is theoretical. It is not clear, conceptually, how Bourdieu would be able to explain the cultural practices of people committed to 'inconspicuous consumption'. To be blunt, Bourdieu is better able to analyse the extravagant, flamboyant and culturally discerning middle classes than the 'boring' semi-detached variety discussed by Whyte, who are wrapped up in the concerns of their employing organisation, and don't appear to be bothered by consumption of any type.

Part of the problem lies in Bourdieu's rather loose concept of 'economic capital'. This is sometimes used in the Marxist sense as property related to ownership of the means of production, but elsewhere is used more vaguely to indicate the 'wealthy', or those on a high income. As a result, his discussions of the attempt to transform cultural capital into economic capital does not distinguish between those simply using their cultural capital to gain a well-paid job, and those actually using cultural capital to acquire capital as property. Furthermore, tied up with Bourdieu's neglect of organisations is his inattention to the state's role both in legitimating cultural and propertied capital, and in affecting the processes by which these two might be converted into each other.

A final weakness in Bourdieu's account is his neglect of household and gender relations, which, as we argued above, may be becoming a more central determinant of middle-class formation as a result of the growing significance of petty property. Bourdieu's work has little explicit discussion of gender, and slides between individual and household analyses of cultural practices and habits.

Hence although Bourdieu's broad framework is exceptionally valuable in helping us examine cultural life, it is not without its problems. It ignores the cultural ramifications of organisation assets, conflating these unhelpfully with economic capital. Yet given the argument that organisation assets fail to convey the security of property because of the problems in storing them, it could very well be argued that differing cultural processes will be found where the two assets can be clearly distinguished – as they can in Britain. This is something we need to rectify as we now turn to examine the cultural practices of the contemporary British middle classes.

103

# A SURVEY OF MIDDLE-CLASS CONSUMPTION PATTERNS

Archetypally the British middle classes have historically conformed to the 'organisation man' portrait. Samuel's (1983a,b) emphasis upon the inter-war middle class's acceptance of their subordinate position, is a typical example. In the past decade, however, a number of writers have argued that a more culturally outgoing middle class has developed, drawing either implicitly or explicitly on Bourdieu's arguments about the significance of cultural capital. Much of this writing is, however, journalistic. We find Leadbeater (1989) writing about the emergence of the new, southern-based professional middle class. After their early morning jog they return home to fresh croissants and real coffee.

> They eat fresh pasta and Italian salami, drink French wine and Spanish beer, admire Italian suits and drive German cars. They may aspire to own a little farmhouse in southern France. They certainly travel more frequently to Spain or Italy than to Newcastle or Liverpool.
>
> (Leadbeater 1989: 21)

Meanwhile a popular image emerging from, say, the pages of *Country Life* is that of an older more staid fraction engaging in slower pseudo-rural ways of life; wearing Barbour jackets, green wellingtons and driving spotless four-wheel-drive Land Rovers in pursuit of their children and horses.

Unfortunately, hurried generalisations of this kind are also a feature of more analytical accounts. Thrift (1989), for example, writes of 'service-class culture', its endorsement of 'countryside' or 'heritage' traditions and its attempts to make nostalgic cultural forms into the accepted priorities of other more subordinate social groups. But these accounts are based on very little conceptually informed survey work. Thus Thrift is reduced to using indicators of 'service-class culture' that are of a somewhat impressionistic nature: maps showing Laura Ashley and Country Casual shops supposedly selling clothes to the 'service class' in the South East (Thrift 1987). But these can be no substitute for knowing how different groups of middle-class women (and men) actually consume. The absence of adequate information is in real danger of reproducing journalistic stereotypes.

To deal with at least some of these problems and to develop our understanding of consumption-behaviour by the contemporary middle classes, we now turn to our analysis of the British Market Research Bureau's 'Target Group Index' (BMRB 1988a). As we shall later make clear, this cannot claim to cover all the areas of social life in which a study of middle-class consumption is interested. Nevertheless, it provides an excellent basis for appreciating some of the main changes in middle-class behaviour and, most importantly, the role of relationships between social groups in bringing about these changes.

TGI is an annual survey of 24,000 adults, with respondents asked to provide details of a large range of consumption habits. The social groups analysed by TGI are not perfect for an analysis of consumption patterns, since they use 'market research' categories which confuse some of the salient distinctions that we have emphasised. The basic classification is as follows (for further details see Appendix 3):

*Social group*

A 'Upper Middle Class': higher managerial, administrative or professional.

B 'Middle Class': intermediate managerial, administrative or professional.

C1 'Lower Middle Class': supervisors or clerical and junior managerial, administrative or professional.

C2 'Skilled Working Class': semi-skilled manual workers.

D 'Working Class': semi- and unskilled manual workers.

E 'Those at lowest level of subsistence': state pensioners and widows, casual and lower-grade workers.

The problems of using market research categories are, however, partly overcome since TGI conduct a separate study of the AB group which allows a more fine-grained analysis. While we shall be partly concerned with the general survey of groups A to E above, we shall be especially concentrating on the AB group. The special AB survey is also conducted annually and it covers approximately 5,500 adults per year. In order to have a sufficiently large base for the analysis of subgroups within the ABs we shall in fact be grouping two such surveys (those for 1987 and 1988), the total number of respondents therefore being approximately 11,000.

Some of the associations between the middle classes and cultural preferences developed by Bourdieu cannot, as we have earlier discussed, be explored with the aid of the TGI survey. His coverage of, for example, taste in paintings and music cannot be explored with the kind of information useful for market research purposes. But the TGI survey, as we shall shortly see, does allow us to examine some of the principal differences in lifestyle (a) as they affect different income groups and (b) between broad occupational groupings within the middle classes. Further divisions are made between ages and genders, the stage at which respondents' formal education was completed and differences between regions.

Our approach to the analysis is to explore the possible patterns we find using the TGI categories, and then to consider how these might relate to our arguments. We shall therefore need to spend some time, as we analyse the figures, thinking about how the largely descriptive categories used by the TGI (e.g. 'government workers', 'arts and sports workers', 'education, health and welfare workers') relate to the sorts of distinctions that we have developed so far (for details of how occupations have been classified in the TGI, see Appendix 3).

The TGI itself (which is used for the main and supplementary survey) is a measure of the extent to which the particular group under study compares with the population as a whole. As such, it is a measure of how one social group is distinguished (or distinguishes itself) from the population at large. For much of the study below, 'the population at large' comprises the ABs – that is, the middle classes as a whole – though occasionally the basis for comparison will be population groups A to E – that is, everyone. For Figures 6.1 to 6.12 the average for the base group is 100. Levels above this figure therefore indicate above-average participation in this activity for the group in question, and those below this level indicate below-average participation. A figure of 150 would indicate that the group is 50 per cent more likely to consume a particular product than the sample as a whole. Furthermore, the band between 80 and 120 is omitted, the objective being to draw out the really distinctive consumption patterns of the group being considered.

Before outlining our findings and conclusions we should avoid confusion by clarifying one particular categorisation made by the TGI survey. As regards women, those in the AB survey take their social grading from their own jobs, not those of their partners. In the larger survey of the whole population, however, the categorisations of women are based on husbands, partners or other dependants. This separation between men and women within the AB group stems largely from the demands of consumer research. These people are, after all, the high spenders and when creating or targeting new products it is important that producers and retailers have a detailed knowledge of the consumption patterns of both genders.

## THE EMERGENCE OF A POST-MODERN LIFESTYLE?

Figure 6.1 provides a preliminary overview of the association between incomes and forms of consumption. It also helps us to introduce our central argument regarding contemporary consumption patterns among the middle classes. The figure shows dramatically and conclusively the extent to which high incomes are associated with a new culture of health and body maintenance. At the same time, however, it demonstrates that this new culture combines with an older 'culture of extravagance' in a contradictory manner. The 'old' culture is one of excess and indulgence largely based on a predilection for foreign eating styles and heavy drinking. Correspondingly, those on low incomes remain largely excluded from both forms of consumption. (The numbers of individuals in the £100,000+ p.a. category are for the most part too small to be reliable. Even so, it is clear that 'Eating

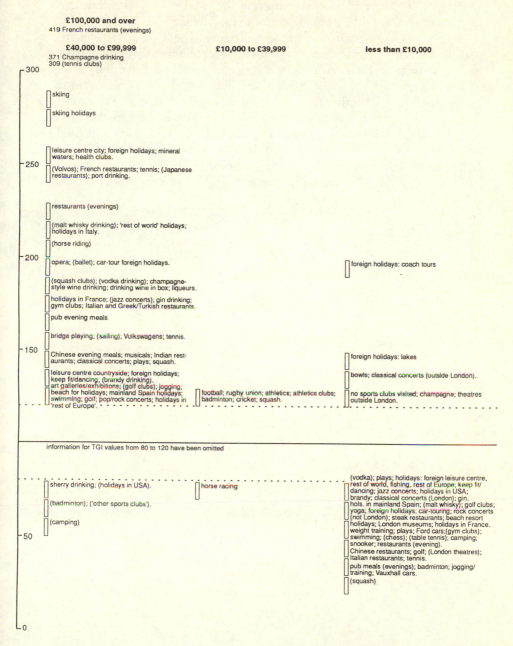

**£100,000 and over**
419 French restaurants (evenings)

**£40,000 to £99,999**        **£10,000 to £39,999**        **less than £10,000**
371 Champagne drinking
309 (tennis clubs)

300

skiing

skiing holidays

leisure centre city; foreign holidays; mineral waters; health clubs.

250

(Volvos); French restaurants; tennis; (Japanese restaurants); port drinking.

restaurants (evenings)

(malt whisky drinking); 'rest of world' holidays; holidays in Italy.

(horse riding)

200   opera; (ballet); car-tour foreign holidays.                    foreign holidays: coach tours

(squash clubs); (vodka drinking); champagne-style wine drinking; drinking wine in box; liqueurs.

holidays in France; (jazz concerts); gin drinking; gym clubs; Italian and Greek/Turkish restaurants.

pub evening meals

bridge playing; (sailing); Volkswagens; tennis.

150

Chinese evening meals; musicals; Indian restaurants; classical concerts; plays; squash.          foreign holidays: lakes

leisure centre countryside; foreign holidays; keep fit/dancing; (brandy drinking).          bowls; classical concerts (outside London).

art galleries/exhibitions; (golf clubs); jogging; beach for holidays; mainland Spain holidays; swimming; golf; pop/rock concerts; holidays in 'rest of Europe'.          football; rugby union; athletics; athletics clubs; badminton; cricket; squash.          no sports clubs visited; champagne; theatres outside London.

information for TGI values from 80 to 120 have been omitted

sherry drinking; (holidays in USA).          horse racing          (vodka); plays; holidays: foreign leisure centre, rest of world, fishing, rest of Europe; keep fit/ dancing; jazz concerts; holidays in USA; brandy; classical concerts (London); gin.

(badminton); ('other sports clubs').          hols. in mainland Spain; (malt whisky); golf clubs; yoga; foreign holidays: car-touring; rock concerts (not London); steak restaurants; beach resort holidays; London museums; holidays in France.

(camping)          weight training; plays; Ford cars;(gym clubs); swimming; (chess); (table tennis); camping; snooker; restaurants (evening).

50          Chinese restaurants; golf; (London theatres); Italian restaurants; tennis.

pub meals (evenings); badminton; jogging/ training; Vauxhall cars.

(squash)

0

*Figure 6.1*  Consumption by income group 1987–88. Uses AB Survey as a base. Vertical axis = Target Group Index (TGI) where the value for Great Britain = 100. Brackets are used when cell counts are too low to produce reliable data.
*Source*: British Market Research Bureau

in French Restaurants' is by some margin the most élitist cultural practice in Britain: the score here (419) is extraordinarily high.)

Figure 6.1 suggests a theme that we will develop below. For some groups within the middle class lifestyles do not fit any coherent single organising principle: instead, high extravagance goes along with a culture of the body: appreciation of high cultural forms of art such as opera and classical music exists cheek by jowl with an interest in disco dancing or stock car racing.[1] This type of lifestyle may best be described – partly tongue in cheek – as 'post-modern', where a binge in an expensive restaurant one night might be followed by a diet the next. This might be seen as a consumer culture 'based upon a profusion of information and proliferation of images which cannot be ultimately stabilized, or hierarchized into a system which corre-

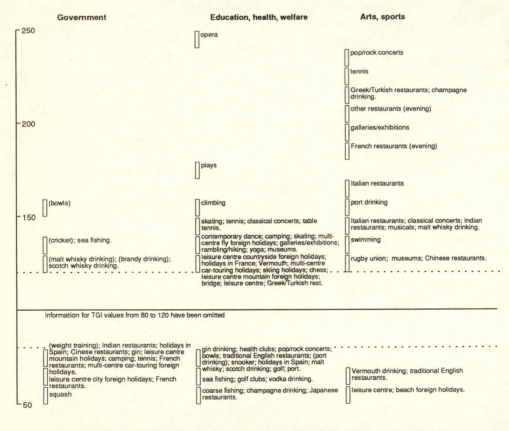

*Figure 6.2* Consumption by type of employment 1987–88. Uses AB Survey as a base. Vertical axis = Target Group Index (TGI) where the value for Great Britain = 100. Brackets are used when cell counts are too low to produce reliable data.
*Source*: British Market Research Bureau

sponds to fixed social divisions' (Featherstone 1982: 55). Let us now see what other evidence there is for the existence of such a lifestyle.

In opposition to the 'post-modern' consumers exists a group of people whose consumption patterns seem to fit more clearly into an 'ascetic' organising principle. Figure 6.2 shows that there is a distinct group of people who operate as standard-bearers for an ascetic lifestyle founded on health and exercise. This group is labelled by the British Market Research Bureau as 'Education, Health and Welfare'. It incorporates teachers in schools and higher education, medical workers of all types and those employed in welfare and social service organisations. This is the group Bourdieu would probably label as 'intellectuals' – people with cultural assets, but not much money, who rely on the state.

Their consumption patterns are quite distinct from those of the AB category as a whole in a number of significant respects. They engage in a number of very active forms of exercise to an extent that is well above the average for ABs as a whole. Thus climbing, skating, table tennis and hiking are well represented. Furthermore, participation in yoga (an activity usually associated with 'healthy' living) is also above average among this group. All this is very much in line with the findings of Bagguley *et al*. (1990), who see 'the state professional sector of the service class' as drawn to a culture of 'authenticity' and the 'natural' (see also Urry 1990).

The asceticism of this class is revealed by the fact that alcoholic drinking is well below average, and they also have below-average participation in sports such as snooker and fishing, which are not seen as conducive to health. Somewhat paradoxically, their membership of health clubs is also below average – perhaps due to the expense of membership, but it may also reflect their individualistic orientation. Indeed, more generally, it is notable that their range of health-giving activities is not associated with team games and organised collective sports. Presumably this group's adoption of an active, healthy, lifestyle is closely related to their above-average involvement in a range of outdoor activities, including camping, multi-centre countryside and mountain holidays.

This is not to say that the group does not engage in more conventional forms of consumption, or older ('pre-Californian') cultural practices. They also show an interest in forms of 'high culture'. Those in Education, Health and Welfare attend plays, classical concerts and contemporary dance performances to a higher extent than ABs as a whole. In this respect they share certain values with a related group of other intellectuals and cultural pace-makers; those working in 'Arts and Sports', also shown on Figure 6.2. Those in 'Education, Health and Welfare' undertake above-average numbers of visits to galleries and classical concerts. Their habits in this respect are a scaled-down version of the activities of those more directly associated with the higher independent professions who are more likely to engage in traditional forms of consumption. Their relative rejection of 'high living' and commercialism in the form of, for example, alcoholic drinking and attendance of rock and pop concerts nevertheless makes them quite distinct from those in the literary and artistic categories.

This ascetic lifestyle can be associated with the 'habitus' of this particular group, one reflecting their often expert knowledge of the body and their separation from the world of business. Thus, their habitus can be seen as simultaneously a product of deliberate choice (one rejecting competitive individualism and marketplace values) while at the same time being a rationalisation of their comparatively low incomes. We have argued above that the body is of crucial importance as the actual vehicle in which cultural assets are stored, and the cultural practices revealed in this survey can be seen as attempts to preserve and manicure the body in various ways. Furthermore, they remain in a relatively poor position to fully participate in the commodified 'high living', even should they wish to become involved in such cultural practices: an ascetic culture has the advantage of being relatively cheap to maintain. They also have a slightly above-average commitment to family relative to career. Their score here is 103, compared with, for example, 90 for the professionals.[2]

There are certain points of contrast between these state welfare professionals and the category of 'Government' employees also shown in Figure 6.2. 'Government' employees, it should be noted here, are administrative workers in national and local government. They are bureaucrats or 'civil servants' – a group distinct from, say, health or education workers due to their greater reliance on organisational careers. With the somewhat curious exceptions of their enthusiasm for bowls and their general aversion to squash, government workers of this type neither engage in nor avoid any distinctive form of consumption. Here we begin to find the stolid 'organisation man' beginning to emerge. These bureaucrats are not really distinctive in anything, and since they are relatively highly career motivated, they score quite low (89) when assessing the importance of family relative to career. This is very much as Whyte would predict!

Such separation from attachment to family and distinctive involvement in civil society by the government workers is perhaps a result of their continuing reliance on large bureaucracies. Their security and lifestyles are, to a much greater extent than other fractions of the middle classes, related to, bound up with and dependent upon their organisations and organisation assets. So while private sector professionals and managers become decreasingly tied to specific firms and rely on contacts made in civil society for further business (the golf club being the classic instance), government workers are more likely to inhabit a closed world, and need few such contacts to achieve security and relatively high rewards.

The general significance of cultural capital in affecting lifestyle is underscored by examining Figure 6.3. The dramatic differences in lifestyles

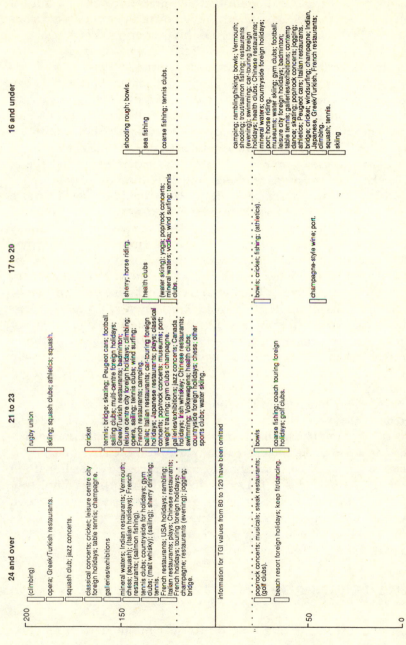

*Figure 6.3* Consumption by age of completion of education 1987–88. Uses AB Survey as a base. Vertical axis = Target Group Index (TGI) where the value for Great Britain = 100. Brackets are used when cell counts are too low to produce reliable data.
*Source:* British Market Research Bureau

between those who left school at 16 or under and those who completed their education at 21–23 or 24+ are self-evident.

Particularly noticeable is the link between high levels of educational attainment and engagement in the new forms of 'body culture' associated with keeping fit (Featherstone 1982). And this of course ties in with one of our principal themes: the promotion of 'self' in the form of fitness and health is, in our terms, an investment in the storing of cultural assets as distinct from property assets or reliance on organisation assets.

Noticeable too, however, is the extent to which these health-giving concerns are combined with other, more exotic forms of consumption. Thus the acquisition of cultural capital also equates with 'things foreign'. Those with higher levels of cultural capital are far more likely to indulge themselves in supposedly more exotic contexts such as French, Chinese, Greek, Turkish and Indian restaurants. Similarly, those with higher levels of cultural capital are far more likely to take their holidays in more 'sophisticated' localities, especially in western Europe. Mineral water – especially a well-known French variety – has also tended to be closely associated with high levels of cultural capital. There are some other important distinctions to be made between those who finished their education between 21 and 23 and those who completed at 24+. Those who stayed on into post-degree education are especially likely to engage in 'older', 'high' forms of culture such as climbing, opera, classical concerts, art galleries and foreign restaurants. These, as Samuel (1983b) suggests, are forms of culture which the middle classes have long shared with the upper classes, including the landed aristocracy. They engage considerably less in competitive sports and the newer hedonistic 'Californian' forms of consumption.

We have briefly touched on variations in the relative commitment to family relative to career. A quite important factor in this respect is the level of credentials accumulated. There is a quite small but nevertheless distinct tendency for career to become increasingly significant relative to family as cultural capital is acquired. Thus those who had received education up to the age of 24+ scored only 81. This compares with 93 for those completing at 21–23, 101 for those completing at 17–20 and 109 (i.e. somewhat above average) for those completing at age 16 or under. In other words, the more qualified people are, the more career oriented they become, and the less important their family is to them.

## MANAGERS, PROFESSIONALS AND THE NEW LIFESTYLE

There has, in Britain, been a long history of anti-intellectualism. The historical formation of cultural capital out of aristocratic cultural forms, discussed in Chapter 3, led to an identification of culture with leisured, amateur pursuits that was antagonistic to any idea of 'learning as a vocation'. In his account of the relationships between the middle classes during the inter-war period Samuel notes a general hostility towards intellectuals:

> Highbrow-baiting was a favourite sport in the millionaire press, and it was taken up with enthusiasm on the golf-links and in the smokerooms of the commercial and county hotels ... Anti-intellectualism was also a matter of pride in the upper-middle-class. In the public schools, notwithstanding a certain weakening in the cult of athleticism, the tyranny of the 'bloods' was unimpaired, and the budding of the artist or poet was liable to be treated with sniggering contempt. In the universities, aesthetes were persecuted by the boat club and rugger scrum hearties, debagging being the favourite Oxford punishment in the 1920s for those too immersed in their books.
>
> (Samuel 1983a: 35)

The relationships between 'intellectuals' and other groups within the middle classes now seems more ambiguous, contradictory and complex. While it can hardly be said that all the values of contemporary 'highbows' are endorsed with alacrity by other middle-class groups, there are some aspects of intellectuals' priorities (especially those which offer long-term economic benefits) which are indeed adopted by those with higher levels of economic capital. This we contend is linked to the growing salience of cultural assets in contemporary Britain.

Our general argument so far suggests that intellectuals act as a vanguard for a new 'healthy' lifestyle. This is the group employed in education and welfare and whose general outlook and circumstances are associated with cultural capital but who do not form a particularly affluent group. 'Healthy life' for these people certainly incorporates yoga, jogging and abstinence from alcohol, but it also includes more established, somewhat less individualistic, forms of exercise such as mountaineering and rambling.

Our main argument, however, is that insofar as this group acts as a standard-bearer for others, the situation has now moved on beyond that outlined by Bourdieu. In brief, a version of the 'healthy lifestyle' is, as we have outlined, now being rapidly adopted by sections of the middle classes who are fully part of the materialistic world which Bourdieu's 'intellectuals' largely reject. What were once the practices of an 'alternative' middle-class minority resisting materialism and the dictates of professionalised medicine have now been adopted on a large scale by those with much greater economic resources. However, in the process it has not replaced other cultural practices but sits alongside them as another one to 'sample'. A 1960s-style counter-culture has been transformed into a 1990s-style postmodern cultural conformity.

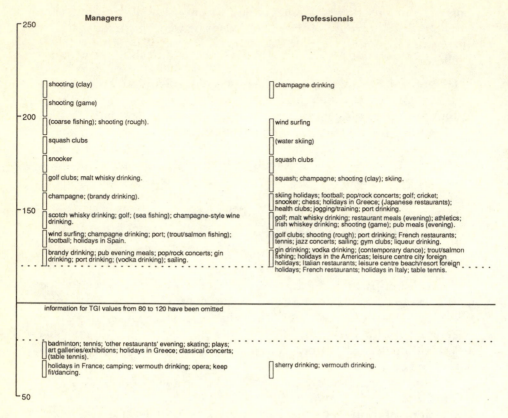

*Figure 6.4* Consumption by managers and professionals 1987–88. Uses AB Survey as a base. Vertical axis = Target Group Index (TGI) where the value for Great Britain = 100. Brackets are used when cell counts are too low to produce reliable data.
*Source*: British Market Research Bureau

What are the reasons for such adoption? Clearly, they are multiple. They include – as implied for example by Jane Fonda's fitness and health regimes – heightened sexual attraction. Clearly such promises have a special relevance to the young professionals who, as we shall see later, are particularly pursuing the supposedly healthy lifestyle. Linked to this, however, are the long-term economic rewards supposedly associated with healthy living. At this stage we can turn to Bourdieu's more general arguments. The attempt is now being made to transform 'cultural capital' as originally owned by specific groups within the middle classes into greater economic rewards. A 'healthy' lifestyle is in effect becoming instrumentally converted into health for increased earning capacity and the accumulation

114

of economic assets. Glassner's comments on the contemporary significance of fitness are therefore particularly apposite. Fitness programmes 'suggest that by exercising and eating correctly, one will achieve professional-quality mastery, not just of one's appearance and health, but of one's position in the labor and mate markets' (1989: 186).

As Figure 6.4 shows, it is indeed the rapidly rising professional workers (defined as professions in law, financial services, personnel, economic advice, computing and data processing, marketing, advertising, public relations, sales and purchasing) who are now adopting a version of the 'healthy' lifestyle previously espoused mainly by the 'education and welfare professionals'. These seem close to Bourdieu's 'new petite bourgeoisie', except that they also include older, more established professions, and are not as economically marginal as in Bourdieu's framework. As Figure 6.4 indicates, the professionals are heavily into a wide range of sports; especially those of the more individualistic, supposedly 'Californian', variety. Thus this group is exceptionally well-disposed towards wind surfing, water skiing, squash, skiing, jogging and (unlike those in teaching and welfare) health clubs. To a lesser extent it is also engaged in the older 'non-Californian' (indeed often peculiarly British) forms of exercise such as football, cricket and golf.

But a central point here (and one we have already alluded to) is that this group is caught up in a major contradiction. While they take up and engage in a very wide range of health-giving activities, their affluence also allows them to indulge in a series of potentially non-health-giving lifestyles. Thus they are among the leading champagne drinkers and, to a lesser extent, port, whisky, liqueur, gin and vodka drinkers. (We should note here that we have transferred TGI's category of 'heavy drinking' into the 'drinking' category shown on the figures.) In short, this group's lifestyle involves a number of tensions. On the one hand, they largely endorse the cultural practices of the intellectuals with their low levels of economic capital. On the other hand, largely since they are also able to market their skills, the professionals have the economic wealth and cultural propensities to engage in precisely those older, supposedly less 'healthy', forms of consumption to which the intellectuals are averse.

The lifestyle of the professionals contrasts with that of the managers, also shown on Figure 6.4. We have seen the distinctive separation of these two classes in Britain. Samuel (1983a) indicates some of the cultural ramifications of this by noting that for the inter-war period the 'deepest division of all' within the middle classes was between these two groups. The former, he argues, were relatively detached from the marketplace; they could rely on secure work-positions, long-term employment in public or private sector employment, and they viewed managers as 'money grubbers' with little sense of a public interest.

Major divisions between the managers' and the professionals' lifestyles still exist, but are now of a rather different sort from that outlined by Samuel. Indeed, the position is now somewhat reversed, it being the managers who indulge in the more staid and conventional sports such as shooting – to which they are particularly drawn – fishing, sailing and golf and the professionals in a more hedonistic, personalised and market-oriented form of consumerism. Insofar as Thrift's emphasis upon the 'countryside' orientation of the 'service class' is borne out by our findings, it is largely the managers who appear to indulge in it. There is little evidence of 'Californian' sports among managers; the exception being the somewhat curious one of windsurfing.

These cultural patterns are closely related to the wider restructuring of the middle classes. The professionals are, as we have indicated in Chapter 4, increasingly likely to apply their personalised skills to a wide range of organisations; moving between firms towards this end and perhaps even operating as small firms themselves. As such, their consumption lifestyles reflect the individualism of their lives in employment. The managers are now those more likely to rely on their place within organisations in attempting to achieve security and identity. In short, self-investment (in the form of body- and skills-maintenance) is of less value to the managers who need to rely on organisation assets.

As we have also seen, managers are becoming increasingly separated from credentialism. As such, their 'habitus' is less likely to incorporate a dedication to what we might term the 'health-with-champagne' practices of the professionals. Notable, too, is the managers' aversion to many of the better-established or 'higher' forms of culture – a tendency which mirrors Bourdieu's findings for 1960s France. These older or higher forms include not only classical music, attendance at theatres, galleries and opera houses but holidays to France and Greece. They seem more prone – as Weiner (1980) argues in a wider historical context for British management – to seek 'escape' in the form of modified versions of country pursuits earlier adopted by the landed aristocracy. For the managers at least the pursuit of a cleaned-up version of the 'heritage' or 'countryside' tradition, as outlined by Thrift, seems apposite. It is almost as if they look for security in the past, in the days when careers could be built upon loyalty.

What distinguishes the lifestyles of the A and B categories (the middle classes as a whole) from those of the 'lower' social groups? We can make some observations here by examining Figure 6.5, showing how the consumption-styles of the ABs and the C1s (the 'lower middle classes' of supervisors, clerks and junior administrative and professional workers) compare with the whole population. To generalise here, we find that the forms of sport, culture and consumption adopted by the C1s are what we might term a 'reduced' version of those of the ABs. That is, whether we are dealing with the 'new' forms of culture (such as skiing holidays) or the 'old' forms (such as classical music, art galleries and theatre) the C1s are

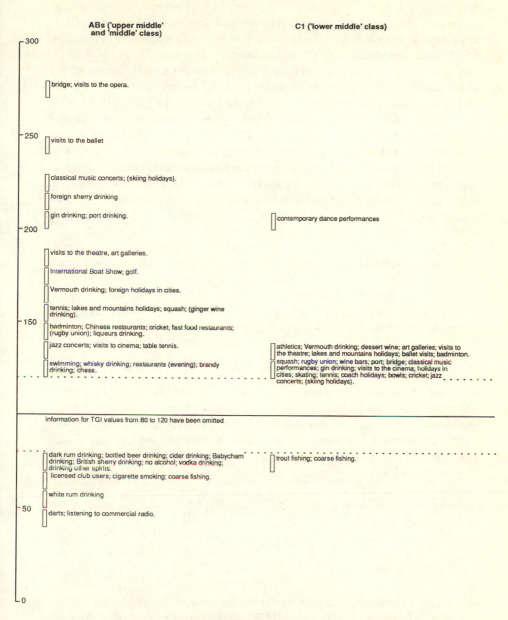

*Figure 6.5* Consumption by social class 1987–88. Uses AB Survey of total population as a base. Vertical axis = Target Group Index (TGI) where the value for Great Britain = 100. Brackets are used when cell counts are too low to produce reliable data.
*Source*: British Market Research Bureau

characterised by the same above-average activities as the ABs, but at a lower level.

A perhaps unexpected exception is the C1s' patronage of wine bars, these being stereotypically linked with the young and affluent. In fact, use of wine bars by the ABs is approximately the same as the average of the whole population while, at 126, the C1s' use of these institutions is well above average. This perhaps indicates that one function of wine bars is as training grounds for young people aspiring towards high levels of social mobility. To put this in more formal terms, it suggests that wine bars may have an important role as finishing schools. Aspirant professionals are investing their (or their parents') money here and, in the process of interacting with others, are developing particular forms of cultural capital. This includes social and work contacts, forms of discourse and class taste, not least taste in alcoholic and non-alcoholic drink. All such cultural capital will presumably be transformed back into economic capital at a later stage in their careers.

Meanwhile, we should also note the ABs' relative aversion to certain types of drinking and culture, such as beer drinking, darts playing and listening to commercial radio. These are engaged in marginally more by the C1s than the ABs, though not on a scale sufficiently large to register on Figure 6.5. At this stage we appear to be entering into the margins of distinctively working-class forms of culture.

## LIFE CYCLE, AGE AND LIFESTYLE

The above discussion suggests that there is a further set of important distinctions not adequately covered by Bourdieu: that of age. Referring to the inter-war period, Samuel (1983a) refers to 'the valorisation of age'. Not only was every schoolchild brought up to respect the elderly but middle age was idealised and equated with all forms of success.

> Age was not only more powerful than youth, it was also, in some sort, more glamorous. The matinée idol, 'suave and elegant', was, by modern standards, middle-aged, a man with grown up children (like Gerald Du Maurier) or, like Ivor Novello, with iron-grey streaks in his hair. Likewise the idealised English lady, represented on stage by the middle-aged Gladys Cooper, was a mature beauty.
>
> (Samuel 1983a: 33)

It would be difficult to argue that our own era is characterised by such valorisation of the elderly or middle aged. Today's 'matinée idols' are predominantly young, and commercialised glamour is primarily organised around the promotion of youth. It is the emphasis upon the young middle class, expressed above all in the term 'yuppie', that has grabbed attention. Figure 6.6 shows that the high-living but health-seeking section of the

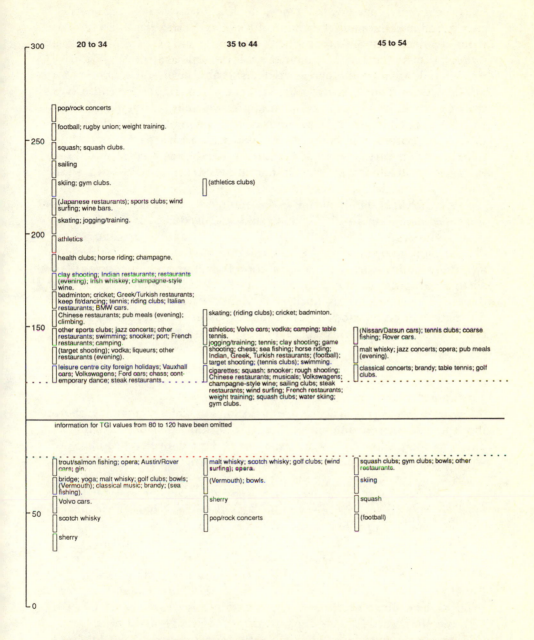

*Figure 6.6* Consumption by age (20–54) 1987–88. Uses AB Survey as a base.
Vertical axis = Target Group Index (TGI) where the value for Great Britain
= 100. Brackets are used when cell counts are too low to produce reliable data.
*Source*: British Market Research Bureau

middle class is indeed a young fraction of this group. The young are, overwhelmingly, engaging in the new 'healthy' lifestyle and it comes as no surprise to find the marketing of health-giving foods, drink, exercise as principally aimed at this group.

Such marketing of health-giving lifestyle towards the young is of course partly a reflection of their high levels of disposable income. To some extent it reflects this group's physical capacities. Clearly, in Figure 6.7, those over the age of 34 are less capable of indulging in many of the supposedly health-giving sports of their younger colleagues. As Figures 6.6 and 6.7 show, increasing age among the ABs is associated with a gradual shedding of the more energetic sports. At the same time, the apparently hedonistic engagement in all forms of entertainment becomes gradually reduced in scale.

Nevertheless, it should of course be remembered that many of those in the older age-groups will not have substantially sampled the 'healthy' lifestyles now associated with the young. The commitment to various forms of consumption by those in the 55+ category and those over retirement age are presumably less a product of lifestyle change and more a result of a habitus originally acquired during the earlier stages of their lives. Figures 6.6 and 6.7 are therefore as much a comment on the values associated with a specific new class (associated with finance, marketing, property and so on) as an indication of the changing values of the same people.

An apparent exception to the association between youth and healthy living is yoga. As we shall see in the next section, women predominantly engage in this activity. It would also appear, however, that women from a wide range of age-groups engage in this activity.

While the young in particular are engaging in 'Californian sports', there is at the same time, as implied earlier, a continuing tension here: that is, adopting the healthy life yet still being considerably over-represented in wine bars, heavy champagne drinking and all forms of foreign restaurant.

Especially notable here (though not especially surprising) is their support of rock and pop music and a corresponding aversion to older forms of 'high' culture such as opera and classical music. Their conscious or subconscious attempts to distinguish themselves spreads to resisting the acquisition of items such as low-status Austin Rover cars and the purchase of more status-giving forms of transport such as BMWs. Some kinds of cars, such as Volvos and to a lesser extent Volkswagens, also offer 'health' and future economic assets in the form of extra physical protection. This form of body-protection is not, however, adopted on any noticeable scale by the ABs until they reach the 35–44 age-group, and by that time, of course, they will probably be considering the well-being of not only themselves but their offspring.

The young also distinguish themselves from their elders by resistance to other activities such as fishing, bridge and bowls. Similarly, their drink-

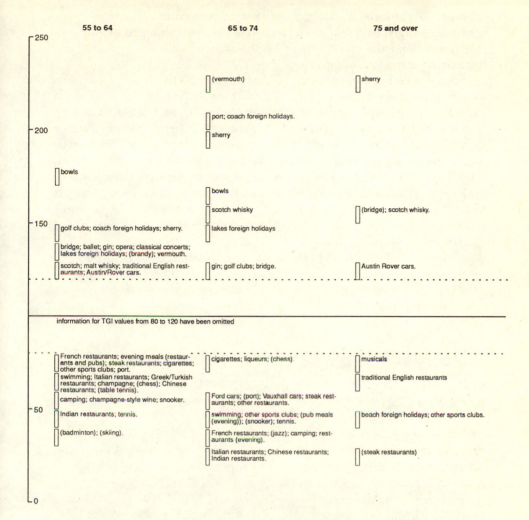

*Figure 6.7* Consumption by age (55 and over) 1987–88. Uses AB Survey as a base. Vertical axis = Target Group Index (TGI) where the value for Great Britain = 100. Brackets are used when cell counts are too low to produce reliable data.
*Source*: British Market Research Bureau

ing of alcoholic liquor is of the distinctive 'prestige' type adopted by the young – meaning that they remain averse to the more conventional types of liquor and alcohol such as whisky, sherry and brandy. Age, or stage in the life cycle, is therefore a central element in explaining the adoption of a version of the new 'health-giving' lifestyle, one convertible into future economic rewards. Equally central, as we shall now discuss, is gender.

## GENDER, HOUSEHOLDS AND CONSUMPTION STYLES

We have earlier mentioned gender and households as important omissions in Bourdieu's work. This is particularly problematic, given the significance of gender relations to processes of middle-class formation. The special contemporary significance of gender starts to be indicated when we examine Figure 6.8, which shows that AB males overwhelmingly engage in the very large array of sports and pastimes that we identified in Figures 6.1 and 6.2. Furthermore, it is to a large extent the AB males who combine these 'health-giving' activities with the various forms of indulgences that

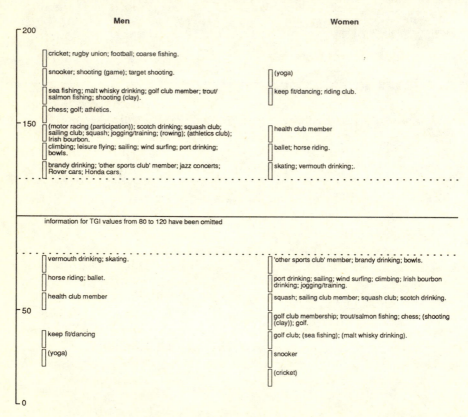

*Figure 6.8* Consumption by gender 1987–88. Uses AB Survey as a base. Vertical axis = Target Group Index (TGI) where the value for Great Britain = 100. Brackets are used when cell counts are too low to produce reliable data. *Source*: British Market Research Bureau

we noted are in part contradiction to the maintenance of health. Thus, not only do they score well above average when it comes to cricket, rugby union, football, fishing, athletics and so forth, but they also score considerably above average in terms of heavy whisky and port drinking. Middle-class men would therefore appear to be receptive to the post-modern lifestyle!

Middle-class women, by contrast, score above average in a limited array of activities – specifically yoga, keep fit/dancing, riding and participation in health clubs, indicating a weak endorsement of the ascetic lifestyle. Another way to see this is in terms of the activities where women's participation is below average. As Figure 6.8 shows, their participation is well below average in activities such as jogging, fishing, golf, cricket and so on. But, despite the more limited range of women's leisure, noticeable here is their lower level of engagement in competitive sports. Yoga, keep fit and so on are of a qualitatively different nature from the sports most engaged in by men, such as cricket, football, rugby and athletics.

Finally, we should note the high contemporary attendance of women in some 'older' forms of culture such as ballet performances. This perhaps indicates the potential significance of considering households rather than individuals. It could be (although the evidence here is by no means conclusive) that a negotiated division of labour takes place between members of households when it comes to consumption practices. Not only do men and women tend to engage in different activities but these differences can be seen as complementary to one another; women now tending to engage more in 'high' culture (as well as in distinctive forms of the newer body culture) with men engaging more in the newer practices in which exercise is combined with physical excess.

Nevertheless, the idea of wholly negotiated distinct forms of 'habitus' for men and women could be seen as an exceptionally voluntaristic form of interpretation. It may be, as suggested above, that the distinctive forms of female culture are a product of active choice. But it may also be that women do not engage in the same forms of consumption as men due to time constraints (including those deriving from childcare), lack of disposable income and active exclusion by men. At the same time, some forms of leisure undertaken by senior white-collar men are presumably linked to the cultivation of business contacts and hoped-for acquisition of further economic assets through, for example, contacts in the golf or squash club. And this may be given as a further rationale for excluding wives and partners.

The causes of these very real differences and distinctions are difficult to define. They are presumably a result of women's active preferences or of men's active exclusion, or a combination of the two.

## REGION AND LIFESTYLE

To what extent can we speak of distinct local cultures, once the social specificity of places is taken into account? Are there different local middle-class cultures? And, given our emphasis upon the singular, and growing,

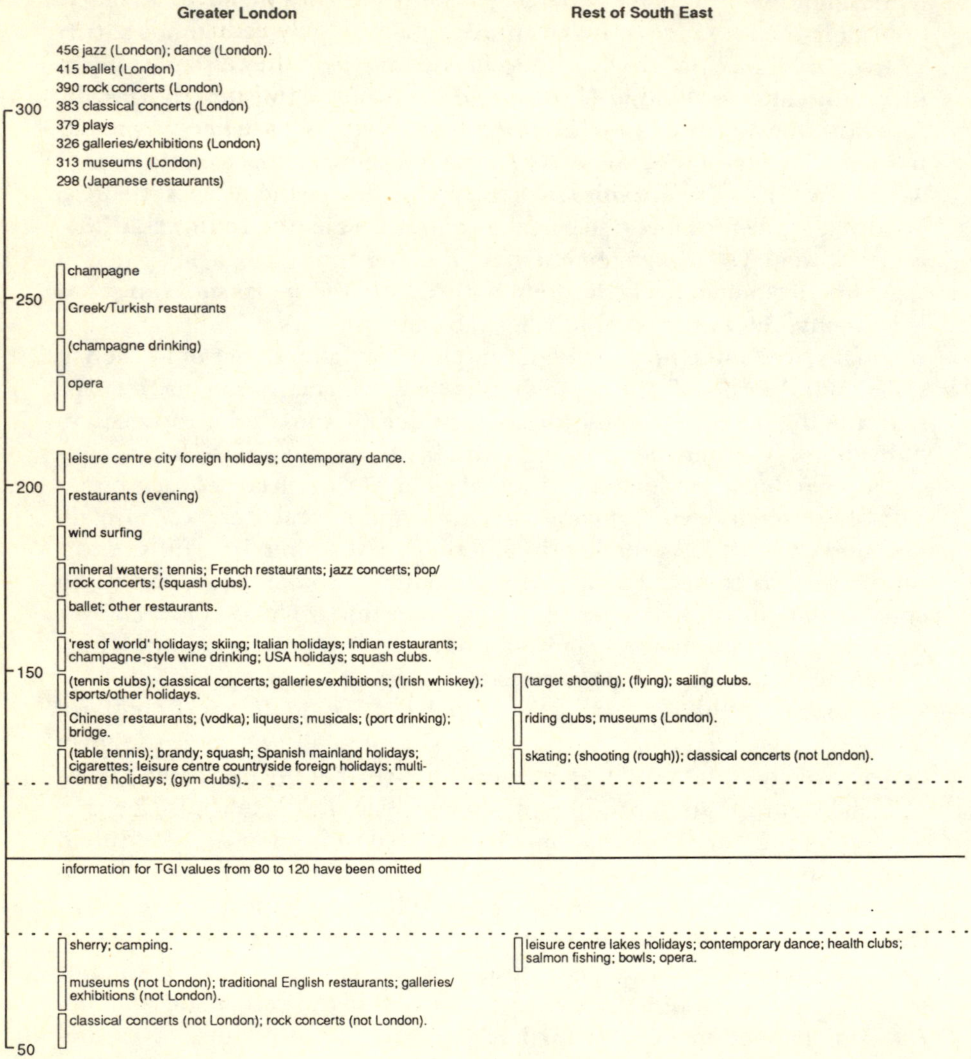

Greater London　　　　　　　　　　　　　　Rest of South East

456 jazz (London); dance (London).
415 ballet (London)
390 rock concerts (London)
300 ── 383 classical concerts (London)
379 plays
326 galleries/exhibitions (London)
313 museums (London)
298 (Japanese restaurants)

champagne

250 ── Greek/Turkish restaurants

(champagne drinking)

opera

leisure centre city foreign holidays; contemporary dance.

200 ── restaurants (evening)

wind surfing

mineral waters; tennis; French restaurants; jazz concerts; pop/rock concerts; (squash clubs).

ballet; other restaurants.

'rest of world' holidays; skiing; Italian holidays; Indian restaurants; champagne-style wine drinking; USA holidays; squash clubs.

150 ── (tennis clubs); classical concerts; galleries/exhibitions; (Irish whiskey); sports/other holidays.　　　　(target shooting); (flying); sailing clubs.

Chinese restaurants; (vodka); liqueurs; musicals; (port drinking); bridge.　　　　riding clubs; museums (London).

(table tennis); brandy; squash; Spanish mainland holidays; cigarettes; leisure centre countryside foreign holidays; multi-centre holidays; (gym clubs).　　　　skating; (shooting (rough)); classical concerts (not London).

information for TGI values from 80 to 120 have been omitted

sherry; camping.　　　　leisure centre lakes holidays; contemporary dance; health clubs; salmon fishing; bowls; opera.

museums (not London); traditional English restaurants; galleries/exhibitions (not London).

classical concerts (not London); rock concerts (not London).

50 ──

*Figure 6.9* Consumption by region (London and South East) 1987–88. Uses AB Survey as a base. Vertical axis = Target Group Index (TGI) where the value for Great Britain = 100. Brackets are used when cell counts are too low to produce reliable data.
*Source*: British Market Research Bureau

124

role of the South East in middle-class formation, can there be distinctive cultural patterns there? Figures 6.9 to 6.12 show conclusively that there is indeed a London lifestyle if we take the AB group as a whole. All forms of culture (whether of the 'new' or the 'old') are much more likely to be engaged in by the middle classes in London. Furthermore, London is well represented when it comes to the new healthy lifestyles we have discussed earlier. We can also see a similar, though considerably reduced, lifestyle for the South East as a whole. This is the area in which they are most likely to adopt the different types of consumption associated with high levels of economic and cultural capital. It is here, too, that they are likely to make an array of contacts that will be useful for future economic success.

Figures 6.9 to 6.12 suggest we need to reassess the stereotype (see Leadbeater 1989) of London and the South East as the setting for fast-

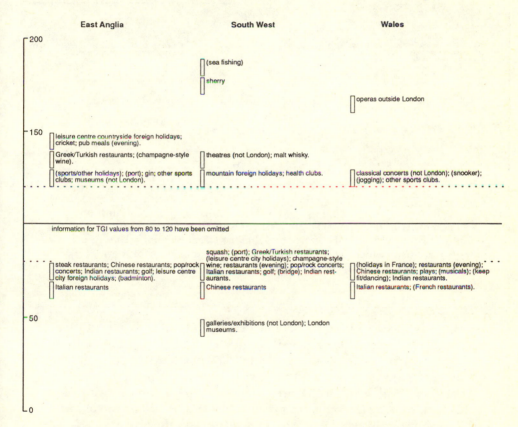

*Figure 6.10* Consumption by region (East Anglia, South West and Wales) 1987–88. Uses AB Survey as a base. Vertical axis = Target Group Index (TGI) where the value for Great Britain = 100. Brackets are used when cell counts are too low to produce reliable data.
*Source*: British Market Research Bureau

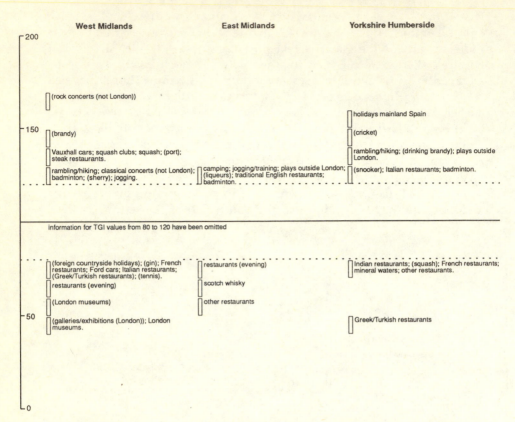

*Figure 6.11* Consumption by region (West Midlands, East Midlands and Yorkshire-Humberside) 1987–88. Uses AB Survey as a base. Vertical axis = Target Group Index (TGI) where the value for Great Britain = 100. Brackets are used when cell counts are too low to produce reliable data.
*Source*: British Market Research Bureau

moving, high-living and cosmopolitan lifestyles. This picture is partly true but it underestimates the extent to which such practices are combined with more ascetic ways of life based on body-maintenance and self-preservation.

Other regions demonstrate distinctive cultures engaged in by the ABs. Golf, salmon fishing and scotch are, unsurprisingly, associated with Scotland. Yorkshire, again confirming popular legend, is well associated with cricket. Similarly, Welsh ABs are more prone to visit the opera. But, apart from some relatively modest jogging, the regions outside London are again relatively under-represented when it comes to the 'new' cultural forms engaged in by the young, mainly male and well-educated, middle classes.

126

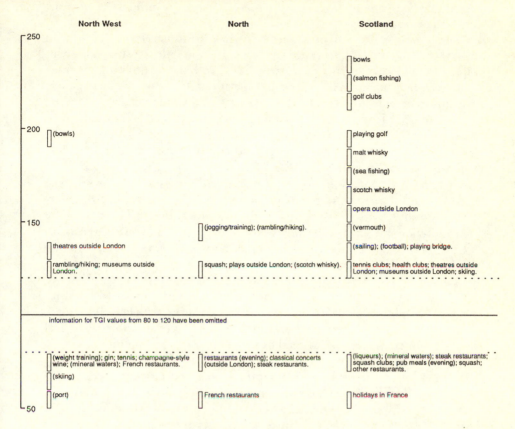

*Figure 6.12* Consumption by region (North West, North and Scotland) 1987–88. Uses AB Survey as a base. Vertical axis = Target Group Index (TGI) where the value for Great Britain = 100. Brackets are used when cell counts are too low to produce reliable data.
*Source*: British Market Research Bureau

## INTELLECTUALS AND THE THEORY OF POST-MODERN CULTURE

The TGI survey indicates three salient types of middle-class lifestyle which we have labelled the *ascetic*, the *post-modern*, and the *undistinctive*. All appear to have a distinct social base within the middle classes: the first among the public sector welfare professionals, the second among the private sector professionals and specialists, and the third among managers and government bureaucrats. But these processes interweave with those of gender, age and location: a young, male, London-based advertising executive is

127

undoubtedly prone to have a post-modern lifestyle, as indeed the 'yuppie' stereotype would suggest.

The 'ascetic' culture of public sector professionals would tie in well with Bourdieu's arguments, since this group is high in cultural, but not economic capital. However, the group associated with the stolid 'undistinctive' – or just plain boring – lifestyle is not mentioned by Bourdieu at all, but appears to be of some significance in Britain. (This will probably not come as a surprise to foreign readers!) The greater separation of cultural from organisation assets in Britain compared to France is almost certainly the cause of this. Finally, Bourdieu would associate the 'post-modern lifestyle' with the 'new petite bourgeoisie'. While we can see echoes of this from our survey, the important point to recognise is that this lifestyle appears to exist throughout the private sector professional middle class, not just the marginal, 'up and coming' elements within it, which Bourdieu sees as the defining characteristics of the 'new petite bourgeoisie'. It would seem, from our survey, that barristers, accountants and surveyors partake in the post-modern lifestyle as much as sex therapists or advertising agents.

The time has come to consider the issue of post-modernism rather more seriously. We have hitherto seen this as a culture of 'health with champagne', a combination of otherwise opposing cultures, which are 'sampled' rather than incorporated into a way of life. This relates to more analytical analyses which argue that instead of single, totalising, discourses (as represented by, for example, fixed notions of 'art' or 'culture') contemporary post-modern culture is pluralist, depthless and self-mocking. Post-modernism, unlike modernism, is said to embrace 'the death of the author' and results from the steady penetration of commerce and the commodity form into the realm of art and culture. Previously well-established cultural traditions are thus increasingly treated in a 'pastiche' way. Previously 'high' or 'unique' culture are mass-produced and treated as just one form of culture along with others. The distinction between 'high' and 'low' culture ('taste' and 'tack') is steadily obliterated as forms of art and culture previously surrounded by a distinct aura stemming from their rarity become just another mass-produced commodity.

There are numerous attempts to explain the rise of post-modern culture. Harvey (1989), echoing Jameson (1984), argues that post-modern culture is the product of capital's needs for rapid turnover. Forms of culture are established only to be immediately destroyed as capital creates a sequence of rapidly changing fads and fashions; the imperative being the rapid turnover of capital. Connor (1989) argues, quite persuasively, that the discovery of 'post-modernism' is largely a belated recognition by academics of forms of behaviour (especially various forms of commercialised consumption) which have actually been in existence for a long time.

More precise attempts to pin down the 'audience' for post-modern culture have been essayed by a number of writers. All are united in seeing it as some kind of middle-class phenomenon, but their specification of its precise location within the middle class varies. Lash and Urry (1987) argue that the 'service class' of senior white-collar workers has a central role both in defining what are 'high' and 'low' cultures and in establishing new kinds of post-modern culture. To relate this to our earlier discussion, Lash and Urry argue that senior white-collar workers have a central position both in determining the form of a dominant type of culture (whether it is skiing, champagne or port drinking) and in breaking down the previously fixed divisions between 'high' and 'low' culture. Furthermore, they remain far less awestruck with certain lifestyles and cultural forms than previous generations. They can as easily engage in ballet, opera, rock music and 'Californian sports', treating none of these as *the* culture, each being an activity to be sampled – albeit in an apparently 'depthless', pastiche, manner.

Clearly Lash and Urry's arguments, while helpful, are not precise enough in distinguising groups within the 'service class'. Pfeil (1988) sees the key group as the highly educated who work in large bureaucracies, and so suffer from the alienation caused by engaging in instrumental, largely meaningless work. But apart from the fact that this tension goes back a long time – it could as easily explain the rise of modernist as much as post-modernist culture – it would appear that Pfeil has wrongly specified the social bases of post-modern lifestyle. Bureaucrats are not drawn to post-modernism, but either to asceticism (if highly educated) or to a mundane lifestyle. Bagguley *et al.* (1990: 160), who also see managerial workers as attracted to post-modernism, are also mistaken here.

Lash (1990), on the other hand, is more accurate in speculating about the role of the 'post-industrial middle classes' in post-modernism. He sees these groups as working on symbols rather than things, so that they 'produce symbols which help realise the value of other symbols' (Lash 1990: 251). It is indeed professional workers in advertising and so forth who appear most prominently as exemplars of the 'post-modern' lifestyle according to our analysis. However, Lash, like Bourdieu – on whose arguments he draws – ignores what to us seems the crucial element, concerning the significance of the public–private sector divide.

The professionally educated workers who work in the private sector appear to be the key constituency for post-modernism. As we explained in Chapter 4, it is especially this group that has come to the fore with the rapid rise of the new service sectors such as financial services, advertising, property and personnel management. This, in turn, suggests that 'post-modern' culture may well be associated with a social group that is becoming culturally, socially and economically dominant in contemporary Britain. This group is discovering, for the first time, that cultural assets need not depend on the legitimacy offered by the state. Cultural assets can be deployed and valorised in the market, and in this respect post-modern culture might be seen as the commodification of cultural assets themselves.

As our data suggest, it is above all this group which indulges in a wide range of disparate consumption practices. As a result, practices considered to have an auratic quality by previous generations become treated in a non-auratic way by the new (young and predominantly male) private sector professional middle class. Opera, classical music, skiing holidays, foreign travel are all cases in point. Similarly, the brash and economically well-endowed young executive buying a new house which cashes in on the 'tradition' of a rural area is guaranteed to raise the hackles of the well-ensconced guardians of 'local culture'. A particularly stunning example of an aura's demise, and one which horrifies older generations, is the treatment by the young male middle classes of long-established forms of alcoholic drink. Champagne and port are now, as the theorists of post-modernism suggest, just one among many drinks – not those to be consumed on rare and special occasions.

This leads us to the debate on post-modernism itself. This should be seen not as a debate within all the middle classes – for there are many of the middle classes, especially those in managerial jobs, who are unlikely either to have heard of it, or to have engaged unknowingly in its practices. Rather, it should be seen as a debate within the narrower middle class relying on cultural assets. The term 'post-modernism' is very much a product of the intellectuals who do not form a central part of the new form of culture (Bauman 1988; Connor 1989). 'Post-modernism', we would argue, is a labelling by intellectuals and others of a form of activity that has broken away from the 'fixed', non-commercialised forms of culture linked to the legitimation offered by the state with which they are closely associated and for which they have long been guardians and gatekeepers. It is a product of the very struggles within the middle classes that we have been discussing in this chapter and elsewhere in the book. The word 'post-modern' refers to a real enough phenomenon; especially the commercialisation of culture and the decline of 'high' or what Benjamin (1973) called 'auratic' art. But at the same time it refers to a set of values which academic and other commentators (with their high levels of cultural capital and their continued adherence to an ascetic culture) find extremely difficult to endorse. But it also reflects the fascination of these groups with the activities of their high-spending professional colleagues. Intellectuals with their comparatively low levels of economic capital remain largely unable to fully engage in post-modern culture even if their adopted ways of life (their habitus) could be extended to allow them to do so, but they can comment on the activities of their friends – with many of whom they graduated – and wonder what might have happened if they had chosen a different career.

In short, the concept of 'post-modernism' does reflect changing cultural practices, in particular the engagement in diverse forms of practice by a new (mainly young, mainly male) social group. On the other hand, the label, 'post-modern', is a category that established intellectuals apply to commercialised cultural forms which they find both difficult to understand and mildly distasteful. At the same time, it serves (as indeed Bourdieu's theory of social dynamics predicts) to label, scarcify and exclusify a particular cultural form.

In this chapter we have begun to move away from considering the changing salience of specific types of assets and have begun to show how the middle-class employees are being formed into three different cultural groups. It is now time, therefore, to tackle the issue of middle-class formation head on. We need to consider exactly how the changes we have elaborated in this and the previous two chapters may have affected the historical patterns of middle-class formation we enumerated in Chapter 3. This thesis is taken up in the remainder of the book.

# 7

# SOCIAL MOBILITY AND HOUSEHOLD FORMATION

In the last three chapters of this book we consider the nature of middle-class formation directly. Since the pathbreaking work of Goldthorpe (1980), drawing upon the theoretical insights of Giddens (1973), it is now widely recognised that processes of social mobility are central to an understanding of how social classes form as 'stable collectivities'. In Giddens' words, 'the greater the degree of "closure" of mobility chances – both inter-generationally and within the career of the individual – the more this facilitates the formation of identifiable classes' (quoted in Goldthorpe 1987: 25).

It is within this vein that this chapter proceeds. We begin by arguing that while Goldthorpe has put the relationship between social mobility and class formation firmly on the research agenda, his own approach to the relationship between social mobility and class formation contains some weaknesses. We therefore suggest a rather different agenda for the study of the relationship between social mobility and class formation, before drawing upon existing research in this area to suggest a series of empirical gaps in previous analyses of social mobility as it affects the middle classes.

In order to address the questions we have set ourselves we need to provide new evidence on patterns of middle-class social mobility, and for this purpose we report our secondary analysis of two, rather different, surveys. Firstly, we analyse the Longitudinal Study (LS), which links together the Census records of 1 per cent of the population between 1971 and 1981 and hence allows a detailed, fine-grained analysis of career mobility. Secondly, we examine social mobility from the British General Election Survey 1987, in order to consider in more detail patterns of inter-generational mobility between parents and children.

## SOCIAL MOBILITY AND CLASS FORMATION

The study of social mobility is one of the most sophisticated branches of empirical sociological enquiry. In Britain three major surveys have pro-

132

vided evidence and set the terms of debate: the LSE study, carried out in 1949 and reported in Glass (1954), but now heavily criticised by Payne (1987a); the Nuffield study, carried out between 1972 and 1974, and reported in Goldthorpe (1980); and the Scottish mobility study carried out in the early 1970s and reported in Payne (1987b).

Of these the most important, both in terms of its conceptual rigour and methodological exactness, is that of Goldthorpe (1980). This study has transformed our understanding of the processes of social mobility in contemporary Britain and has been rightly hailed as one of the most important works of post-war British sociology (Marshall 1990b). It will be clear to many readers that we have learned a great deal from Goldthorpe's work – not least the very idea that class formation is primarily about the creation of 'stable class collectivities'. Nonetheless, we believe that Goldthorpe's approach to social mobility is more geared to understanding how 'open' societies are than it is to throwing light on processes of class formation, and therefore his approach needs modification.

Goldthorpe argues that studies of social mobility address two rather different issues of sociological concern. Firstly, they allow us to probe the openness of any particular society by comparing the mobility chances of different groups within the population, in order to assess whether any groups are more advantaged than others. Secondly, they allow us to throw light on the processes of class formation, by examining how certain classes may be more or less self-recruiting, and hence more or less socially cohesive. The more any class recruits from outside its own ranks, the less likely it is that it will emerge as a stable social collectivity. And, he claims, the former issue (the degree of social openness) can best be studied by examining relative mobility rates – the mobility chances of members of one class relative to those of another class. The latter issue (class formation) should focus on absolute mobility rates – the proportion of any one class who are recruited from outside that class.[1]

In this elegant formulation Goldthorpe appears to resolve many of the ambiguities and uncertainties in earlier studies of social mobility. By using different techniques sociologists can use the same set of data to throw light on two rather different issues. However, in our view Goldthorpe overlooks one major difference between the two purposes of inquiry, which reduces its value for the study of class formation.

If we are interested in the degree of openness in any society, the crucial issue is to examine social mobility *between* differing classes. Usually this involves considering the extent to which individuals can move between social classes that differ unequally in the life chances they convey. One of the merits of Goldthorpe's approach, however, is that he also examines horizontal mobility between social classes who enjoy similar market and work situations but have differing employment relationships in the class structure. Nonetheless, the prime focus is on mobility between differing sets of class positions.

However, if we are interested in issues of class formation – the development of stable social class collectivities in Goldthorpe's own terms – it is by no means clear that mobility between classes is of such over-riding importance. Arguably, what is of equal importance is intra-class mobility, the mobility within classes which, in Goldthorpe's terms, may have similar types of employment relations. It might be the case, for instance, that if there is a high degree of occupational closure between similar types of occupations – with children of doctors becoming doctors and children of barristers becoming barristers, for instance – then there will be relatively little mobility between quite similar types of occupations, and this might affect the degree to which these different occupations are formed into a wider social class collectivity.

The problem surfaces in Goldthorpe's treatment of the service class, which, as we have seen, includes employers, professionals, administrators and managers (Penn 1981; Payne 1987a: 118–22), although he does distinguish junior from senior members of this class in some of his analyses. Goldthorpe's class schema prevents him from systematically examining the extent of internal, horizontal mobility within the service class (though, as we shall see presently, he does provide some asides on this issue) to see how this affects its class formation: he is largely restricted to assessing this issue simply in terms of vertical mobility into or out of the service class.

Using Goldthorpe's criteria there is a high degree of mobility into (though not out of) the service class. Only 37 per cent of the upper service class in his sample had fathers in the service class, compared with 72 per cent of unskilled manual workers whose fathers were manual workers (Goldthorpe 1987: Table 2.1). Hence, he argues that the service class is not cohesively formed and cannot be expected to engage in class-based action, while the working class is. But this does not follow. Some groups within the 'service class' may have much higher rates of self-recruitment, in which case there is no reason why they are not able to engage in class-based action. Historically, we have seen that this appears to be true for the professional middle classes. On the other hand, within the largely self-recruiting working class, it may be that there are a number of differing self-recruiting groups – for instance, based around particular industries – so it may not be possible to talk of the 'maturity' of the working class, as Goldthorpe does, on the basis of inter-class mobility alone.

This point is especially pertinent in the light of the theoretical framework we have developed, since we believe that some groups within Goldthorpe's 'service class' are much better able to store and transmit their assets than others. Those with cultural capital, often working in professional jobs, may well be much more self-recruiting than those working in managerial or administrative jobs. We have seen in Chapters 3 and 4 the way in which the professional classes have carved out a distinctive place for themselves in British society, while managers have developed as a subordinate class, dependent to a much greater extent on their employers. While they may be able to gain an advantaged economic position through their superordinate positions in organisational hierarchies, the difficulty in storing this outside their employing organisation may well mean that their advantages cannot be passed on to their children.

The problem, however, in attempting to examine this argument lies in the fact that most sample surveys simply will not have enough cases to allow analysis of occupational or internal mobility in the way we deem important. It is in this respect that the secondary analysis of the Longitudinal Study is of major importance. This links together the Census records of 1 per cent of the English and Welsh population between 1971 and 1981, and hence has over half a million people in its sample. Thus it contains over 34,000 individuals in 'service-class' jobs in 1971, over three times the number in the entire Nuffield social mobility study, permitting it to deal with mobility at a fine-grained level.

We analyse this survey by concentrating on absolute mobility rates and on patterns of career (work-life) mobility. These decisions also followed from an unease with Goldthorpe's own preferred approach. Goldthorpe, more than any other contemporary writer in the field of social mobility, has been concerned with developing a class-based approach to social mobility (in distinction to American work, which has characteristically been more concerned with examining the sorts of factors that allow people to 'get ahead'). However, Goldthorpe analyses social closure largely in terms of relative social mobility. In other words, he regards changes to the occupational structure as changes that need to be controlled and excluded from analysis so that class advantages and patterns of social closure can be revealed in a 'pure' form through the analysis of 'mobility regimes' as shown by the application of log linear models. But this is unduly restrictive, since it assumes occupational change has nothing to do with the dynamics of class conflict. In fact class processes affect the occupational structure itself: the case of the defeat of the National Union of Mine-workers in 1984–85 on the number of coal-mining jobs being only a dramatic instance of this.[2] As a result, the analysis of absolute rates of mobility also bears upon class processes, and we shall hence focus our analysis on absolute rates of social mobility to indicate not only processes of class formation, but also to suggest tentatively the relative propensities of different middle-class groups to store and transmit their advantages.[3]

Another problem in Goldthorpe's account is that his prime focus of social mobility is inter-generational, between parents and children. Career, or work-life, mobility is important mainly in elaborating patterns revealed in the more basic tables, and most of his discussion in *Social Mobility and the Class Structure in Modern Britain* is concerned with how a consideration of career mobility affects the findings about the more fundamental 'inter-generational' patterns. We follow Sorenson (1986), however, in arguing that career mobility is of greater significance than this suggests. Any analysis of inter-generational mobility 'freezes' two individuals at an arbitrary stage in their work-lives. It is hence better to begin by examining typical patterns of career mobility so that we learn about typical work-life trajectories before examining inter-generational patterns. This emphasis upon career mobility is of particularly great significance for us since we have argued, in Chapter 2, that the distinction between differing career strategies is of major importance in distinguishing managers from professionals.

Finally, Goldthorpe has defended the 'conventional view', whereby the class position of women is derived not from their own labour market position but from that of their husbands or fathers (Goldthorpe 1983, 1984). Whatever the merits of Goldthorpe's view in a period when women's labour market involvement was of limited duration, it is clearly inappropriate today when nearly half the workforce is female, and when Dex (1987, 1988) has shown that women have distinct careers of their own and have a definite commitment to the workforce. All our analyses of social mobility are based upon individuals rather than households. Goldthorpe's more recent advocacy of the 'dominance' approach (Goldthorpe 1987) – whereby the class location of all the household's members is determined by the labour market position of the best-placed household member, male or female – appears to make some concessions to the growing numbers of women in 'middle-class' employment. We have argued in Chapter 5, however, that specific types of household structure are of increasing salience in middle-class formation, and it is therefore necessary to examine how individuals, with differing types of labour market position, come together to form specific types of household. For this reason we complement our analysis of social mobility with an examination of household structure among the middle classes at the end of this chapter.

## SOCIAL MOBILITY WITHIN THE MIDDLE CLASSES

The crucial issue then is not just inter-class mobility but intra-class mobility. While this has not been systematically investigated before, we are not working entirely in the dark. Goldthorpe, in particular, does occasionally refer to horizontal 'situs' divisions within the service class, though he never elaborates the precise status of the concept 'situs'. He draws these situs divisions between professional workers on the one hand, and administrative and managerial workers on the other. This appears to be a useful distinction in the light of our earlier findings about the differential development of the managerial and professional middle class in Britain. We also have assorted comments of Heath (1981) and Payne (1987b) to draw upon.

The existing work does suggest three points which indicate the salience of our earlier arguments. Firstly, it would appear that there is a fair degree of internal closure between managerial and professional groups, so suggesting that they have rather different patterns of social mobility. Secondly, it would appear that there is some evidence that there is greater career social mobility out of managerial jobs, indicating the relative insecurity of organisation assets. Finally, there are some indications of differences in patterns of inter-generational mobility between the two situses. We shall address each of these in turn.

The first point seems flatly contradicted by Goldthorpe's own statement that:

> for one thing, mobility between these situses would appear to be fairly frequent, both in the course of working life and inter-generationally. In the former case, the most notable tendency is for professionals eventually to take up administrative and managerial positions; while conversely, in the latter, it is for the sons of administrators and managers to be, if anything, more likely to be found in professional occupations than in ones similar to their fathers.
>
> (Goldthorpe 1982: 178–9)

Goldthorpe here claims that internal mobility is common, and hence that there tends not to be social barriers internal to the service class which might affect class formation. But let us put this in perspective. Our reworking of Goldthorpe's figures on career movement between professional and managerial 'situses' (Goldthorpe 1987: Figures 5.1, 5.11 and 5.12) suggest that for those whose first and current jobs were in the service class, 81 per cent of professionals stayed in professional ranks, and 75 per cent of managers stayed in managerial jobs. This seems to indicate that both professionals and managers tend to remain in their particular 'situses' and do not move with great frequency between them.[4]

Further inspection of his Table 5.1 indicates that of the 24.4 per cent of men who started their working lives in the intermediate classes (III–V), 32 per cent of them moved into the service class in the course of their working lives. In other words, there appears to be more work-life movement into the service class from the outside, than between professional and managerial groups within it. At the very least, the issue clearly needs further elaboration than Goldthorpe's cursory statement suggests.

As to the second issue, Goldthorpe is insistent that 'men who enter service-class occupations ... have a very low probability of thereafter leaving such occupations. This finding, one would suggest, results in part from the character of the service relationship' (Goldthorpe 1982: 175). But it is not clear how Goldthorpe's method of analysis allows this point to be demonstrated. His analysis of career mobility is rather restricted since it measures mobility between first and current job alone. This procedure is likely to underestimate downward career mobility, since even if a worker is demoted in later life, that person may still end up in a 'higher' job than the first one he or she took when entering the labour market.[5] In fact, one survey of managers (Crockett and Elias 1984) did, *pace* Goldthorpe, find a high level of downward intra-generational social mobility from managerial ranks.

Finally, what about patterns of inter-generational mobility? Do all the middle-class groups have an equal likelihood of being self-recruiting, or does it vary by situs? And, conversely, do the children of managers have as much chance of staying in middle-class work as the children of professionals, as Goldthorpe suggests? Goldthorpe does not break down inter-generational mobility by situs anywhere in his book. Heath (1981), working on the same data, does so however, and these reveal contrasting patterns. Over half of industrial managers have working-class fathers, compared with 43 per cent of senior administrators, 39 per cent of professional employees, and 24 per cent of the professional self-employed (Heath 1981: Table 2.3), which seems to suggest some significant differences. The professional middle class does appear to be more self-recruiting.

Payne (1987b) also considers this issue of the transmission of middle-class positions inter-generationally in more detail. He notes, from the Scottish mobility study, that 29 per cent of the sons of professionals move into the professions, compared with another 17 per cent who move into other parts of the 'upper middle class' (a grouping similar to Goldthorpe's 'service class', but excluding property owners). In other words, 63 per cent of the sons of professionals who remain in the 'UMC' remain within professional ranks. The picture is different for the sons of managers, however: 18 per cent of their sons become managers, while another 26 per cent move into other parts of the 'UMC'. This supports Goldthorpe's contention that significant numbers of children of managers move into professional occupations. Rather than being able to pass on their own organisation assets to their children, the assets need to be translated into educational assets which allow entry to professional work. As Payne himself notes,

> there is no evidence to suggest that managers *per se* presently consti-
> tute a new closed group with inherited privilege. Less than one in
> five managers' sons have become second generation managers ...
> Even if writers on industrial and post industrial society were correct
> about the significance of technical expertise and the division of
> ownership and control, these UMC managers have yet to show any

signs of consolidating their economic power into dynastic security of the kind presumably enjoyed by the owners.

(Payne 1987b: 85)

Payne goes on to note that relatively few sons of professionals move into management, and while the overall proportions of sons of professionals and managers being downwardly mobile are similar, those managers' sons who are downwardly mobile usually move further down than the sons of professionals (Payne 1987b: 85–6). The crucial point is that while the sons of professionals appear able to follow their fathers' footsteps into professional employment with reasonable regularity, managers' sons are less likely to follow their fathers into managerial work. Their fathers' organisation assets have to be traded in, as it were, for educational credentials if they are to remain part of the middle classes. This reveals once again the specific insecurity of the managerial middle classes, and is a point to which we shall return.

## INTRA-GENERATIONAL MOBILITY

We have a few clues, then, but clearly we need to go further than the rather fragmentary treatment that can be found in existing work. We need to probe patterns of internal mobility with much more exactitude than has been the case in the past to discover how the different middle-class assets we have specified affect patterns of middle-class formation.

In this section we concentrate on four simple tables (inflow and outflow, men and women) showing absolute rates of work-life mobility between 1971 and 1981 using the LS. The LS is a good tool for studying career mobility, as we can see how individuals moved between jobs during the period 1971 to 1981, or moved into or out of the labour market. The best method of analysis is to 'open up' the middle classes, as it were, and inspect patterns of mobility within them. The easiest way of doing this is to examine mobility between OPCS Socio-Economic Groups (SEGs). We shall be using SEGs in the remainder of the book, and Appendix 2 provides full information on their derivation. Their advantages are that they allow us to look inside the middle classes since there are enough SEGs (six within the 'service class' for example) to examine internal as well as intra-class mobility, but few enough to be manageable and to avoid being overwhelmed by detail. There is one important rider, however. The dominant capitalist class of large property owners is probably found in SEG 1.1. However, the numbers of the sample in SEG 1.1 are very small, and it is not possible to investigate the social mobility of this dominant capitalist class through the use of the LS, or indeed any other sample survey.

Table 7.1 is an 'outflow' table for men showing mobility within the middle classes as well as between different social classes. The table indicates

*Table 7.1* Outflow table: men's work-life mobility, 1971–81

| 1971 SEG | 1.1 | 1.2 | 2.2 | 3 | 4 | 5.1 | All SC | PB | Others* | N= |
|---|---|---|---|---|---|---|---|---|---|---|
| | | | | 1981 SEG | | | | | | |
| 1.1 | 3.7 | 9.3 | 13.0 | 3.7 | – | 5.6 | 35.2 | 25.1 | 15.6 | 54 |
| 1.2 | 0.0 | 32.6 | 17.6 | 4.2 | 3.4 | 3.8 | 52.7 | 3.1 | 18.1 | 5,008 |
| 2.2 | 0.0 | 13.6 | 34.4 | 0.5 | 1.8 | 2.8 | 53.2 | 9.8 | 21.6 | 6,790 |
| 3 | – | 1.0 | 3.0 | 55.5 | 12.6 | 4.5 | 76.6 | 3.7 | 2.7 | 1,118 |
| 4 | 0.0 | 9.3 | 8.6 | 5.6 | 40.0 | 11.1 | 74.4 | 2.0 | 13.3 | 5,497 |
| 5.1 | – | 10.9 | 4.4 | 0.4 | 8.6 | 41.6 | 65.9 | 2.1 | 16.9 | 6,373 |
| All SC | 0.0 | 15.2 | 16.2 | 4.1 | 12.8 | 14.8 | 63.1 | 4.5 | 16.9 | 24,849 |
| PB | 0.0 | 0.7 | 6.2 | 0.3 | 0.3 | 1.6 | 9.3 | 50.2 | 22.7 | 10,671 |
| PWC | 0.0 | 7.7 | 9.5 | 0.3 | 3.0 | 4.9 | 25.4 | 4.2 | 50.6 | 17,062 |
| PBC | 0.0 | 1.5 | 2.3 | 0.0 | 0.9 | 1.7 | 6.5 | 4.7 | 69.8 | 69,170 |
| UE | – | 1.0 | 2.6 | 0.3 | 1.1 | 2.2 | 7.3 | 6.5 | 62.3 | 4,528 |
| Total LM | 0.0 | 5.0 | 6.3 | 0.9 | 3.5 | 4.7 | 20.4 | 8.5 | 61.1 | 126,277 |

* Others in different labour market groupings (PWC, PBC, UE).

*Notes*: (a) For a 1% sample of men in England and Wales who were in the labour market in 1971.

(b) Percentages do not match to 100%, since the balance have left the labour market between 1971 and 1981 (usually through retirement).

(c) Classification:
- 1.1 = Large employers
- 1.2 = Managers, large establishments
- 2.2 = Managers, small establishments
- 3 = Self-employed professionals
- 4 = Professional employees
- 5.1 = Ancillary workers
- All SC = All service class
- PB = Petite bourgeoisie (SEGs 2.1, 11, 13)
- PWC = White-collar proletariat (SEGs 5.2, 6, 7)
- PBC = Manual working class
- UE = Unemployed
- Total LM = Total labour market

(See Appendix 2 for more details.)

*Source*: LS ASTF011 (Longitudinal Study 1990) (Crown Copyright reserved).

the 1981 destinations of individuals in 1971 SEGs, thus allowing us to see if any middle-class groups appear to have more social mobility into other social groups.

The easiest way to unravel Table 7.1 is to start by looking at the diagonal values, since these report the proportions persisting in the same grouping, and hence indicate stability between 1971 and 1981. Of all the diagonal values, the highest is for SEG 3, where 56 per cent of those in SEG 3 in 1971 are still in SEG 3 in 1981. This is revealing since SEG 3 comprises the professional self-employed: in other words, those who are likely to draw on *both* cutural and property assets. Next highest comes the petite bourgeoisie (with property assets alone), with a 50 per cent survival rate, followed by professional employees at 40 per cent (who have cultural assets alone), but the managerial groups have much lower survival rates.

All this seems to conform to our expectations: property assets and cultural assets appear to convey greater security than organisation assets. Let us now turn to consider mobility out of the middle classes between 1971 and 1981. This is best examined by looking at the mobility into the column headed 'Others', indicating other employment outside the middle classes. There is negligible mobility out of SEG 3 (3 per cent), but reasonably high rates for the managerial SEGs (18 per cent and 22 per cent) and the petite bourgeoisie (23 per cent). Goldthorpe's belief that there is no downward mobility from the service class seems to stretch the evidence. And if we look at the figures under the column 'All SC' we can see that only half of managerial workers stay in the 'service class', but three-quarters of professionals do.

Examining mobility within the middle classes, Table 7.1 partly supports Goldthorpe's observation that work-life movement from professional to managerial jobs is not uncommon. Nearly 18 per cent of SEG 4 (professional employees) had moved into the managerial SEGs between 1971 and 1981, and, in line with Goldthorpe's observations, the figures for managers moving into professional work are much lower. Professionals hence have opportunities of entering managerial jobs, while managers have far less prospect of moving in the opposite direction. This is consistent with the arguments we developed in Chapter 4 concerning the way in which organisations restructure to allow their managerial posts to be filled by professional specialists. This is a well-known trend in accountancy, in particular (Armstrong 1987).

Let us now look at the rows at the bottom of Table 7.1 which allow us to consider the mobility of non-middle-class men into the middle classes between 1971 and 1981. If we look at the PWC – routine white-collar work – there is a reasonably high degree of mobility into managerial work – 17.2 per cent of them move into the managerial groups by 1981. But the rate of entry into professional jobs is far smaller. Similarly, although a smaller proportion of manual workers entered the middle classes, those who did tended to enter managerial rather than professional ranks.

Finally, what of the self-employed? Of considerable interest here is the relatively high degree of mobility into the petite bourgeoisie from managerial groups, especially SEG 2.2. Ten per cent of small managers in 1971 had become small employers by 1981 – a much higher proportion than those who had moved into professional ranks. This fits in with our argument in Chapter 4 that managers' main career strategy is to convert organisation assets into property assets through entrepreneurship.

It seems clear that the patterns revealed by Table 7.1 fit our expectations closely. Those with organisation assets alone – managerial groups – have the most downward mobility. Those with both property and cultural assets have the least. And it does seem that there is far more mobility into the managerial groups than into the professional ones. Two career flows that we discussed in Chapter 4 – the movement of professionals into organisational hierarchies, and the movement of managers into self-employment – seem to be present in significant numbers.

What of women's career mobility? The issue to concentrate on here is whether women can draw upon the three assets in an identical way to men, or whether their mobility patterns vary systematically, linked to the possibility that some of these assets may be more gender neutral than others. Goldthorpe (1987), discussing women's inter-generational mobility, argues that the inclusion of women makes very little difference to analyses of social mobility, but we have argued above that organisation assets in particular are more 'patriarchal' than cultural assets, since organisational hierarchies, as they have developed in modern Britain, depend upon the subordination of female labour. We would hence expect to find differences between men's and women's mobility within the middle class. Table 7.2 provides the evidence on this point.

The first point to establish, in contrast to Table 7.1, is that there are far fewer middle-class women, and most of them are overwhelmingly concentrated in SEG 5.1. This group (which comprises the so-called 'semi-professions' such as nursing and teaching) contains 70 per cent of middle-class women compared to only 26 per cent of men.

Table 7.2 also clearly reveals that middle-class women are less likely to stay in the middle class than men. In all cases, except SEG 5.1, the diagonals

*Table 7.2* Outflow table: women's work-life mobility, 1971–81

| 1971 SEG | 1.1 | 1.2 | 2.2 | 3 | 4 | 5.1 | All SC | PB | Others* | N= |
|---|---|---|---|---|---|---|---|---|---|---|
| | | | | *1981 SEG* | | | | | | |
| 1.1 | – | – | – | – | – | – | – | – | 33.3 | 3 |
| 1.2 | – | 17.4 | 8.3 | – | 0.8 | 8.0 | 34.6 | 1.3 | 19.3 | 827 |
| 2.2 | – | 4.1 | 16.0 | 0.1 | 0.4 | 4.7 | 25.4 | 4.3 | 25.5 | 1,607 |
| 3 | – | 1.0 | 3.3 | 37.0 | 14.1 | 7.6 | 63.0 | 4.3 | 7.6 | 92 |
| 4 | – | 3.3 | 7.0 | 3.8 | 18.4 | 16.6 | 49.1 | 1.7 | 16.7 | 603 |
| 5.1 | – | 3.3 | 1.3 | 0.0 | 1.3 | 47.1 | 52.9 | 1.1 | 11.4 | 7,566 |
| All SC | – | 4.5 | 4.4 | 0.6 | 2.2 | 35.6 | 47.2 | 1.7 | 14.4 | 10,698 |
| PB | 0.0 | 0.6 | 3.5 | 0.0 | – | 2.5 | 6.7 | 23.9 | 21.6 | 2,845 |
| PWC | 0.0 | 1.3 | 2.0 | 0.0 | 0.1 | 2.6 | 6.1 | 1.6 | 47.7 | 39,100 |
| PBC | – | 0.3 | 0.6 | 0.0 | 0.1 | 1.6 | 2.7 | 1.1 | 47.8 | 21,666 |
| UE | – | 0.7 | 1.4 | 0.0 | 0.3 | 6.1 | 8.5 | 1.7 | 36.1 | 2,477 |
| Total LM | 0.0 | 1.4 | 1.9 | 0.1 | 0.4 | 6.4 | 10.6 | 2.3 | 40.5 | 76,696 |

*Notes*: (a) 1% sample of all women in England and Wales in the labour market 1971.
(b) Otherwise as for Table 7.1.
*Source*: Table ASTF014 (Longitudinal Study 1990) (Crown Copyright reserved).

are lower for women than for men. However – and this is a striking point – a rather smaller proportion of women moved into lower social class employment: 14 per cent compared to 17 per cent of men. The disparity is largely explained by the number of women leaving the labour market by 1981. Particularly low numbers of women left SEG 5.1 to move into 'other' employment. This supports the arguments of Dex (1987) and Crompton and Sanderson (1990) that professional employment can serve as a niche which prevents women from moving *down* the class hierarchy. However, whereas men often move out of SEG 5.1 into other 'service-class' employment in SEGs 1–4, few women do. Almost one-quarter of men moved out of SEG 5.1 into higher SEGs by 1981, but only 6 per cent of women. 'Niche' employment may protect women from downward mobility, but it also acts as a barrier to upward mobility.

Against this consider the extraordinarily few managerial women who remained in managerial work – around a third or less. And a very small proportion of self-employed women continued as self-employed between 1971 and 1981. It is also much rarer for middle-class women to move into self-employment than is the case for middle-class men.

This leads us to a crucial observation: cultural assets appear to be more important for women than for men. For men, cultural capital is clearly very important in helping them to stay within the middle classes, but they can also do this by being self-employed, and organisation assets – while not as effective – are still better than nothing. For women the relative importance of cultural capital over property and organisation assets seems much more marked. But even when they obtain a professional occupation, it appears difficult for this to lead to further career progress, in the way seen for male professionals who may move into management. We shall return to this point later.

The true nature of gender inequality within the middle classes can best be gauged by considering the extent of career mobility into the middle classes between 1971 and 1981. Whereas a large proportion of men (25 per cent) gained promotion out of routine white-collar work, only around 6 per cent of women did. A simple calculation shows that if men and women were to be promoted out of routine white-collar work indiscriminately, only 8 per cent of men would enter the managerial SEGs compared with the 17 per cent who actually made that transition between 1971 and 1981. Male mobility is dependent upon female immobility, in the way discussed by Crompton (Crompton and Jones 1984; Crompton 1986). It also underlines our point that women are crucially dependent upon educational credentials, and hence cultural capital, while men find it easier to draw upon other assets in order to reach and retain middle-class positions.

So, we have established that at least in terms of career mobility, it does seem important to relate patterns of mobility to the possession of certain assets, and that these assets appear to offer gender specific benefits. Now

*Table 7.3* Inflow table: men's work-life mobility, 1971–81

| 1971 SEG | 1.1 | 1.2 | 2.2 | 3 | 4 | 5.1 | All SC | PB | Others* |
|---|---|---|---|---|---|---|---|---|---|
| | | | | *1981 SEG* | | | | | |
| 1.1 | 5.1 | 0.0 | 0.0 | 0.1 | – | 0.0 | 0.0 | 0.1 | 0.0 |
| 1.2 | 5.1 | 22.2 | 9.0 | 1.5 | 2.6 | 2.1 | 8.5 | 1.2 | 0.9 |
| 2.2 | 15.4 | 12.5 | 24.0 | 2.6 | 1.9 | 2.1 | 10.6 | 5.3 | 1.5 |
| 3 | – | 0.1 | 0.3 | 45.2 | 2.2 | 0.5 | 2.5 | 0.3 | 0.0 |
| 4 | 2.6 | 6.9 | 4.8 | 22.3 | 33.5 | 6.7 | 12.0 | 0.9 | 0.7 |
| 5.1 | – | 9.4 | 2.9 | 1.7 | 8.4 | 29.0 | 12.3 | 1.1 | 1.0 |
| All SC | 28.2 | 51.2 | 41.1 | 73.5 | 48.6 | 40.4 | 45.8 | 8.9 | 4.3 |
| PB | 28.2 | 1.1 | 6.7 | 2.7 | 0.5 | 1.9 | 2.9 | 42.3 | 2.5 |
| PWC | 12.8 | 17.9 | 16.6 | 3.5 | 7.8 | 9.1 | 12.7 | 5.7 | 8.7 |
| PBC | 20.5 | 14.1 | 16.3 | 2.6 | 9.2 | 13.0 | 13.0 | 25.9 | 48.9 |
| UE | – | 0.6 | 1.2 | 1.1 | 0.7 | 1.1 | 1.0 | 2.3 | 2.9 |
| Total LM | 89.7 | 85.0 | 82.0 | 83.4 | 66.9 | 65.5 | 75.4 | 85.1 | 67.1 |
| N = | 39 | 6,368 | 9,758 | 1,372 | 6,541 | 9,125 | 34,203 | 12,664 | 98,829 |

*Notes*: (a) A 1% sample of men in England and Wales who were in the labour market in 1981.
(b) Percentages do not tally to 100% since the balance were outside the labour market in 1971 (usually in education).
(c) Classifications as for Table 7.1
*Source*: LS ASTF011 (Longitudinal Study 1990) (Crown Copyright reserved).

let us consider the picture the other way round, using an 'inflow' perspective. Here we look at the 1971 origins of people in certain SEGs in 1981, and this allows us to judge the degree to which the respective groups are self-recruiting. It is hence of vital importance in considering the nature of class formation.

Table 7.3 should be read vertically (down the columns), rather than horizontally (across the rows). If we look first at the diagonals, we find fairly much the same pattern as we saw in Table 7.1; the professional self-employed being more likely to have been in the same group in 1971, followed by the petite bourgeoisie, the professional employees and finally the managerial groups. The overall figures are, however, much smaller: indeed it is striking to note that less than half of the 1981 'service class' were in the 'service class' in 1971: this supports Goldthorpe's general argument about the instability of the service class, and hence its weak 'class formation'.

The crucial issue is to see how much mobility there is into the respective middle-class groups from people who were in the labour market in 1971, but not in the middle classes. A comparison of the row 'all service class' with 'total labour market' shows that about 34 per cent of managers of large industries, and 41 per cent of managers of small industries were in the labour market, but outside the middle classes, in 1971 – a remarkably high proportion. A very high proportion of managers have worked in working-

Table 7.4  Inflow table: women's work-life mobility, 1971–81

| 1971 SEG | 1.1 | 1.2 | 2.2 | 3 | 4 | 5.1 | All SC | PB | Others* |
|---|---|---|---|---|---|---|---|---|---|
| | | | | *1981 SEG* | | | | | |
| 1.1 | – | – | – | – | – | – | – | – | 0.0 |
| 1.2 | – | 8.5 | 2.5 | – | 0.9 | 0.5 | 1.7 | 0.4 | 0.2 |
| 2.2 | – | 3.9 | 9.3 | 1.7 | 0.9 | 0.6 | 2.4 | 2.3 | 0.6 |
| 3 | – | 0.0 | 0.1 | 28.1 | 1.6 | 0.0 | 0.3 | 0.1 | 0.0 |
| 4 | – | 1.2 | 1.5 | 19.0 | 14.1 | 0.9 | 1.7 | 0.3 | 0.1 |
| 5.1 | – | 14.8 | 3.4 | 0.8 | 12.0 | 30.8 | 23.6 | 2.9 | 1.2 |
| All SC | – | 28.5 | 16.9 | 49.6 | 29.5 | 32.9 | 29.8 | 6.0 | 2.2 |
| PB | 25.0 | 0.9 | 3.6 | 0.8 | – | 0.6 | 1.1 | 22.5 | 0.9 |
| PWC | 38.0 | 29.6 | 29.0 | 2.5 | 6.6 | 8.8 | 14.0 | 21.3 | 26.3 |
| PBC | – | 4.7 | 4.7 | 0.8 | 1.8 | 3.0 | 3.4 | 7.8 | 14.8 |
| UE | – | 1.0 | 1.3 | 0.8 | 0.9 | 1.3 | 1.2 | 1.4 | 1.3 |
| Total LM | 63.0 | 64.7 | 55.4 | 54.5 | 38.7 | 46.7 | 49.5 | 59.0 | 45.0 |
| N = | 8 | 1,694 | 2,764 | 121 | 790 | 11,571 | 16,948 | 3,013 | 70,798 |

Note: Classifications as for Table 7.1
Source: LS ASTF011 (Longitudinal Study 1990) (Crown Copyright reserved).

class or routine white-collar jobs in the early stages of their careers. However, only 10 per cent of the professional self-employed, 18 per cent of professional employees, and 25 per cent of 'ancillary workers' came from this location. Once again it appears that our expectations concerning the fundamental difference in patterns of recruitment between managerial and professional jobs are borne out. Goldthorpe is clearly aware of these differences (e.g. 1987: 125ff), but does not give them the theoretical emphasis they deserve. In our view it suggests that his arguments about the service class are confusing because they do not distinguish these two very different groups, each relying on differing class assets with varying causal powers.

Table 7.4 provides an inflow analysis for women. It indicates that very few women in middle-class occupations in 1981 can be regarded as stable middle class: only 30 per cent were also in middle-class occupations in 1971. Around 36 per cent of large industrial managers and 39 per cent of small industrial managers were recruited from lower social classes, figures quite similar to those for men. Only around 5 per cent of the professional self-employed, 9 per cent of professional employees, and 14 per cent of the semi-professionals came from these locations, however – figures that are considerably smaller than for men. It would therefore appear that women professionals are actually rather more homogeneous than their male counterparts: very few appear to have worked outside the middle classes, whereas significant, though still small, numbers of men have.

We have seen then that there are three distinct types of career mobility, each relating to the assets we have developed above. Professionals are largely closed to those already in the labour market and professional workers have good prospects of maintaining their middle-class position. Managerial groups are more open, since they recruit from those already in the labour market, and they also offer less security, with relatively high proportions being downwardly mobile. The petite bourgeoisie is also relatively closed, and it tends to recruit a high proportion of its members from the working class, but is less closed than the professionals, and attracts a reasonable number of managerial workers.

If we consider the effects of career mobility on patterns of class formation it seems evident that the professional classes can be said to be much more cohesively formed than managerial groups. Managers are drawn from a wide variety of backgrounds, and there is also considerable mobility between the different managerial groupings (SEG 1.2 and 2.2). The petite bourgeoisie appears to have a core that is highly stable, but there is also a high degree of mobility into and out of peripheral self-employment. The professions, however, are much more stable, and offer greater security to their members. Hence Goldthorpe's conclusions concerning the formation of the service class need revision. Goldthorpe argues that because the service class has expanded so rapidly it is composed of people from a great variety of backgrounds, and hence it has not formed as a stable social class. Our findings suggest that while this is true enough for managerial groups, it does not hold true for the professional classes. Two examples of particular occupations reinforce this point, at least in terms of career mobility. Of those doctors in 1971 who were still in the labour market in 1981, around 90 per cent were still practising doctors in 1981, and only 2 per cent had moved down into working-class occupations. For lawyers, the corresponding figures were 82 per cent and slightly over 2 per cent. Around 1 per cent of doctors in 1981 had been in working-class occupations in 1971, though this was the case for a rather higher proportion of lawyers (7 per cent). These figures are not perhaps surprising, but they do starkly reveal the degree of work-life closure that strong professional groups are able to achieve.

## INTER-GENERATIONAL MOBILITY

We now turn to consider how class formation occurs inter-generationally. We need to examine whether the same processes that operate at the intra-generational level also work here. But here the LS is of less use. It does link the records of individuals in 1981 with those of their family in 1971 if they were residing with them. For younger people, under the age of 27 in 1981 (who would therefore have been under 17 and hence probably resident with their parents in 1971) this does allow the analysis of inter-generational social mobility. And, even though this severely narrows down the sample, given the overall size of the LS, there are still over 6,000 individuals under the age of 27 in 1981 who were in 'service class' occupations, so permitting refined analysis.

Nonetheless it is unwise to base our arguments entirely on this, since it only includes the young, and is hence unrepresentative, especially since, as we have seen, managerial workers tend to be promoted later in life. We therefore begin by using a secondary analysis of the British General Election Survey 1987. The BGES has been used by Heath (1981) and Goldthorpe (1987) to inquire into social mobility and its reliability hence seems to be well established. It is, however, a small survey of only 3,565 people, which makes it difficult to carry out reliable analyses for each SEG as we did for intra-generational mobility. Hence we decided to aggregate the SEGs into three middle-class groupings reflecting the basic distinctions we uncovered earlier. This is not a perfect procedure: it would be nicer to look inside the middle classes in a much more open way, and try to make sense of the patterns revealed for each SEG, rather than to use predefined classifications. But, we believe that it is still a useful exercise to carry out a simple analysis of inter-generational social mobility along the lines we propose, and we shall use the LS to 'check' our findings by SEG later on.

Table 7.5 presents a table showing the social class destinations of all the children of fathers in various social classes. It can either be read as an outflow table, by looking at the row percentages, or an inflow table, by looking at the column percentages. Looking first at the outflow figures *it is clear that at this inter-generational level there are more similarities between the mobility patterns of professionals and managers than were evident in our examination of career patterns.* Thus, we can see that 75 per cent of the children of

*Table 7.5*  Middle-class inter-generational mobility, 1987

| Father's group | Child's group | | | | |
|---|---|---|---|---|---|
| | Managerial | Professional | Petite bourg. | Others | N = |
| Managerial | 19.3 | 23.4 | 6.1 | 51.2 | 295 |
| | 17.3 | 15.0 | 7.7 | 6.8 | |
| Professional | 13.6 | 36.7 | 7.2 | 42.5 | 221 |
| | 9.1 | 17.5 | 6.9 | 4.2 | |
| Petite bour. | 10.4 | 15.6 | 14.7 | 59.4 | 443 |
| | 14.0 | 15.0 | 27.9 | 11.9 | |
| Others | 8.6 | 10.6 | 5.9 | 74.9 | 2,276 |
| | 59.6 | 52.5 | 57.5 | 77.0 | |
| N = | 329 | 461 | 133 | 2,212 | |

*Notes*: (a) Outflow mobility in top left corner; inflow mobility bottom right corner.
(b) Managerial SEGs = 1.1, 1.2, 2.2; professional SEGs 3, 4, 5.1; Petite bourgeoisie = 2.1, 11, 13.
*Source*: British General Election Survey 1987.

147

'other', non-middle-class fathers are themselves outside the middle class, but that this figure is considerably less for the three middle-class groups we have specified. Yet it is also clear that the children of professionals are the most advantaged: 57 per cent of these stay in the middle classes, compared with 49 per cent of the children of managers, and 41 per cent of the children of the petite bourgeoisie.

Similarly, if we look at the diagonals which indicate the direct inheritance of father's class, then the professionals emerge as substantially the most closed in inter-generational terms. Over one-third of professionals' children move directly into professional work, yet only 19 per cent of managers' children become managers, and – more surprisingly – only 15 per cent of the children of the petite bourgeoisie have become self-employed. In other words, it would appear easier for cultural capital to be directly transmitted inter-generationally than either organisation assets or property assets.

But the important finding is the very large numbers of managers' children who cross the 'situs' divide, and retain middle-class position by becoming professionals. This is precisely the point made by Goldthorpe (1982), and echoed by Payne (1987b). Indeed, more children of managers become professionals than managers: 23 per cent of managers' children become professionals compared with 19 per cent who become managers. And this is a crucial issue: managers' children are still advantaged over the children outside the middle classes, but in order to retain a place in the middle classes it would appear that they have to 'trade in' their organisation assets for educational credentials and entry to professional work.

If we look at Table 7.5 as an inflow table the fusion of professional and managerial backgrounds also becomes clear. 15 per cent of current professionals come from managerial fathers, and 18 per cent from professional fathers, only a minor difference. More managers are from managerial backgrounds than professional backgrounds (17 per cent compared to 9 per cent). In the inflow tables the petite bourgeoisie emerges as the most cohesive social class, with 27 per cent of its members being recruited from petit bourgeois fathers.

We have a general picture of the fusion of organisation and cultural assets at this inter-generational level. And, as we have seen, the crucial process allowing this is the large numbers of managers' children who move into professional work. Before attempting to explain how this happens we shall pursue the subject a little longer to gain a precise understanding of the basic mobility patterns. We shall do this firstly by considering how gender impacts on these findings, and secondly we shall use our information from the LS to consider mobility between SEGs to obtain a more fine-grained breakdown of mobility patterns.

On the first point, Table 7.6 provides an outflow table for women only. Comparison with Table 7.5 reveals some striking findings.

*Table 7.6*  Middle-class inter-generational mobility, 1987: women only

| Father's group | Daughters' group | | | | |
|---|---|---|---|---|---|
| | *Managerial* | *Professional* | *Petite bourg.* | *Others* | *N =* |
| Managerial | 9.8 | 23.8 | 2.8 | 63.6 | 143 |
| | 17.3 | 15.0 | 7.1 | 7.2 | |
| Professional | 6.9 | 39.7 | 2.6 | 50.9 | 116 |
| | 9.9 | 20.3 | 5.4 | 4.7 | |
| Petite bour. | 6.0 | 15.4 | 7.3 | 71.4 | 234 |
| | 17.3 | 15.9 | 30.4 | 13.3 | |
| Others | 40.0 | 9.8 | 2.8 | 83.4 | 1,131 |
| | 55.6 | 48.9 | 57.1 | 74.8 | |
| *N =* | 81 | 227 | 56 | 1,260 | |

*Notes*: As for Table 7.5
*Source*: British General Election Survey 1987.

The daughters of professional fathers emerge as much the most likely to retain a middle-class position themselves, and 40 per cent of them become professionals – albeit mostly in SEG 5.1, or the 'semi-professions'. As we suggested above, cultural assets appear to be of particular importance for women. Only 7.3 per cent of the daughters of self-employed fathers become self-employed, and only 10 per cent of managers' daughters become managers, figures that are well below the equivalents for men. Yet more professionals' daughters than sons become professionals.

Finally, Table 7.7 is an inflow table providing information on the SEGs of the fathers of young men in differing middle-class groups in 1981. In this case the professional SEGs seem more closed than the managerial ones: 48 per cent of the male professional self-employed and 41 per cent of the male professional employees come from service-class backgrounds. Yet in both of these cases a higher proportion come from managerial backgrounds. SEG 1.2 – managers in large organisations – are especially well represented here. Table 7.7 confirms the findings of the BGES that inter-generational mobility between managerial and professional ranks is of major significance.

So, how do we conclude this discussion? Looking at social mobility inter-generationally, it does appear that Goldthorpe's stress on the distinctive advantages of the children of the service class over the children of other classes seems substantially correct. It is true that the children of professional fathers – and especially their daughters – have slightly higher chances of staying in the middle class than the children of managers, but we should not exaggerate the differences.

But, what we find of particular interest are the different routes that the children of professionals and managers follow. The children of

Table 7.7   Inflow table: 1981 sons and 1971 fathers*

| 1971 fathers | 1981 sons | | | | | |
|---|---|---|---|---|---|---|
| | 1.2 | 2.2 | 3 | 4 | 5.1 | All SC |
| 1.1 | 0.4 | 0.2 | – | 0.1 | – | 0.1 |
| 1.2 | 9.1 | 8.0 | 13.0 | 11.7 | 7.0 | 8.8 |
| 2.2 | 7.3 | 12.7 | 8.7 | 9.2 | 7.3 | 9.1 |
| 3 | 1.5 | 1.3 | 8.7 | 2.4 | 1.5 | 1.7 |
| 4 | 6.9 | 5.2 | 8.7 | 11.4 | 5.9 | 7.3 |
| 5.1 | 5.4 | 4.2 | 8.7 | 6.3 | 9.7 | 6.9 |
| All SC | 30.6 | 31.6 | 47.8 | 41.2 | 31.4 | 34.0 |
| PB | 8.6 | 11.0 | 8.7 | 6.3 | 8.8 | 8.7 |
| PWC | 11.0 | 11.2 | 21.7 | 8.6 | 11.6 | 10.7 |
| PBC | 32.8 | 32.3 | 13.0 | 30.5 | 35.7 | 33.0 |
| UE | 1.7 | 4.2 | 4.0 | 0.9 | 1.3 | 1.4 |
| Total LM | 84.7 | 87.7 | 95.7 | 87.6 | 88.8 | 87.7 |
| N = | 464 | 860 | 23 | 920 | 1,265 | 3,535 |

* Table for sons aged 17–27 in 1981, living with parents in 1971.
Notes:   (a) There were only three sons in SEG 1.1: one had a father in SEG 2.2, another in PWC, and the other was outside the labour market.
(b) Classifications as in Table 7.1.
Source: LS ASTF021 (Longitudinal Study 1990) (Crown Copyright reserved).

professionals tend to follow their fathers directly into professional work, but the children of managers are less likely to follow directly into managerial work and tend to move into professional occupations. One possible explanation of this may be that the figures actually conceal the degree of professional self-recruitment. This might be due to the fact that, as we saw in Table 7.1, significant numbers of professionals become managers in the course of their careers, and hence some of the ostensible children of managers may actually be brought up in households where the father was initially employed in professional work. In this sense the return of their children to professional employment may be a form of 'counter mobility'.

This is, however, entirely speculative and is unlikely to account for the tendency of managerial children to become professionals in its entirety. It would appear that managerial fathers can attempt to trade in their 'organisation assets' in order to fit out their children with educational credentials. They obviously succeed in doing this, but the question is how? We turn to consider this by examining the role of education in middle-class formation.

## EDUCATIONAL ATTAINMENT AND MIDDLE-CLASS FORMATION

It is at this point that the nature of educational provision may be of particular significance. The role of the education system in processes of middle-class formation is, as we suggested in Chapter 1, one of Bourdieu's central arguments, and led him to develop the concept of 'cultural capital' itself. But if it is the case that the children of largely unqualified managerial fathers, who have attained middle-class ranks by slow career progress, can perform well at school and move into professional employment, then it suggests that cultural capital is either less significant in affecting educational performance, or can be more easily acquired than Bourdieu suggests.

This is indeed the position of Halsey *et al.* (1980) who argue that large numbers of children from social backgrounds in which one would not expect to find much cultural capital have nonetheless succeeded in gaining qualifications. For Halsey *et al.* (1980: 88), 'the twentieth century history of secondary school expansion, at least in Britain, draws attention to the accumulation and dissemination of cultural capital as much as to its preservation and concentration'. As they show, the crucial factor governing levels of educational attainment is less the parents' educational background than the type of school attended.

This point is particularly salient in view of the argument developed in Chapter 2, where we showed that while processes in the labour market tended to fragment the middle classes according to the different types of career they pursued, those based around family structures and neighbourhood tended to unify them. Hence middle-class schools, which might see the mixing of differing middle-class children, may allow cultural capital to be acquired by the children of managerial groups, so allowing them to gain a high level of educational attainment in turn. In this sense schools may be a vital force in forming a wider 'service class' out of two otherwise rather different middle classes.

It is therefore worth pointing out that most work on educational inequality rarely distinguishes different middle-class groups. There is, however, one important exception, in the work of Basil Bernstein. In a seminal paper he distinguishes between visible and invisible pedagogies, claiming (Bernstein 1975) that an 'old middle class' relies on a visible pedagogy where rules of educational transmission are open and explicit. The 'new middle class' – largely composed of professionals – on the other hand relies upon an 'invisible pedagogy' where rules are implicit. 'In the old middle class socialisation is into strong classification and strong framing, where the boundaries convey, tacitly, critical condensed messages. In the new middle class, socialisation is into weak classification and weak frames' (Bernstein 1975: 125). He sees the rise of nursery education as being linked to the rise of the invisible pedagogy, and we might extend his arguments to suggest that comprehensive education – which does not have *explicit* rules of selection and hierarchy – is also, in this sense, related to an invisible pedagogy.

If this is true it suggests that the demise of the tripartite system may be

*Table 7.8* Social class of father and educational achievement of child, by age group (column percentages)

| Educational attainment | Father's group | | | | |
|---|---|---|---|---|---|
| | Managerial | Professional | Petite bourg. | Others | All SC |
| *Respondent under 30 years old* | | | | | |
| None | 3.2 | 2.2 | 16.8 | 19.7 | 15.1 |
| Vocational | 44.1 | 22.6 | 36.8 | 36.8 | 35.9 |
| 'O', 'A' level | 29.0 | 33.3 | 29.5 | 32.7 | 31.9 |
| Professional | 6.5 | 8.6 | 7.4 | 3.2 | 4.8 |
| Degree | 17.2 | 33.3 | 9.5 | 7.6 | 12.2 |
| *N* = | 93 | 93 | 95 | 462 | 745 |
| *Respondent 31–55 years old* | | | | | |
| None | 18.9 | 11.3 | 43.1 | 43.8 | 39.4 |
| Vocational | 27.9 | 28.9 | 29.3 | 29.7 | 29.4 |
| 'O', 'A' level | 22.1 | 24.7 | 12.6 | 15.0 | 16.0 |
| Professional | 18.0 | 13.4 | 8.6 | 6.6 | 8.3 |
| Degree | 13.1 | 21.6 | 6.3 | 4.9 | 6.9 |
| *N* = | 122 | 97 | 174 | 1,027 | 1,420 |
| *Respondent over 56 years* | | | | | |
| None | 28.9 | 34.0 | 56.8 | 67.8 | 61.4 |
| Vocational | 18.9 | 17.0 | 14.8 | 15.9 | 16.0 |
| 'O', 'A' level | 23.3 | 19.1 | 14.8 | 7.2 | 10.2 |
| Professional | 17.8 | 14.9 | 11.8 | 7.4 | 9.3 |
| Degree | 11.1 | 14.9 | 1.8 | 1.7 | 3.0 |
| *N* = | 90 | 47 | 169 | 779 | 1,085 |

*Notes*: (a) Vocational = trade apprenticeship, RSA, commercial qualification, City and Guilds, BEC/TEC.
(b) 'O', 'A' levels = either 'O' levels or 'A' levels but no other qualification.
(c) Professional = teacher training certificate, nursing qualification, 'other technical, professional or business qualification'.
*Source*: British General Election Survey 1987.

of some importance in altering the relationship between schooling and middle-class formation. All the pupils who succeeded in gaining entry to grammar schools under the old system may have been able to benefit from the greater resources they possessed, regardless of the precise educational background of their parents. On the other hand, comprehensive schools, by formally removing principles of selection, may actually maximise the advantages of those children who can bring resources to schools in the form of cultural capital: they may, in short, increase the advantages of professional children over managerial ones, as well as over working-class ones.

What this suggests is that character of educational provision is itself a battleground within the middle classes as well as between middle and working classes, in which those already endowed with cultural capital are engaged in conflicts with those who have not. The latter seek to use the educational system to acquire credentials, while the former seek to use it to transform pre-existing cultural capital into educational qualifications. Comprehensive schools, since they operate more with an 'invisible pedagogy', by not selecting through entrance examinations, actually might confer more benefits on those children with cultural capital.

Table 7.8 uses evidence from the BGES to support our argument, showing the educational attainments of the respondents, broken down by their fathers' social class. The results, we contend, are striking. The oldest age group will largely have been educated before 1944, when the elementary school was the main form of schooling available outside the private sector. They show that the children of managers and professionals are both more likely to gain qualifications than those outside the middle classes. Whereas 61 per cent of the sample had no formal qualifications, this was true for 29 per cent of managers' children and 34 per cent of professionals' children. The children of the petite bourgeoisie are much more similar to 'others' than they are to professionals and managers.

Those aged between 31 and 55 were largely educated under the tripartite system. There is a dramatic increase here in the overall number of qualifications gained, and a significant gap in the attainments of professionals and managers begins to emerge. The children of professionals are significantly more likely to gain degrees than the children of managers. On the other hand 18 per cent of managers' children received professional training – usually teaching certificates or nursing qualifications – a higher proportion than professionals' children.

It is in the youngest age group that we find the starkest differences. Many of these children will have been educated in the comprehensive system, yet it is here that the advantages of the children of professionals over managers emerges most strikingly. Fully one-third of professionals' children get degrees, yet only one in six of managers' children do. Managers' children appear to have the motivation to gain qualifications, judging from the very high proportions gaining vocational qualifications, but higher education appears to be increasingly the province of the children of professionals.

Table 7.8 suggests that the patterns revealed in the LS, and in the Nuffield mobility study of the early 1970s, where managers' children move into professional work, usually via high levels of educational attainment, may be under threat. Under the tripartite system, and before this in the elementary schools, it was evidently possible for managers' children to perform well and gain educational credentials, usually to much the same standard as the children of professionals. But, it would appear that the rise of the comprehensive school, because it has removed formal inequalities from the selection processes in secondary schools, may have actually enhanced the significance of cultural capital for the acquisition of educational qualifications. As a result, one of the main routes by which the children of managers may retain their middle-class position may be lost. The result, we would claim, may well increase the self-recruiting nature of the professional middle class, and lead to the marginalisation of managerial groups.

## HOUSEHOLDS AND MIDDLE-CLASS FORMATION

We now turn to consider the evidence concerning the salience of the household structure as a determining feature of middle-class formation, a point we have developed in Chapter 5. The potential importance of women's entry to middle-class employment for patterns of class formation has not, however, attracted much interest in British research (though see Dex 1987; Crompton and Sanderson 1990). Most research has focused upon the internal relationships and the household circumstances of the male middle-class employee and the housewife – many pointing to the continuing strong gendered segregation of activities, and the continued subordination of women, in these households (Pahl and Pahl 1971; Edgell 1980; Finch 1983). More pertinently, Crompton and Sanderson (1990: 166) point out that since middle-class men and women frequently form households together this will tend to accentuate patterns of social inequality, as dual career households enjoy even more marked advantages *vis-à-vis* other households. This point can also be seen by considering the work of American researchers on the rise of the 'dual career family' (Rapoport and Rapoport 1971). The crucial issue they pointed to was not that there was any marked shift towards equality within the household – the evidence for this is very limited – but the ability of dual career households to draw upon a greater range of assets. In particular it allowed security to be combined with entrepreneurship.

> The husbands saw various work contexts as advantageous for their wives in different ways. In some instances a wife's career within an organisational structure was associated with the feeling that the husband could take greater risks in his own work ... in other instances there was the feeling that if he pursued a more secure occupational career for himself, he could encourgage entrepreneurial activity by his wife.
>
> (Rapoport and Rapoport 1971: 291–2)

The potential for the deployment of organisation assets and property assets, for instance, by different members of the same household, opens up. In this case different types of middle-class household may become of major significance in allowing different types of assets to be used and transformed, and hence middle-class formation becomes crucially dependent upon household type and structure.

Table 7.9 considers the structure of middle-class households in 1987.

As we argued in Chapter 2, whatever their other differences, those with organisation and cultural assets tend to have common gendered relations: the distinction between professionals and managers is of only marginal importance here, and the most apparent of these – the higher proportion of single, male professionals – can probably be explained by the fact that professionals tend to be younger than managers.

*Table 7.9*  Household relationships among the middle classes, 1987 (column percentages)

| Partner | Managerial | Professional | Petite bourg. | Others | All SC |
|---|---|---|---|---|---|
| | | Men | | | |
| Managerial | 7.4 | 4.8 | 1.8 | 1.8 | 3.1 |
| Professional | 9.5 | 13.3 | 5.4 | 2.4 | 5.6 |
| Petite bour. | 3.2 | 2.7 | 8.4 | 0.6 | 2.4 |
| Others | 28.6 | 21.3 | 29.5 | 37.0 | 32.2 |
| At home | 39.1 | 32.5 | 39.1 | 27.7 | 31.8 |
| No partner | 12.2 | 25.5 | 15.7 | 30.4 | 24.8 |
| N = | (189) | (188) | (166) | (667) | (1,210) |
| | | Women | | | |
| Managerial | 23.6 | 15.0 | 2.6 | 9.6 | 11.1 |
| Professional | 7.3 | 22.2 | 10.5 | 6.1 | 9.2 |
| Petite bour. | 9.1 | 5.2 | 55.3 | 7.6 | 9.3 |
| Others | 14.5 | 22.2 | 7.9 | 39.8 | 33.8 |
| At home | 9.1 | 7.2 | 2.6 | 8.7 | 8.1 |
| No partner | 36.4 | 28.1 | 21.1 | 28.2 | 28.4 |
| N = | (55) | (153) | (38) | (635) | (881) |

*Notes:*  (a) Occupational groupings derived from collapsed version of SEGs. See Tables 7.1 and 7.5 for fuller discussion of our procedures here.
(b) 'At home' includes all headings where the respondent is not employed in the labour market.
*Source*: British General Election Survey 1987.

Table 7.9 shows important tendencies towards middle-class endogamy. For men, it is still more common to have a conventional family – with wife at home – than to belong to a dual career family. Around 17 per cent of male managers have 'service class' partners, while 19 per cent of professionals do – numbers that are significant, though not overwhelming. Compared, however, to the petite bourgeoisie and 'other' men (who have 7 per cent and 4 per cent married to service-class women) these are very high proportions. Furthermore, there is considerable inter-marriage between professionals and managers, suggesting that different assets may indeed be combined within one household.

Petit bourgeois men, on the other hand, show patterns much closer to other social classes, and have a particularly high proportion of their wives at home, a finding consistent with our argument about the singular nature of gender relations in these households. Generally it is clear that the hegemony of the 'conventional family' for middle-class men is certainly not well marked. Table 7.9 shows an even division of service-class men into four household types: single men; men with partners at home; men with partners in non-middle-class work; and 'dual career' families.

If we examine the household structure of middle-class women we find a rather different pattern. Table 7.9 shows that higher proportions of middle-class women live with middle-class men than vice versa: 30 per cent of managerial and 37 per cent of professional women live with middle-class partners. Around a fifth of 'service-class' women have male partners employed in lower occupational groups. And the proportion of single women is around the average for all women among professionals, but slightly higher for managers.

In short, Table 7.9 shows the considerable fragmentation of middle-class household types. There is no longer a 'typical' middle-class family, and this fragmentation may well be an important force by which 'service-class' formation is forestalled. The nuclear family, with women being confined to the home, which Davidoff and Hall show was central to middle-class formation, is no longer of overwhelming numerical importance. But it seems important to take this issue further in order to consider the extent to which household type makes a difference to levels of income, and hence household circumstances more generally.

*Table 7.10*  Middle-class household structure and income, 1987 (row percentages)

| Household type | Household income | | | | |
| | Under £8,000 | £8,000 – £12,000 | £12,000 – £20,000 | Over £20,000 | N = |
|---|---|---|---|---|---|
| Both MC | 1 | 6 | 32 | 61 | 127 |
| Husband MC, wife Emp | 3 | 10 | 52 | 35 | 193 |
| Wife MC, husband Emp | 7 | 20 | 43 | 30 | 102 |
| Husband MC, wife at home | 22 | 23 | 32 | 23 | 211 |
| Wife MC, husband at home | 32 | 24 | 28 | 16 | 25 |
| Single MC man | 8 | 23 | 33 | 35 | 60 |
| Single MC woman | 30 | 24 | 17 | 30 | 54 |
| All | 12 | 17 | 37 | 35 | 772 |

*Notes*: (a) MC = in professional or managerial SEG (1.1, 1.2, 2.2, 3, 4, 5.1).
(b) Emp = employed outside the middle classes.
*Source*: British General Election Survey 1987.

Table 7.10 therefore indicates the proportion of differing middle-class households earning different levels of income. The findings are startling. By some distance the wealthiest households are the 'dual career' families, where 61 per cent had household incomes of £20,000 or more in 1987. This is not perhaps surprising given the obvious earning power of these households, but the scale of their clear economic supremacy over other middle-class households is worth emphasising.

The poorest middle-class families, on the other hand, tend to be female headed (single, middle-class women, or middle-class women with a partner at home), and also – which is particularly striking – conventional house-holds with a middle-class man and his partner at home. Less than a quarter of these 'conventional' middle-class families earn more than £20,000. Looking at the figures another way, over half of 'poor' middle-class families earning under £8,000 p.a. are of the 'conventional' type. Single middle-class men and women, on the other hand, are well represented among the highest bracket of household income earners.

Clearly the diversity of household types leads into major differences in levels of household income. And, the 'conventional' middle-class family, which Parsons and Goode celebrated, must now be regarded as being of relatively minor importance, both in terms of numbers, and in terms of any strategic position its wealth might give it within the middle class as a whole. The process of class formation will increasingly depend not simply on the assets on which an individual can draw, but on the assets on which a household can draw. The three work strategies (organisational, occupational and entrepreneurial) we discussed in Chapter 2 can be combined in differing ways, so increasing the potential for the fragmentation of the middle-class ranks.

## SUMMARY

The analysis of mobility patterns revealed in this chapter show that patterns of career mobility, in particular, are very strongly affected by the types of assets on which people can draw. Those with property and cultural assets are clearly best able to retain middle-class position and pass it to their children. It is also clear, however, that people are not passive. They can attempt to trade in assets, in order to convert them to a more valuable currency. We have seen managerial groupings do this in two ways. A reasonable number of managers move into self-employment in the course of their careers. The children of managers appear to be able to move into professional work in large numbers, an example of the inter-generational 'trading-in' of organisation for cultural assets. This situation is, however, premised upon a particular education system, and the rise of the com-prehensive school, we suggest, may reduce the chances of the children of managers *vis-à-vis* professionals from attaining high levels of educational rewards.

The fragmentation of the middle classes by household type is also striking. The decline of the hegemony of the nuclear family has increased the range of middle-class household types. Further, it is clear that household type is of major importance in determining that household's general prosperity. The rise of the 'dual career' household is of major significance here, yet the number of single middle-class households is also noteworthy.

# 8

# REGIONAL CONTEXT
# AND SPATIAL MOBILITY

In older studies of the middle classes, analyses of spatial mobility were centre stage. Spatial metaphors were frequently used as a means of distinguishing types of middle class, as in Gouldner's cosmopolitans and locals, or Watson's spiralists and burgesses. The relationship between processes of spatial and social mobility was of major concern (Whyte 1957; Watson 1964; Blau and Duncan 1967), yet in the studies on social mobility discussed in the previous chapter such concerns are noticeably absent. They all measure social mobility within national boundaries, and do not consider the extent of spatial variations within these boundaries, or the way in which migration affects processes of social mobility.[1]

There are several reasons for this recent neglect. In Goldthorpe's case it is probably to be explained by his rejection of the 'status attainment' approach to social mobility, which had been concerned to isolate the factors that allowed an individual to 'get ahead'. In this view migration could be another factor to be included in the models, but it might direct attention away from basic class divisions, which Goldthorpe placed at the heart of his preferred 'class structural approach'. It was probably also due to the pragmatic need for log linear models to have large sample sizes, so necessitating the use of the whole – national – sample in all analyses.

But it also reflected the fact that the study of migration was generally becoming a specialist area focused around entirely demographic concerns, in which the wider social implications of migration were becoming increasingly marginalised. It is indeed noteworthy that the development of Marxist geography in the 1970s drew hardly at all on work concerned with migration (e.g. Harvey 1982; Massey and Meegan 1979; Massey 1984). Its main focus, on the geography of capitalist forms of production, was more concerned to examine the spatial mobility of capital and capitalist organisations than it was to examine the spatial mobility of people. Further, the growing concern to establish the significance of the capital–labour relation as the crucial factor affecting the geography of production led to a growing concern with the nature of local labour markets, to which workers were seen as being largely fixed as if they had no prospect of moving elsewhere (e.g. Urry 1981; Cooke 1983). This perspective is, however, clearly inadequate in coming to terms with the scale of mobility – especially for the middle classes – and its crucial role in affecting processes of class formation.

In this chapter we consider the relationship between regional context and middle-class formation. We argue against the idea that this can best be understood simply in terms of the types of jobs in a particular region. The role of the South East in the wider processes of middle-class formation is vital, but is not revealed by simply seeing it as an area where middle-class employment is based. We argue instead that its role is best understood as an 'escalator region'. The South East is a region in which young middle-class individuals are often trained, formed, and then move away later in their career. As a result the influence of the South East on middle-class formation is not restricted to the South East, and it can be said to permeate middle-class formation in many parts of Britain. As in Chapter 7, we draw heavily upon the Longitudinal Study (LS) which is an excellent source by which to examine how processess of spatial mobility and social mobility intertwine.

## THE ROLE OF THE SOUTH EAST IN MIDDLE-CLASS FORMATION 1900–90

It is commonplace to regard the South East as a middle-class region (e.g. Thrift 1987). This argument has characteristically been based on observations about the role of the South East within the spatial division of labour (e.g. Massey 1984). In Massey's particularly concise formulation of the issue, the South East has become dominant as an area where 'control functions' – research, planning, financing, marketing and so forth – are concentrated, while subordinate functions are carried on elsewhere, such as the older manufacturing regions of the north, west, Scotland and Wales. And, since 'class is understood to be importantly (though not solely) defined by places within the relations of production, then the geography of those relations and the places within them, which spatial structures illuminate, begin to define a geography of class' (Massey 1988b: 264). As a result, managers, professionals, administrators and technicians become focused in the South East, as these are the people who carry out the 'control functions'.

There is, of course, nothing new about the dominant role of the South East in Britain's spatial division of labour. We saw in Chapter 3 how London came to occupy a pivotal role for the professional middle classes during the course of the nineteenth century. But this role has changed in the course of the twentieth century, and it has been argued that the rise of 'Post-Fordism' has marked a new phase, leading to possibly even more accentuated patterns (Martin 1988). While the 'Fordist' period of the mid-twentieth century saw London and the South East become the centre for 'control' functions within organisational hierarchies, the 'Post-Fordist' period has seen the externalisation of functions, and a range of specialist professionals have developed in the South East to 'service' the large firms.

While London's distinctive position in the nineteenth century was based around its place as the centre of government, commerce, and financial and professional services, during the first part of the twentieth century it also became important as the centre from which 'Fordist' organisational hierarchies were organised (see Ward 1988; Pollard 1962; Scott and Griff 1984). Law (1981) shows that a third of top manufacturing firms had headquarters in London by 1919 and over half by 1930. These large organisations provided an alternative, less spatially restricted co-ordinating device to the previous concentration of associated firms in regional economies (see, generally, Storper and Walker 1989). As a result, semi-autonomous regional economies began to lose their distinctive regional service centres, accentuating the relative decline of central urban sites such as Manchester or Glasgow The British economy became increasingly organised on a national basis in which the South East came to play a dominant role (Lash and Urry 1987; Allen 1988a).

It is against this backdrop that it has been argued that more recent changes have increased the significance of the South East within the British economy. As firms increasingly externalise functions on the market (see Chapter 4), there is a growing demand for specialist producer services, and these tend to centre in the South East, where they can deal with head offices and government departments. The growing employment of professional specialists in services is hence becoming concentrated in the South East, especially in producer services. J. Marshall *et al.* (1988) show how private producer services are more unevenly distributed than public consumer services – a point also developed by Allen (1988b, 1988c) – and that this employment is centred in the South East since this is where the demand is based. Two-thirds of the 860,000 jobs created in the service sector between 1979 and 1986 were located in the South East, South West and East Anglia. As a result of these changes, 'the groups which have been growing fastest of all have been the wide range of private sector "professionals"' (Massey 1988b: 266). Leyshon and Thrift (1989) and Leyshon *et al.* (1988) have shown the concentration of those in producer services and financial services in and around London, while the concentration of 'hi-tech' professionals in the 'Western crescent' in the Home Counties is also well documented (Hall *et al.* 1987; Savage *et al.* 1988).

The crucial question is, however, to consider just what the implications of these geographical patterns of job change actually have for middle-class formation. Massey is cautious on this point. She follows the distinction between 'places' and 'persons' endorsed by Wright and Goldthorpe, and argues that the types of people who fill these jobs is contingent and cannot be read off from economic changes alone.

Thrift (1987) is similarly emphatic that the geography of the 'service class' cannot be read off from the geography of employment. He notes – as does Massey – that in some ways the line of causality works the other way, and that the jobs move to where the service class chooses to live. This focus suggests that the role of the South East in middle-class formation is as much cultural as economic. This view is endorsed by Massey, who refers to the cultural role of the South East whereby residence in this regions is 'a means of asserting social arrival' (Massey 1988b: 268).

Despite this, these views continue to see the crucial role of the South East in terms of the *density* of middle-class population there. We believe this is a mistaken view for two reasons: firstly, it exaggerates the concentration of middle-class employees in the South East; and, secondly, it pays inadequate attention to the migration process. We develop this point by arguing that the South East's role in middle-class formation is best understood in terms of its role as an 'escalator' region, where young middle-class workers tend to congregate, are formed, and are then exported elsewhere.

## THE MIDDLE CLASSES AND REGIONAL CHANGE 1971–81

Many commentators have argued that as the South East's role as a region where 'control functions' are centred becomes more marked, so will its share of 'control workers': managers and professionals (Hamnett 1986, 1990; Owen and Green 1984). In fact this over-representation of the middle classes in the South East is not as dramatic as is sometimes supposed. Furthermore, there is clear evidence that what over-representation there is has a long history, and if anything the proportion of the middle classes living in the South East has been declining. Hamnett (1986) shows that the increase in professional, managerial and intermediate class was of the order of 46.7 per cent between 1961 and 1981 in the South East, but 48.2 per cent in Enlgand and Wales as a whole. Owen and Green also conclude that

> the stability of the pre-existing regional differentials – with the overrepresentation of non-manual workers in the South and East and an overrepresentation of manual functions in the North and West – during the period 1971–81 is the major conclusion derived from this analysis.
>
> (Owen and Green 1984: 19; see also Savage and Fielding 1989)

Even the existing over-representation of middle-class employees in the South East can be exaggerated. Data from the LS can be used to examine the spatial concentrations of workers in 1981. This shows that there is no

Table 8.1 Regional class structures and changes in regional class structures relative to England and Wales. The values are percentage point differences from the England and Wales figures

| | South East | | | East Anglia | | | South West | | |
|---|---|---|---|---|---|---|---|---|---|
| | 1971 | 1981 | 1981 –1971 | 1971 | 1981 | 1981 –1971 | 1971 | 1981 | 1981 –1971 |
| SC | +3.6 | +4.2 | +0.6 | −1.4 | −0.7 | +0.7 | +0.1 | −0.1 | 0.2 |
| PB | −0.2 | −0.2 | 0.0 | +1.9 | +1.9 | 0.0 | +3.7 | +3.5 | −0.2 |
| WC | +4.3 | +3.7 | −0.6 | −2.2 | −1.8 | +0.3 | +0.6 | +0.6 | 0.0 |
| BC | −7.0 | −5.7 | +1.3 | +1.7 | +1.9 | +0.2 | −4.0 | −2.6 | +1.4 |
| UE | −0.6 | −2.1 | −1.5 | +0.1 | −1.3 | −1.4 | −0.3 | −1.5 | −1.2 |

| | East Midlands | | | West Midlands | | | Wales | | |
|---|---|---|---|---|---|---|---|---|---|
| | 1971 | 1981 | 1981 –1971 | 1971 | 1981 | 1981 –1971 | 1971 | 1981 | 1981 –1971 |
| SC | −2.7 | −2.5 | +0.2 | −2.2 | −2.5 | −0.3 | −1.5 | −2.9 | −1.4 |
| PB | −0.1 | 0.0 | +0.1 | −1.1 | −0.9 | +0.2 | +2.4 | +1.0 | −1.4 |
| WC | −3.6 | −3.1 | +0.5 | −3.5 | −3.1 | +0.4 | −4.2 | −2.6 | +1.6 |
| BC | +6.9 | +6.5 | −0.4 | +7.2 | +4.6 | −2.6 | +2.6 | +2.1 | −0.5 |
| UE | −0.3 | −0.9 | −0.6 | −0.2 | +1.9 | +2.1 | +0.8 | +2.4 | +1.6 |

| | Yorkshire/Humberside | | | North West | | | Northern | | |
|---|---|---|---|---|---|---|---|---|---|
| | 1971 | 1981 | 1981 –1971 | 1971 | 1981 | 1981 –1971 | 1971 | 1981 | 1981 –1971 |
| SC | −2.9 | −3.4 | −0.5 | −1.5 | −1.9 | −0.4 | −3.3 | −4.4 | −1.1 |
| PB | −0.1 | −0.4 | −0.3 | −0.6 | −0.6 | 0.0 | −2.0 | −1.8 | +0.2 |
| WC | −2.9 | −2.4 | +0.5 | −1.1 | −1.3 | −0.2 | −2.0 | −2.7 | −0.7 |
| BC | +5.7 | +4.9 | −0.8 | +2.5 | +1.6 | −0.9 | +5.4 | +5.2 | −0.2 |
| UE | +0.3 | +1.2 | +0.9 | +0.8 | +2.2 | +1.4 | +1.9 | +3.5 | +1.6 |

Note: SC = service class; PB = petite bourgeoisie; WC = white collar; BC = blue collar; UE = unemployed.
Source: OPCS Longitudinal Study (Crown Copyright reserved).

question that, in aggregate terms, the middle classes are concentrated in the South East. In 1981 the South East contained 40 per cent of the middle classes, and 42 per cent of middle-class employees,[2] a proportion significantly above its share of the total workforce (35 per cent). The three southern regions (the South East, East Anglia, the South West) together contain 53 per cent of middle-class employees and have 47 per cent of the workforce. The petite bourgeoisie is, however, rather less concentrated here, and the South East's share of the total (34 per cent) is somewhat below its share of the total workforce. These regional figures are shown in Table 8.1, which maps the class distributions of the nine standard regions in terms of their percentage point differences from the structure for England and Wales.

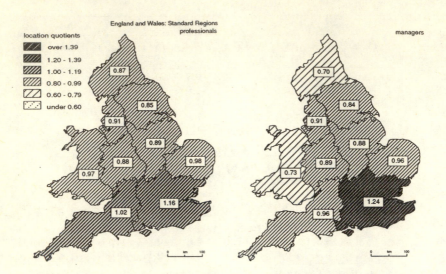

*Figure 8.1* The regional distribution of professionals in 1981 (England and Wales: Standard Regions)
*Source*: OPCS Longitudinal Study (Crown Copyright reserved)

*Figure 8.2* The regional distribution of managers in 1981 (England and Wales: Standard Regions) (key as in Figure 8.1)
*Source*: OPCS Longitudinal Study (Crown Copyright reserved)

*Figure 8.3* The regional distribution of the petite bourgeoisie in 1981 (England and Wales: Standard Regions) (key as in Figure 8.1)
*Source*: OPCS Longitudinal Study (Crown Copyright reserved)

Figures 8.1 to 8.3 reveal the bias of the South East towards middle-class employees. Managers emerge as slightly more concentrated than professionals: 11.4 per cent of the South East workforce are managers compared to 9.2 per cent nationally, while the figures for managers are 14.6 per cent compared to 12.6 per cent. These produce location quotients (LQs) of 1.24 and 1.16 respectively.[3] No other region has a proportion above the England and Wales percentage in the case of managers, and only one region (the South West) in the case of professionals. This is clearly in line with the way in which 'control functions' for the British economy are concentrated in the South East of England. Nonetheless, the percentage point differences between the South East and other regions can be exaggerated, and are always in single figures. The middle classes do live everywhere!

The petite bourgeoisie is, however, located according to different principles. The South West has the highest LQ here, of 1.53, followed by East Anglia, with an LQ of 1.29, while the South East has an LQ of 0.97. These figures probably reflect the role of family farming in the respective regions.

The vital point to emphasise is that these regional class structures are not static. They shift over time, in ways that we would anticipate on the basis of our earlier discussion. In the period between 1971 and 1981 the England and Wales occupational structure shifted from blue-collar manual occupations towards middle-class employment and unemployment in a very marked fashion. Manual occupations declined from 45 per cent in 1971 to 38 per cent in 1981, while the percentage of middle-class employees rose from 17 per cent to 22 per cent, and unemployment doubled, from 4 per cent to 9 per cent. Table 8.1 provides the shifts in regional distributions, measured in percentage points above and below the figures for England and Wales.

Table 8.1 shows that the relatively slow growth of unemployment in the three southern regions was matched by relatively slow decline of blue-collar employment here, reflecting the better performance of manufacturing here. In the South East and East Anglia there was also a marked increase in the proportions of middle-class employees.

The LS also shows that professionals increased in England and Wales by just over 25 per cent, *but by slightly under this in the South East* (22 per cent). In East Anglia, the South West and the East Midlands their rates of increase were well above average (+37, +35 and +34 per cent respectively). The pattern is similar for managers. These increased in England and Wales by 33 per cent, but again the South East stands a little lower at 32 per cent, while East Anglia, East Midlands and the South West head the field with rates of 67, 48 and 41 per cent respectively. The petite bourgeoisie actually declined slightly by 2 per cent, and the only regions to record significant growth are East Anglia (+9 per cent), the South West (+5 per cent) and the East Midlands (+4 per cent). Clearly it is the lowland rural regions of southern and eastern England, containing a small number of large free-sized cities and very many small and medium-sized towns, that have seen the most rapid increases in their middle-class populations during this period.

These broad figures show that, at least by 1981, there was little sign that the professional middle classes had become more distinctive in the whole of the South East. Rather, the South East was seeing a faster growth in the number of managers, but even here change was not dramatic. In short, regional differentiation of changes in shares of middle-class employment, while certainly present, should not be overestimated, but share of employment alone tells us relatively little about how these jobs are filled and how classes form, or don't form. It is to this issue that we now turn.

## SOCIAL AND SPATIAL ORIGINS AND DESTINATIONS OF THE THREE MIDDLE CLASSES

We have seen that the role of the South East as a key region for the location of middle-class personnel, while clear cut, was undergoing fairly modest change, at least between 1971 and 1981. However, we now turn to consider the social and spatial mobility of middle-class personnel, where we shall argue that the LS shows the South East to have a key role as an 'escalator region' for the middle class.

The vital theoretical point to bear in mind is that one cannot read off processes of class formation from aggregate employment changes alone. If middle-class jobs are expanding in one region they might be filled locally, by local entrants from manual work, for instance, or they might be filled by turning to local school leavers, or to local women, or the jobs might be filled by 'importing' labour from elsewhere. The character of class formation can be expected to be different in any of these cases. On the other hand, even if middle-class jobs are static in numbers, there may be differing ways in which people are recruited to them which will affect their cohesiveness and solidarity.

The processes of migration are hence of major importance in affecting processes of class formation. Yet relatively little is known about it. Aggregate levels have been declining (Devis 1983), and there is some evidence that for the first time the spatial mobility of managers and professionals is polarising. Savage (1988a) shows that in 1966 both managerial and professional SEGs had rates of migration well above those for the population as a whole. By 1981, however, the rates for managerial groupings had dropped considerably – being only slightly above the average for the population as a whole – while those for professionals stayed high. Consistent with this, Salt (1990) shows that the most mobile middle-class groupings in the 1980s were in the educational and health services, and in the civil

*Table 8.2* Inter-regional migration, social class and housing tenure, England and Wales, 1971–81
The data refer to people who were in England and Wales at both dates. 1.096% sample

| | Class tenure in 1981 | % | Inter-regional migration rates: England and Wales = 100 | | |
| | | | In labour market in 1981 | In labour market in 1971 & 1981 | In same class/ tenure in 1971 & 1981 |
|---|---|---|---|---|---|
| (i) *Social class* | | | | | |
| Service class | 45,988 | 21.1 | 194 | 188 | 222 |
| Petite bourgeoisie | 14,451 | 6.6 | 91 | 97 | 54 |
| White collar | 57,501 | 26.4 | 92 | 94 | 99 |
| Blue collar | 82,197 | 37.7 | 55 | 56 | 55 |
| Unemployed | 17,834 | 8.2 | 98 | 110 | 104 |
| | 217,971 | 100.0 | 100 | 100 | 100 |
| (ii) *Housing tenure* | | | | | |
| Owner-occupiers | 137,669 | 63.2 | 111 | 117 | 129 |
| Council tenants | 58,364 | 26.8 | 42 | 41 | 27 |
| Other tenants | 21,938 | 10.1 | 182 | 145 | 115 |
| | 217,971 | 100.0 | 100 | 100 | 100 |

*Source*: OPCS Longitudinal Study (Crown Copyright reserved).

service. This growing disparity between the migration patterns of professionals and managers seems to support our argument concerning the declining salience of the organisational career. Managers are either asked to move less by their employers, or are more reluctant to do so. In the first case employers may be less interested in moving internally promoted workers around their firm. In the latter, managers themselves may be more reluctant to base their career strategies around their firms' prerogatives.

In the remainder of this chapter we therefore clarify the relationship between social class and migration in order to show how spatial mobility may affect class formation. We start with simple descriptive tables, before examining migration flows between different regions of England and Wales.

Table 8.2 shows the proportions of the LS sample falling into particular social class and housing tenure groupings.[4] The last three columns indicate whether the particular group is over-represented or under-represented in terms of their degree of inter-regional mobility between 1971 and 1981. A figure above 100 indicates that the group was more likely, while if it falls below 100 it is less likely. Table 8.2 shows the extremely high level of spatial mobility characteristic of middle-class employees. The third column (in labour market 1981) shows that middle-class employees in 1981, with an index figure of 194, were nearly twice as likely to have migrated inter-regionally than the population as a whole. Blue-collar workers, on the other hand, with an index of 55, emerge as being far less likely to migrate.

Furthermore, if we only consider those in the same class in 1971 and 1981 (the right-hand column) then the differences become even more marked, with the 'service class' of professionals and managers being well over twice as inter-regionally mobile as the wider population. The petite bourgeoisie, on the other hand, emerge as immobile as the manual working class. Owner-occupiers also emerge as more mobile than tenants, and council tenants, in particular, tend not to migrate between regions.

Table 8.3 gives similar index readings, but this time of people moving between class groupings between 1971 and 1981, so that it becomes possible to see if socially mobile people also tend to be spatially mobile. The highest rates are for those figures lying off the diagonal – that is to say, not remaining in the same class grouping. The exceptions to this are people staying in the service class, who enjoy higher rates of mobility than members of the service class moving into other class groupings. The two highest figures for migration rates are for unemployed and blue-collar

*Table 8.3* The association between inter-regional migration and changes in social class and housing tenure, England and Wales, 1971–81
The data refer to people who were in the labour market in England and Wales at both dates

| | Migration rates: England and Wales = 100 | | | | | |
|---|---|---|---|---|---|---|
| | *Standardised by social class and housing tenure in 1971* | | | | | |
| | *(i) Social class* | | | | | |
| | *Social class in 1981* | | | | | |
| *Social class in 1971* | *Service class* | *Petite bourg.* | *White collar* | *Blue collar* | *Unem-ployed* | *Total* |
| Service class | 103 | 117 | 89 | 73 | 115 | 100 |
| Petite bourgeoisie | 185 | 69 | 161 | 100 | 190 | 100 |
| White collar | 165 | 163 | 77 | 77 | 157 | 100 |
| Blue collar | 209 | 168 | 136 | 75 | 133 | 100 |
| Unemployed | 215 | 104 | 113 | 79 | 70 | 100 |
| | *(ii) Housing tenure* | | | | | |
| | *Housing tenure in 1981* | | | | | |
| *Housing tenure in 1971* | *Owner-occupiers* | *Council tenants* | *Other tenants* | *Total* | | |
| Owner-occupiers | 94 | 121 | 232 | 100 | | |
| Council tenants | 192 | 37 | 337 | 100 | | |
| Other tenants | 141 | 67 | 63 | 100 | | |

*Source*: OPCS Longitudinal Study (Crown Copyright reserved).

*Table 8.4* The status in 1971 of those who had professional, managerial or petite bourgeoisie jobs in 1981: origins

|  | *In same region in 1971* | *In another region in 1971* | *In another country in 1971* |
|---|---|---|---|
| In labour market in 1971 | Stayed in same class | Stayed in same class | Immigrants from outside England and Wales |
|  | Moved from other middle class | Moved from other middle class |  |
|  | Moved from working class | Moved from working class |  |
| Not in labour market in 1971 | Entered from education | Entered from education |  |
|  | Entered from other | Entered from other |  |

*Table 8.5* The status in 1981 of those who had professional, managerial or petite bourgeoisie jobs in 1971: destinations

|  | *In same region in 1981* | *In another region in 1981* | *In another country in 1981* |
|---|---|---|---|
| In labour market in 1981 | Stayed in same class | Stayed in same class | Emigrants to outside England and Wales |
|  | Moved to other middle class | Moved to other middle class |  |
|  | Moved to working class | Moved to working class |  |
| Not in labour market in 1981 | Exited to retirement | Exited to retirement |  |
|  | Exited to other | Exited to other |  |
|  | Died | Died |  |

individuals moving into the 'service class'. The lowest figure of all is for individuals staying in the petite bourgeoisie.

It is clear then that inter-regional migration is highly class specific, and is particularly common when moving between social classes. It is this which exercises a profound impact on patterns of middle-class formation in different regions of Britain. Rather than each region having its own distinct 'middle class', the processes of migration tend towards a circulation of people around the country, leading to a more homogeneous national middle class.

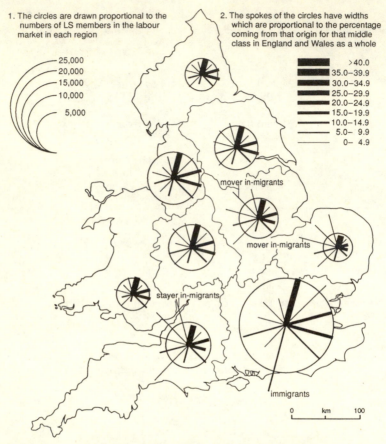

1. The circles are drawn proportional to the numbers of LS members in the labour market in each region

2. The spokes of the circles have widths which are proportional to the percentage coming from that origin for that middle class in England and Wales as a whole

3. The position of the spoke on the circle specifies the origin of the 'flow' into the middle class. Those above the centre line were in the labour market in 1971, those below (except for immigrants whose former status is unknown) were not. Those to the right of the centre line were resident in the same region in 1971, those to the left of the centre line were either inter-regional or international in-migrants between 1971 and 1981

in-migrants in labour market | non-migrants in labour market
stayer in-migrant | stayer non-migrant
mover in-migrant from mc | mover non-migrant from mc
mover in-migrant from wc | mover non-migrant from wc
entry in-migrant from ed | entry non-migrant from ed
entry in-migrant from other | entry non-migrant from other
immigrants
in-migrants out of labour market | non-migrants out of labour market

mc=middle class;  wc=working class;  ed=education.

*Figure 8.4* The social and geographical origins in 1971 of those who were in professional occupations in 1981 (England and Wales: Standard Regions)
*Source*: OPCS Longitudinal Study (Crown Copyright reserved)

170

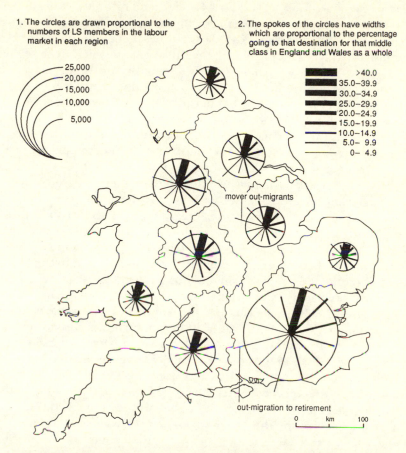

1. The circles are drawn proportional to the numbers of LS members in the labour market in each region

- 25,000
- 20,000
- 15,000
- 10,000
- 5,000

2. The spokes of the circles have widths which are proportional to the percentage going to that destination for that middle class in England and Wales as a whole

| | >40.0 |
| | 35.0−39.9 |
| | 30.0−34.9 |
| | 25.0−29.9 |
| | 20.0−24.9 |
| | 15.0−19.9 |
| | 10.0−14.9 |
| | 5.0− 9.9 |
| | 0− 4.9 |

mover out-migrants

out-migration to retirement

0    km    100

3. The position of the spoke on the circle specifies the destination of the 'flow' out of the middle class. Those above the centre line were in the labour market in 1981, those below (except for emigrants whose latter status is unknown) were not. Those to the right of the centre line were residents in the same region in 1981, those to the left of the centre line were either inter-regional or international out-migrants between 1971 and 1981

out-migrants in labour market | non-migrants in labour market
stayer out-migrant | stayer non-migrant
mover out-migrant to mc | mover non-migrant to mc
mover out-migrant to wc | mover non-migrant to wc
exit out-migrant to ret | exit non-migrant to ret
exit out-migrant to other | exit non-migrant to other
emigrants | death
out-migrants out of labour market | non-migrants out of labour market

mc=middle class;  wc=working class;  ret=retirement.

*Figure 8.5* The social and geographical destinations in 1981 of those who were in professional occupations in 1971 (England and Wales: Standard Regions)
*Source*: OPCS Longitudinal Study (Crown Copyright reserved)

Let us now develop this account by specifying the sorts of migration that take place between regions, in order to consider if any typical routes of migration can be ascertained. Tables 8.4 and 8.5 indicate how we examined this issue by developing categories allowing us to probe the 1971 origins of people in 1981, and the 1981 destinations of people in 1971. We distinguish three types of spatial mobility: those who stay in a given region (non-migrants); those who move within Great Britain (migrants); and those who move to or from another country. Secondly, we distinguish those in the labour market from those not in the labour market at one or other of the dates. And finally, for those in the labour market we distinguish whether they were in the same occupational grouping (stayers), a different middle-class grouping (movers), or were outside the middle class altogether. Tables 8.4 and 8.5 clarify these definitional points.

Figures 8.4 to 8.12 provide an overview of the patterns revealed by the LS. The data have been expressed as LQs in order to help comparison between regions. To give an example, in Figure 8.4(a), the stayer non-migrants (professionals in differing regions in 1981 who were also professionals in the same region in 1971) have an LQ of 1.02 in the South East. This means that this group is slightly over-represented in the South East compared to other regions, but only by 2 per cent.

If we consider firstly the origins and destinations of professionals (Figures 8.4 and 8.5), it is clear that the South East has a particularly distinctive pattern due to the size of immigration from abroad and its within-region shifts from the other middle classes into professional ranks. The 1981 professionals in the South East hence have a more diverse set of 1971 origins than is common elsewhere (see the LQ of 1.19 for non-migrants who have come from other parts of the middle class). But, on the other hand, they also have a slightly higher proportion of stayer non-migrants (i.e. people in the same region and class in 1971), and of non-migrant entries from education (people who left education and moved into professional employment without changing region). In-migrant LQs are low: it seems that very few professionals move into the South East from other regions, and furthermore relatively few migrate into the South East when moving from non-employment or other occupations. The one exception to this – and it is an important one – involves people in education in the regions in 1971 (many at an institute of higher education) but in professional work in the South East in 1981. This is a key point to note. The South East of England does not draw many professionals from outside: rather, people move into these jobs from within the region and from abroad. *The South East is not a magnet drawing professionals to it from outside the region.*

A rather different pattern occurs in East Anglia, South West and East Midlands. Here the rates of in-migration are exceptionally high, though immigration from abroad was consistently low. In these regions the level

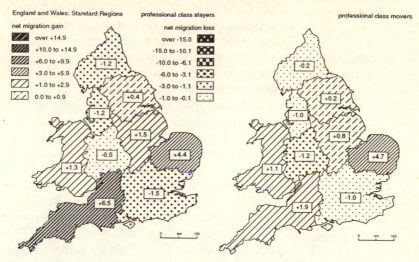

(a) Net migration rates for those who
were in professional occupations in
1971 and 1981

(b) Net migration rates for those who
were in the labour market in 1971
and 1981 but who moved into or out
of professional occupations

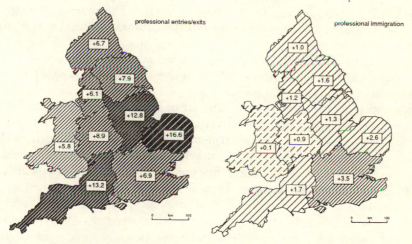

(c) Net migration rates for those who
entered or left the labour market
between 1971 and 1981 as they
entered or left a professional
occupation

(d) Estimated net immigration rates
for professionals 1971-81

*Figure 8.6* Net migration and immigration rates: professionals, 1971–81
(England and Wales: Standard Regions)
*Source*: OPCS Longitudinal Study (Crown Copyright reserved)

of recruitment and retention within the region is low, especially in East Anglia. These are the areas that appear to be attracting already established professionals: the magnet areas. In contrast again the northern and western regions tend to recruit from within the region, and they recruit relatively high numbers from outside the middle classes. These areas appear to be characterised by more localist forms of recruitment, as found by Bagguley *et al.* (1990) who show that very few of the service class in Lancaster had migrated from distant regions.

What about the figures for 1981 destinations of people in 1971? In the South East many professionals move into other middle-class work, or emigrate. This latter point, along with the complementary findings about the high proportions of immigrants into professsional work, clearly suggests the role of London as a 'world city' tied to international labour markets (see more generally, Hamnett 1990). It is especially striking to note the very high numbers of professionals in the South East in 1971 who migrated and retired to other regions in 1981. This movement has been widely discussed (Newby 1980), and is confirmed by these figures.

East Anglia, South West and East Midlands have high out-migration rates as well as high in-migration rates. This is surprising in some ways, but testifies to these regions as high turnover areas. The exception here is the South West, where out-migration proportions are low. Retirees in the South West tend to remain in the same region. The same applies to the professionals of the northern and western regions, who tend to stay there in retirement.

Relative figures such as LQs are in some ways misleading, and Figure 8.6 provides the net migration effects of these flows. The South East loses personnel who are in the middle class, but it gains vast numbers of new entrants – many from education and from abroad. The South East hence does not appear to be a magnet for the already established middle class who tend to leave it, but it has large numbers of new entrants, or movers within the middle classes who are moving to or from managerial work. *It is the region where young aspirants or those trying to change careers are concentrated.* Here we have the germ of the idea of the escalator region, to which we shall return in due course. The East Midlands, South West and East Anglia are the areas that appear to be the magnet regions – they attract those who are already established in professional work or are moving somewhere to retire. But there is a slow drift of professionals from the northern and western regions.

In Chapter 2 we argued that managers and professionals tended to have similar rates of spatial mobility as they each pursued their career development, and hence high levels of spatial mobility tend to draw them together into a more cohesive class. Figures 8.7 and 8.8 show that managers do tend to migrate in similar sorts of directions to professionals (though it should be noted that these figures do not record the amount of migration at the

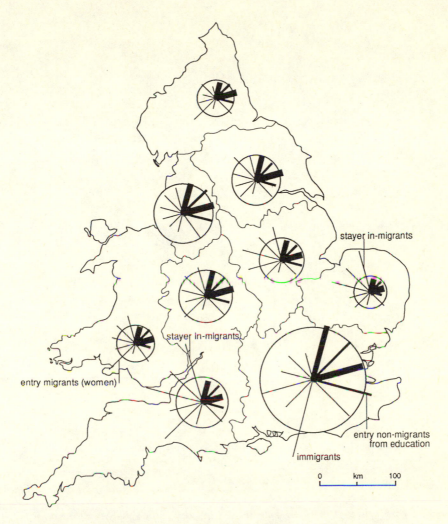

*Figure 8.7* The social and geographical origins in 1971 of those who were managers in 1981 (England and Wales: Standard Regions) (key as in Figure 8.4)
*Source*: OPCS Longitudinal Study (Crown Copyright reserved)

aggregate level for different social groups – we have already seen that the two groups have increasingly different profiles here). The South East region again does not appear to be a magnet: rather it recruits from inside the South East and from education. This point is particularly interesting

175

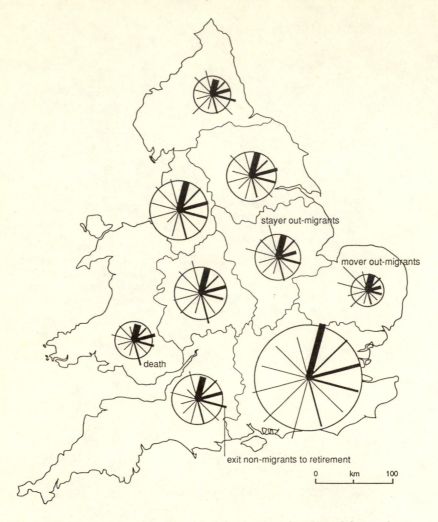

*Figure 8.8* The social and geographical destinations in 1981 of those who were managers in 1971 (England and Wales: Standard Regions) (key as in Figure 8.5)
*Source*: OPCS Longitudinal Study (Crown Copyright reserved)

here: we saw in Chapter 5 that people tend to become managers only after having worked elsewhere in the labour market. Entrants from education have become managers in less than ten years and are hence the likely 'high fliers', and it is noteworthy that they are concentrated in the South East. The growth regions around the South East also have high rates of in-migration from other regions (especially stayer in-migrants to East Anglia

176

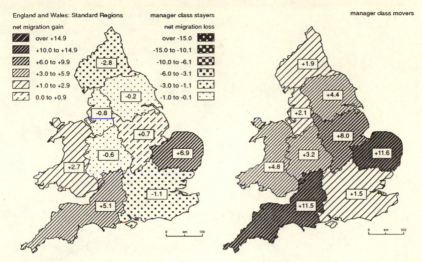

(a) Net migration rates for those who were managers in both 1971 and 1981

(b) Net migration rates for those who were in the labour market in 1971 and 1981 but who moved into and out of managerial occupations

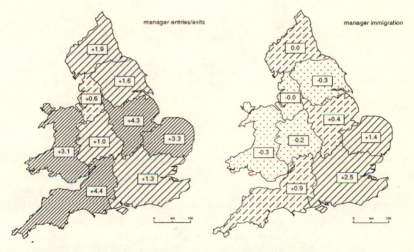

(c) Net migration rates for those who entered or left the labour market between 1971 and 1981 as they entered or left a managerial occupation

(d) Estimated net immigration rates for managers 1971-81

*Figure 8.9*   Net migration and immigration rates: managers, 1971–81
(England and Wales: Standard Regions)
*Source*: OPCS Longitudinal Study (Crown Copyright reserved)

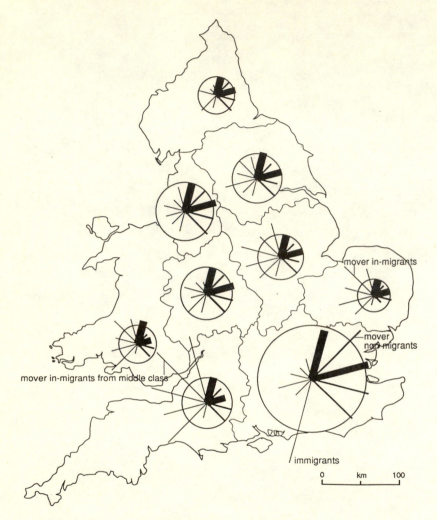

*Figure 8.10* The social and geographical origins in 1971 of those who were
members of the petite bourgeoisie in 1981 (England and Wales: Standard
Regions) (key as in Figure 8.4)
*Source*: OPCS Longitudinal Study (Crown Copyright reserved)

and the South West). The Midlands and North see small numbers from
abroad, but higher proportions entering managerial work from the working class.

The destinations of managers are also fairly similar to those of the
professionals, with the South East's managers tending to be very fixed
except for emigration. In the case of managers, however, the out-migration

178

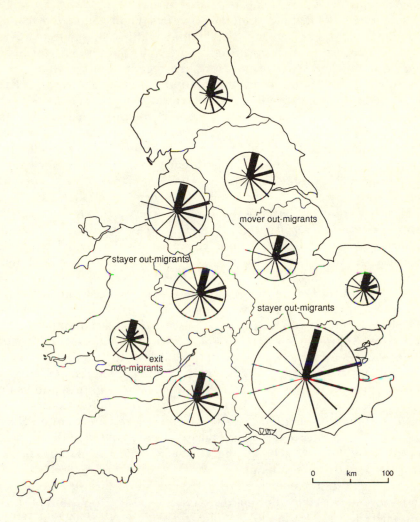

*Figure 8.11* The social and geographical destinations in 1981 of those who were members of the petite bourgeoisie in 1971 (England and Wales: Standard Regions) (key as in Figure 8.5)
*Source*: OPCS Longitudinal Study (Crown Copyright reserved)

from the South East to retirement in other regions is a much less developed feature than it is for professionals. Managers in high growth regions tend to have high turnover, but this is slightly less marked than for professionals. A new feature is the high out-migration of stayers and movers from the Northern region: indeed the out-migration of managers is quite a distinctive feature of several northern and midland regions, possibly testifying to the declining manufacturing bases of these areas.

The patterns of net migration for managers (Figure 8.9) are revealing. For those who stay as managers the situation is little different than it is for professionals, except that East Anglia and Wales gain more, and South West less, and the losses of the Northern region are of a whole order greater. For movers, however, the situation is different. The South East, West Midlands, North West and Northern regions gain managers where they lose professionals, and the rates of gain in East Anglia, South West, and East Midlands are quite exceptionally high. For entrants from education the gains of the South East are much more modest than was the case for professionals, reflecting the longer time it takes to become a manager.

Managers and professionals tend to have similar types of spatial mobility, and many of the differences between them are an artefact of their differing age distributions. But the situation is very different for the petite bourgeoisie (Figures 8.10 and 8.11). They do not tend to stay in the South East region; instead their 1971 numbers were more than usually recruited from class movers within the region, from new entries and from immigration. Particularly high are the LQs from movement from middle-class employees (LQ of 1.27), and from migrants (1.62). Once again, the South East emerges as a region of above-average career change within the middle classes. In common with the professionals and managers, in-migrants are very poorly represented within the South East, but in the case of the petite bourgeoisie four of the LQs are exceptionally low, at around 0.4.

The high turnover regions (East Anglia, South West and East Midlands) show a characteristically high recruitment from in-migrants, and in this respect the petite bourgeoisie is certainly like other middle-class groups, but the stayer non-migrants are also strongly represented. In the North and West the sources of the petite bourgeoisie are not that different from the other middle classes, though the Northern region has an unusually low proportion of stayer in-migrants.

Looking at destinations it is clear that the South East has a relatively high movement to the other middle classes, and the proportion of stayer non-migrants is quite low compared to the figures for managers and professionals. But they do share the common propensity to migrate out of the South East to retire in other regions. The South East and West Midlands have exceptionally high value LQs for their petite bourgeoisie stayer out-migrants, while East Anglia, South West, the Northern region and Wales have unusually low values.

Figure 8.12 shows that the patterns of net migration for the petite bourgeoisie are remarkably similar to those of the professional and managerial middle classes, except in two respects. The first is the low figures of net gain (and in the cases of the South East and North West, net losses) for the entries and exits. This reflects the older average age of the petite

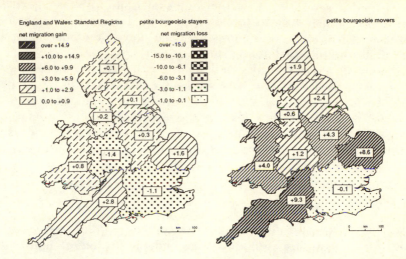

(a) Net migration rates for those who were members of the petite bourgeoisie in both 1971 and 1981

(b) Net migration rates for those who were in the labour market in 1971 and 1981 but who moved into or out of the petite bourgeoisie

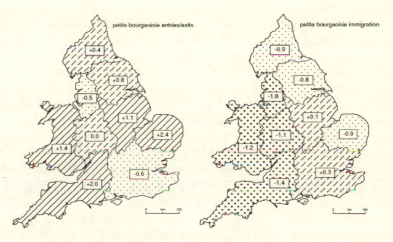

(c) Net migration rates for those who entered or left the labour market between 1971 and 1981 as they entered or left the petite bourgeoisie

(d) Estimated net immigration rates for the petite bourgeoisie 1971–81

*Figure 8.12*  Net migration and immigration rates: petite bourgeoisie, 1971–81
(England and Wales: Standard Regions)
*Source*: OPCS Longitudinal Study (Crown Copyright reserved)

bourgeoisie, and in this respect there are similarities with managers. The second exception concerns the low figures for international migration. Here the petite bourgeoisie shows net gains only in the South East and East Midlands, with high rates of loss elsewhere.

It is clear from our discussion that the South East does not appear to draw already established middle-class people to it from other regions. In fact, the patterns of migration tend to work the other way, with the established middle classes leaving the South East. Any notion that residence in the South East is necessary for middle-class status gains little support. Rather, the evidence is consistent with the idea of the South East as an 'escalator region'.

## THE SOUTH EAST AS AN 'ESCALATOR REGION'

The South East has a distinctive role in processes of middle-class formation. It is clear from our discussion that it has high proportions of middle-class switching: professionals becoming managers, managers becoming petit bourgeois and so on. It is an area where there appears to be a high degree of fluidity between the specific middle classes. It is also an area where a relatively high proportion of the working class enter the middle classes. But the established middle classes do not appear to be attracted to the South East, and tend to move out of it, to other regions.

These findings indicate how the South East can be seen as an 'escalator region'. Three specific characteristics stand out. Firstly, the South East attracts to itself a large number of young potential recruits to middle-class work from the education system. Secondly, it promotes these young in-migrants together with its own young people at accelerated rates into positions of responsibility based upon qualifications and experience. Thirdly, it sends out a significant number of the now established middle classes into other regions as their careers mature, or as they begin to retire. The South East is hence a kind of machine for upward social mobility, in which people at the bottom are promoted relatively quickly, and those at the top disperse elsewhere, so allowing more promotions to take place from within.

It should be emphasised that the South East's role as an escalator region is entirely consistent with our observations concerning the relative lack of growth in middle-class jobs here, compared to the national pattern. As the established middle classes migrate away from the South East this may open up opportunities for others, so allowing early promotion. Hence, even in a situation where employment levels were static, this situation is likely to allow a reasonable degree of fluidity.

To what extent does evidence from the LS confirm this argument? The use of LQs sometimes clouds the issues, as it does not always control for the marginal totals in the way necessary to demonstrate these points. Let us, therefore, go through the three pieces of evidence that would be necessary to demonstrate our argument with some care. Firstly, to support our argument, the LS would need to show that the South East did manage to draw an especially large number of those in education in 1971 into its professional and managerial ranks by 1981. Using the 'origins' data discussed above, it may seem that the LS does not confirm this, since the LQ is only 0.95, rather than over 1.0. However, this is misleading, since it is an artefact of the fact that the South East is, by a considerable margin, the most populous region in Britain. Therefore, it is almost certain, *pari passu*, to have a lower proportion of in-migrants than less-populated regions, where short-distance migration will account for more of the apparent inter-regional mobility, while long-distance migration within the South East (say, from London to Bournemouth) will not show up in the figures. And in fact the in-migrant LQ for entrants from education to the South East is well above that for other categories of in-migrant. If one examines the absolute figures for gains to the South East the pattern is much clearer. For those moving from education to professional or managerial work, the South East made a net gain of +46 per thousand for professionals and +16.7 per thousand for managers, indicating a very sizeable net attraction of such people.

The second piece of evidence required would be that those in the South East would gain accelerated promotion implied by the notion of 'escalator'. Here, once again the LS data are at first glance somewhat equivocal. In support of this view it shows that for those non-migrants leaving education there is a greater than average movement into professional and managerial work (LQs of 1.02 and 1.14 respectively). If the LQs are calculated on the basis of those leaving education (rather than entering these forms of employment), these LQs are increased substantially to 1.19 and 1.45 respectively. But for those in working-class employment in 1971 moving into middle-class jobs by 1981, the LQs are not quite 1.0. The reasons for this lie in the fact that since a smaller proportion of the workforce is manual in the South East, this tends to drag down the LQs compared to those found in the working-class regions of the north. If we calculate the LQs in terms of those leaving the working class in 1971 and moving into the middle class by 1981, the South East LQs rise to 1.21 for professionals and 1.29 for managers. This indicates the substantially better chances for working-class individuals to move into middle-class work in the South East than elsewhere. It also suggests that any simple idea of the South becoming more internally polarised between the middle and working classes might need further consideration.

The final piece of evidence required relates to the 'stepping off' stage – that is, the movement of mid and late career professionals and managers away from the South East. In fact, the LQs for stayer out-migrants from the South East are only 0.83 for professionals and 0.80 for managers. Once again the LQs are affected by the density effect, with bigger regions tending to record lower rates of out-migration due to purely artefactual reasons. If one looks at the net figures, a different story is told. The net out-migration figures here are −15 per thousand for professionals and −10.5 per thousand for managers. Significantly, more people remaining in managerial or professional work left the South East than entered it. There are also particularly high LQs for movement of professionals and managers into retirement in another region: 1.25 for professionals and 1.07 for managers. The net figures are −10.3 per thousand and −13 per thousand respectively.

All the elements of the escalator region idea – the inflow of young professionals and managers, the accelerated internal promotion of those living in the South East, and the outflow of mid to late career professionals and managers – are therefore confirmed by LS evidence for the period 1971–81.

Given our argument, a number of conclusions follow. Firstly, the middle classes in the South East are likely to be very socially diverse, due to the high levels of job changing and accelerated promotion. As a result, if anything, the middle classes are likely to be more fragmented in the South East than elsewhere. Savage and Fielding (1989) show that ony 40 per cent of middle-class employees in the South East in 1981 were middle-class employees in the South East in 1971. This high level of turnover explains the distinct 'cosmopolitan' nature of London, but it also suggests that it is erroneous to see it as a region with a cohesive middle class (see Savage and Fielding 1989 for further discussion on this point).

Secondly, and linked to this, the fusion between managers and professionals seems to be most developed in the South East. It is here that movement between these two groups is most over-represented, and hence the distinction between these two classes in the South East might be eroded, and a more cohesive service class might possibly form. It is more unusual to move between professional and managerial work in other regions, or when migrating.

Thirdly, these changes might well be undermining the pervasive distinction between the metropolitan and the provincial middle classes, which we hinted at in Chapter 3, or at least be changing its boundaries somewhat. This division goes back a long way, and was related to the existence of differing, autonomous regional economies in the Victorian period, in which local professionals and financiers all had distinct roles serving a regional market. The patterns we have uncovered suggest that a rather different situation has developed by the 1970s, however. Many regions will have a number of ex-southerners in their middle classes. Many of the children of middle-class parents throughout Britain will spend time in London and the South East. Rather than there being a permanent split between Londoners and provincials, the circulation of the southern middle classes to the regions – and of their children to the South East – may allow the social and cultural practices associated with the London middle classes to be more widely disseminated. Admittedly, these circulation tendencies are more pervasive in the regions around the South East than in those of the North and West, and we should not exaggerate the extent of the types of migration we have discussed. Nonetheless, the general cohesiveness of the middle classes may well be enhanced by such a development, but paradoxically, not in the South East!

Fourthly, while the middle classes within the South East may be less characterised by a sharp division between professional and managerial workers, these splits may be increased elsewhere, since people moving between these situses tend to do so only in the South East. Doctors, academics, managers and salespeople might socialise together in London, but in Humberside or, perhaps, Manchester they live apart.

Finally, it would appear that much of the migration we have uncovered above is related to changes in household circumstances. In particular there is a high degree of migration associated with entering and leaving higher education; retirement; to prepare for retirement by taking a less pressured job; or to have children. On the other hand, the importance of routine, work-based migration, in order to gain promotion, is probably in decline (see Savage 1988a; though Salt 1990 and Forrest and Murie 1990 have a different emphasis). The patterns emphasise the growing salience of household type and structure as a determinant of migration, which once more is shown to have an important impact on processes of class formation.

In general, while the middle classes appear to be increasingly socially fragmented, they are becoming more nationally homogeneous. Most of the regional cultural differences we uncovered in Chapter 6 can be explained by the 'escalator' effect – for instance, the concentration of 'fitness regimes' and the like among the younger middle classes in the South East of England. For this reason the idea of the middle-class 'cosmopolitan' standing in opposition to the working-class 'local' still has a great deal of currency (see, further, Forrest and Murie 1990).

# 9

# CLASS FORMATION AND POLITICAL CHANGE

The point of class analysis, we have insisted, is to be able to show how social classes form as stable social collectivities and hence help cause historical change. In this chapter we examine the relationship between middle-class formation and political alignments in contemporary Britain. It is therefore the centrepiece of our argument – the chapter the other chapters have been leading to. But as we have seen earlier, there are differing tendencies at work affecting middle-class formation: some fragmenting the middle classes, others unifying them. Class formation is a fluid process and the way in which political alignments are based in class divisions is always complex, testifying to the variety of causal processes and contextual conditions at work.

We begin therefore on distinctly treacherous ground. A great deal has been written about specific facets of middle-class politics – in analyses of voting patterns, 'new social movements', and so forth. Yet there are fundamental disagreements about the character and importance of middle-class political mobilisation. We therefore begin by clarifying the existing debate on middle-class politics, which we show are based on a series of *ad hoc* arguments. Secondly, we show how voting patterns can be affected by the types of divisions we have developed in this book: the salience of the distinction between organisation and cultural assets, the role of the state in middle-class formation, and the significance of social mobility on class formation. We draw upon a secondary analysis of the British General Election Survey 1987, to back up our arguments.

Having indicated the general relevance of our approach we then move on to consider the relationship between Thatcherism and the middle classes. We shall argue that while much of the debate has been concerned with the impact of Thatcherism on the working classes, some of the most significant developments have been related to the growing disaffection of parts of the professional middle classes from Conservatism. We shall argue that the past ten years have seen an intensification of the potential divisions within the middle classes that we have examined in the course of this book, and that this may constitute one of the most significant – if unheralded – political changes in contemporary Britain.

## CONCEPTUAL ISSUES

There are two types of accounts of middle-class politics: speculative and contingent. Speculative accounts are concerned with considering the general political propensities of the middle class. Here, two accounts stand opposed. One, associated with Marxists such as Mallet (1975) and the Ehrenreichs (1979), sees middle-class politics as having a radical, anti-capitalist potential, while the opposing view, argued with particular clarity by Goldthorpe (1982), claims that the 'service class' is a conservative force. The former view points to the existence of 'new social movements' such as environmentalism or pacifism among professional workers, while the latter points to the tendency for the middle classes to vote for right-wing parties, and more generally to support the status quo.

There are two unsettling elements in such accounts. The first concerns the way in which politics is linked to a 'left wing–right wing' axis related to capitalist exploitation alone. This point is sometimes made explicit, as in Carter's (1985) argument that middle-class politics is crucially affected by its wider relationship to capital and labour. In this book we have argued for multiple forms of exploitation, in which that based around property ownership is only one – albeit an important one. To relate middle-class politics entirely to those social conflicts that arise between capital and labour prevents a recognition of the other axes on which classes are formed and on which political mobilisation may occur.

Secondly, most writings in this area are speculative because they argue about an imputed future pattern of middle-class politics rather than its current nature: they examine the potential, rather than the reality of middle-class politics. This is as true of John Goldthorpe – who claims to be a critic of 'historicist' sociology – as it is of Marxists such as Mallet and the Ehrenreichs. Whereas Mallet sees the growing proletarianisation of middle-class jobs leading to the future radicalisation of the middle class, Goldthorpe argues that 'the service class ... as it consolidates, will constitute an essentially conservative element within modern societies' (Goldthorpe 1982: 180). The use of the future tense is instructive here.

Yet the immediate problem faced by such accounts is the diversity of contemporary middle-class politics. There appear to be virtually no forms of politics in which the middle classes are not centrally involved. In party politics the emergence of the middle-class Labour activist has been demonstrated in a number of studies (Hindess 1967; Gyford 1985), and the middle-class basis of the Conservative and Liberal parties is also clear. Barton and Doring's (1986) figures of the social class of delegates at party conferences show that a 'service class' grouping accounts for 79 per cent of Conservative Party and Liberal Party delegates, 82 per cent of the SDP's delegates, and 59 per cent of Labour Party delegates. In pressure group politics the middle classes are heavily involved. Well over half of Cotgrove and Duff's (1980) sample of environmentalists were middle class, and many public sector professionals have been involved in the peace movement (Mattausch 1987; Day and Robbins 1987). A recent study of urban politics in Lancaster found that all the salient social actors struggling around issues of urban development were from different groups within the service class (Bagguley *et al.* 1990).

It is for this reason that speculative accounts soon become contingent and *ad hoc*. Since they are unable to account for the fragmentation of 'actually existing forms of middle-class politics' writers are forced to draw upon a variety of *ad hoc*, empirical factors which account for the existing fragmentation of middle-class politics. These types of explanations have the effect of preventing an adequate consideration of the 'causal powers' of the middle classes, in preference to a study of the contingencies that appear to associate with varying forms of middle-class political practice. We can detect three major types of such explanation: social mobility accounts, sectoral accounts and cultural accounts.

The idea that social mobility is a crucial determinant of middle-class politics is particularly important, since it enables an explanation of middle-class political differentiation. The point developed in different ways by Abramson (1972), Ingleheart (1971), Goldthorpe (1982) and G. Marshall *et al.* (1988) is that the high degree of absolute social mobility into the middle classes is such as to prevent it reaching any political consensus. Since so many of the middle classes have been recruited from working-class origins and hence continue to bear the cultural stamp of their upbringing, it is inevitable that middle-class politics remains fragmented until such a time that the service class is largely self-recruiting. For instance, Abramson argued that middle-class Labour voting was largely the product of working-class children moving into the middle class, while Ingleheart argued that it explained the development of a 'new left'.

Another frequent argument is the idea of 'sectoral cleavages': that the middle class is divided along various structural lines. The most commonly mentioned of these is between public and private sectors, with the employees in the former sector being more radical than those in the latter (Dunleavy 1980; MacAdams 1987). There is no question that in most western capitalist countries there is a significant association between sector of employment and voting preference, but it is not clear why this is the case. Against the commonsense notion that the public sector middle class vote left wing for instrumental reasons – to defend their jobs – it might be argued that middle-class people with certain political views may choose to work in the public or private sector. For instance, Parkin (1967) argues that radicals choose to work in the public sector in the 'welfare and creative professions' where they feel that their political views may have more impact.

This suggests a third factor: cultural and ideological divisions within the middle classes. Marshall (1987) argues that ideological factors are particularly important in shaping middle-class politics, and that the stances adopted by political parties and trades unions may influence their members. There is also evidence that religious divisions retain a considerable pertinence among the middle classes (Heath *et al.* 1991). Yet while there is no doubt of the salience of ideological divisions within the middle classes, such accounts leave us with no way of going any further, or of relating them to the types of cultural assets we have explored in this book.

The problem is that since most accounts of middle-class politics are speculative they give no purchase on empirical patterns, and hence a variety of *ad hoc* explanations are used. It is more useful, however, to consider the issue in relation to the distinctions between property, organisation and cultural assets. It is not that one can naïvely link a particular type of politics to each of these. It is the way in which the state is involved in mediating the relationship between these assets, and in facilitating particular types of class formation based on them, which determines the terrain on which middle-class political mobilisation operates. And, as we have seen in the British case, the state has historically played a particularly important role in forming a distinct professional middle class, while petty property owners have historically been opposed to state intervention. Subordinate managerial groups have, however, had a much more ambiguous relationship to the state: they have rarely depended upon it directly, yet, as we saw in Chapter 5, the education system has played a crucial role in allowing managers' children to retain their places within the middle classes.

This account is in danger of becoming speculative as well! Before elaborating our argument we shall establish its prima facie plausibility by examining voting patterns from one election, that of 1987, in order to indicate how our theoretical account makes more sense of divisions in political allegiance than any of its rivals. After this we shall then be in a position to refine and develop our argument.

## MIDDLE-CLASS VOTING PATTERNS 1987

There is a growing consensus that the adoption of the Nuffield class schema is of major value in clarifying the relationship between class and voting in contemporary Britain (Heath *et al.* 1985; Goldthorpe 1987; G. Marshall *et al.* 1988). Proponents of this view claim that the apparently declining association between class and vote (Crewe and Sarlvik 1981) was an artefact of a theoretically naïve class schema, in which the manual/non-manual divide was given unwarranted importance (see the exchange between

Crewe 1986 and Heath 1987). The Nuffield class schema, with its distinction between the service class, the petite bourgeoisie and the intermediate classes, seemed to offer a more refined tool for analysis.

There is no question that the Nuffield class schema was far more rigorous than any of its predecessors, especially in its treatment of the working and intermediate classes. However, as we argued in Chapter 1, its rationale for specifying a distinct 'service class' is somewhat more doubtful, since in our view this conflates the operation of three different class assets. And indeed, studies of voting using this Nuffield class schema have shown that the 'service class' does not possess a distinctive, uniform, politics. In Heath *et al.*'s (1985) study only 54 per cent voted Conservative in 1983 (and a similar proportion in 1987), which is by no means an overwhelming figure, especially given Goldthorpe's stress on it being the most advantaged class in terms of its work and market situation. It is indeed identical to the proportion of non-manual workers as a whole who voted Conservative in the same election. Its voting profile is nothing like as distinctive as the voting profile of the working class. In 1983, 49 per cent of the working class voted Labour, 75 per cent more than the overall proportion of the electorate who voted Labour. The service class's vote for the Conservative Party was only 28 per cent higher than that of the electorate as a whole.

This fragmented service-class politics has, of course, been widely recognised (see the wider discussion in Savage 1991b). The point to note, however, is that this is then explained in the *ad hoc* way that we have seen to be typical of much theorising about middle-class politics. Goldthorpe (1982) makes much of the significance of high rates of social mobility into the middle classes as a factor preventing it from being overwhelmingly Conservative, while Marshall (1987) emphasises its ideological fragmentation. Yet a more obvious point has received only scant attention: that the fragmentation is linked to the differing causal powers of cultural and organisation assets.

This is not to say that the authors concerned do not recognise the significance of divisions within the 'service class' which might correspond to those we have developed here. Heath *et al.* (1985, 1991) discuss this issue while Goldthorpe (1982, 1980) recognises 'situs' divisions between professional and managerial workers. But these are seen as variations within the service class rather than as fundamental axes of political division.

The easiest way of indicating the importance of divisions within the middle classes is to provide a breakdown of voting patterns not by the Nuffield class schema but by SEG, along the lines we used in Chapter 7, which allows a more detailed examination of the voting patterns of middle-class groups along the managerial–professional axis while also allowing comparison with the Nuffield class schema (for further elaboration of this data, see Savage 1991b).

Table 9.1(a)  Voting patterns (men), 1987 General Election, by socio-economic group (percentages)

| SEG* | Conservative | Labour | Alliance | Others | N = |
|------|-------------|--------|----------|--------|-----|
| 1    | 63.3  | 11.5 | 24.5 | 0.7  | 139   |
| 2.1  | 71.3  | 12.5 | 15.0 | 1.3  | 80    |
| 2.2  | 60.0  | 14.4 | 23.3 | 2.2  | 90    |
| 3    | 50.0  | 12.5 | 37.5 | –    | 16    |
| 4    | 51.6  | 9.9  | 37.4 | 1.1  | 91    |
| 5.1  | 38.7  | 30.1 | 30.1 | 1.1  | 93    |
| 5.2  | 46.9  | 9.4  | 34.4 | 9.4  | 32    |
| 6    | 45.3  | 22.6 | 30.7 | 1.5  | 137   |
| 7    | 15.4  | 61.5 | 23.1 | –    | 13    |
| 8    | 38.7  | 41.3 | 18.7 | 1.3  | 75    |
| 9    | 29.0  | 47.0 | 22.1 | 1.9  | 362   |
| 10   | 32.5  | 43.5 | 23.5 | 0.5  | 206   |
| 11   | 24.4  | 66.7 | 8.9  | –    | 45    |
| 12   | 62.5  | 25.0 | 12.5 | –    | 72    |
| 13   | 100.0 | –    | –    | –    | 6     |
| 14   | 42.9  | –    | 42.9 | 14.3 | 7     |
| 15   | 61.5  | 23.1 | 15.4 | –    | 13    |
| 16   | 100.0 | –    | –    | –    | 5     |
| Total | 43.8 | 31.1 | 23.7 | 1.4  | 1,476 |

*  See Appendix 2 for details of Socio-Economic Groups.

Table 9.1(b)  Voting patterns (women), 1987 General Election, by socio-economic group (percentages)

| SEG* | Conservative | Labour | Alliance | Others | N = |
|------|-------------|--------|----------|--------|-----|
| 1    | 57.8  | 20.0 | 20.0 | 2.2  | 45    |
| 2.1  | 61.9  | 14.3 | 21.4 | 2.4  | 42    |
| 2.2  | 50.0  | 14.7 | 32.4 | 2.9  | 34    |
| 3    | 50.0  | –    | 50.0 | –    | 2     |
| 4    | 52.6  | 21.1 | 26.3 | –    | 19    |
| 5.1  | 41.8  | 24.0 | 31.6 | 2.6  | 196   |
| 5.2  | 55.8  | 15.4 | 26.9 | 1.9  | 52    |
| 6    | 54.3  | 23.5 | 21.0 | 1.2  | 586   |
| 7    | 39.3  | 36.6 | 23.0 | 1.1  | 183   |
| 8    | 25.0  | 41.7 | 33.3 | –    | 12    |
| 9    | 33.9  | 44.6 | 21.4 | –    | 56    |
| 10   | 28.6  | 55.2 | 15.3 | 1.0  | 203   |
| 11   | 24.6  | 46.5 | 28.1 | 0.9  | 114   |
| 12   | 47.4  | 10.5 | 36.8 | 5.3  | 19    |
| 14   | 100.0 | –    | –    | –    | 2     |
| 15   | 37.5  | 18.8 | 43.8 | –    | 16    |
| 16   | 100.0 | –    | –    | –    | 3     |
| Total | 44.8 | 30.6 | 23.3 | 1.4  | 1,584 |

*  See Appendix 2 for details of Socio-Economic Groups.

Tables 9.1(a) and 9.1(b) indicate the basic findings for voting patterns in the 1987 General Election, broken down by gender. These tables clearly indicate that divisions within the 'service class' are systematically organised around a division between professional and managerial groups.[1]

If we firstly examine the figures for men (Table 9.1(a)) we can find systematic differences among the middle classes: whereas 63 per cent of large employers and managers (SEG 1) vote Conservative, only 39 per cent of ancillary workers (SEG 5.1) do; whereas only 10 per cent of self-employed professionals (SEG 3) vote Labour, 30 per cent of ancillary workers (SEG 5.1) do; and while only 23 per cent of small employers and managers vote for the Alliance, 38 per cent of self-employed professionals do. The percentage point differences are never less than 15 per cent and reach over 20 per cent for Conservative voting.

Further scrutiny of Table 9.1 also indicates an interesting fact. The voting pattern of SEGs 1 and 2.2 is quite similar to that of the petite bourgeoisie (SEGs 2.1 and 12), except that the own-account workers have a slightly greater propensity to vote Labour. Generally the managerial and employing groups are more similar to the petite bourgeoisie than they are to their professional counterparts within the 'service class'. It would appear that managerial groups, who tend to rely upon organisation assets, have fairly similar voting patterns to the petite bourgeoisie, a further indication, perhaps, of the weakness of their assets for distinct-class formation.

If the figures for women are considered (Table 9.1(b)) it becomes clear that middle-class women are generally more partisan to the Labour Party than their male equivalents. This is especially true in SEG 4 (professional employees) and SEG 1 (large employers and managers). Middle-class women tend to be less attracted to the Conservative Party, though this is not true for those in the two 'professional' groupings SEGs 4 and 5.1. Differences between managers, professionals and the petite bourgeoisie are less apparent among women than men. Middle-class women appear to exhibit more political uniformity than do middle-class men.

Table 9.2 combines the figures for men and women to show the overall proportions of each SEG voting for the three main parties. At this aggregate level, the clear differences between professional and managers are manifest. The professional SEGs are distinctive in the high level of support they give to the Alliance, though they are also more likely to vote Labour than the other middle-class groups.

So, it would appear that examination of the voting patterns of differing socio-economic groups within the 'service class' does allow us to to make more sense of middle-class political fragmentation. The picture we get is of a broad difference between managerial and professional occupational groups – though this division is less salient for women. We do not claim any degree of novelty in this observation. Other researchers, such as Heath *et al.* (1985), have pointed out occupational differences within the 'service

*Table 9.2*  Voting patterns, 1987 General Election, by socio-economic group (percentages)

| Nuffield class* | SEG † | Conservative | Labour | Alliance | N = |
|---|---|---|---|---|---|
| SC | 1 | 62.6 | 13.7 | 23.6 | 182 |
| PB | 2.1 | 69.2 | 13.3 | 17.5 | 120 |
| SC | 2.2 | 58.7 | 14.9 | 26.4 | 121 |
| SC | 3 | 50.0 | 11.1 | 38.9 | 18 |
| SC | 4 | 52.3 | 11.9 | 35.8 | 109 |
| SC | 5.1 | 41.7 | 26.5 | 31.8 | 283 |
| SC | 5.2 | 55.0 | 13.8 | 31.3 | 80 |
| INT | 6 | 53.2 | 23.7 | 23.1 | 714 |
| INT | 7 | 38.1 | 38.7 | 23.2 | 194 |
| SUP | 8 | 37.2 | 41.9 | 20.9 | 86 |
| SK | 9 | 30.2 | 47.4 | 22.4 | 411 |
| UNSK | 10 | 30.8 | 49.8 | 19.5 | 400 |
| UNSK | 11 | 24.7 | 52.2 | 22.8 | 158 |
| PB | 12 | 60.0 | 22.2 | 17.8 | 90 |
| PB | 13 | 100.0 | | | 6 |
| PB | 14 | 62.5 | | 37.5 | 8 |
| UNSK | 15 | 48.3 | 20.7 | 31.0 | 29 |
| SK | 16 | 100.0 | | | 8 |
| Total | | 44.9 | 31.3 | 23.8 | 3,017 |

*Notes*:
(a)  Votes for other parties are excluded.
(b)  Figures for individuals (not head of households).
(c)  SEG based on last occupation if not currently employed.
*  The Nuffield class schema relates to SEGs in the following way:
   SC       Service class (classes 1 and 2)
   PB       Petite bourgeoisie (class 4)
   INT      Intermediate non-manual workers (class 3)
   SUP      Manual supervisors (class 5)
   SK       Skilled manual workers (class 6)
   UNSK   Semi- and unskilled manual workers (class 7)
†  The Socio-Economic Groups are listed in Appendix 2.
*Source*: British General Election Survey 1987 (unweighted figures).

class', but they have not fully recognised the implications of these divisions because they have adopted inappropriate theoretical ideas. Thus while they clearly point to the differences between the voting patterns of SEG 2.2 and SEG 5.1 in the 1983 General Election, they argue that these are caused by the rise of new 'staff' occupations, such as those supposed by the 'new working-class' theorists of the 1960s. Occupations in SEG 5 are more likely to be proletarianised, and hence members of this class are more likely to vote Labour or Alliance. However, it seems rather strange to ground voting differences between SEG 2.2 and 5 in this particular theoretical perspective. The 'new working-class' theory was designed to apply to technicians and scientific workers. Most of SEG 5.1 are not in these groups:

indeed the majority are teachers and nurses. A brief scrutiny of the voting patterns for specific occupational groups in the BGES 1987 (there are far too few cases in any specific occupational group for extensive analysis, but the figures are instructive) shows that the 'new working-class' occupations do not in fact seem especially radical: the 11 electrical and electronic engineers voted 9 Conservative, 2 Alliance; 17 systems analysts and computer programmers voted 9 Conservative, 7 Alliance, 1 Labour; 13 draughtspersons voted 9 Conservative, 4 Alliance.

In their analysis of the 1987 General Election, Heath *et al.* (1991) have abandoned their stress on the 'new working-class' thesis, and have instead argued for the significance of the 'creative and welfare professions' as a relatively more radical group within the service class. This is a much more acceptable line of argument, and is clearly apposite to the arguments we have developed concerning the way in which cultural assets may be the basis for distinctive political profiles. This group of 'creative and welfare professionals' are also the group we have found to be culturally distinctive in Chapter 6, and this suggests that the 'ascetic lifestyle' goes hand in hand with a relatively radical politics.

## THE STATE AND MIDDLE-CLASS POLITICS

Why do the professional middle classes have such a different set of voting patterns to the managerial and entrepreneurial middle classes? The answer, we believe, is related to the role of the state in their respective class formation. The crucial role of the state as a 'moral regulator' and as the key agent in educational provision makes state intervention of direct importance for the effectivity of cultural capital. Any attempt to undermine the role of the state will not be supported by those with cultural assets. Yet we have also argued that those with cultural assets tend to have an ambiguous relationship with the state, since there is the persistent danger that their cultural distinctions will be routinised and downgraded if they serve the state too directly.

For those with property assets the situation is much simpler. Clearly the state has a policing and law enforcing role to play in their eyes, but apart from this it has no direct place in their class formation. A politics of minimal state intervention is much more attractive than it is for the professional middle class. For those with organisation assets the situation is more complex, however. While not usually relying directly upon the state for employment or for their career advance, as we saw in Chapter 5, their children frequently use the (state) educational system to move into the professional middle class in order to preserve their middle-class position. It is this dynamic – the way in which the state is tied in to different processes of class formation – that helps explain the fractured politics of their middle class.

194

There is a great deal of evidence to support our case. The association between voting patterns and state employment is well known, with public sector workers being consistently less likely to vote Conservative. Edgell and Duke (1986) argue that 'public sector controllers' have been radicalised in recent years. G. Marshall *et al.* (1988: 251) point out that the sectoral effect is stronger among non-manual classes, and show quite dramatic differences in the voting patterns of the service class according to their sector of employment. Of the upper service class in the private sector, 63 per cent would have voted Conservative according to their survey, compared with only 32 per cent in the public sector (1988: Table 9.17).

Heath *et al.* (1985: Table 5.2) also point to the existence of sectoral divisions within the service class (as does Robertson 1984), though they appear to be considerably less significant than in Marshall *et al.*'s survey, and they argue that for some particular socio-economic groups (SEG 5.1) they disappear altogether. Heath *et al.* (1991) make a similar point in their analysis of the 1987 election, where they argue that an apparent association between sector and vote largely disappears once occupational differences within the service class are taken into account.

Heath *et al.* (1991) argue their case, however, only by using a simple dichotomy between the 'public sector' and the 'private sector'. They do not distinguish the nationalised industries from public services (though Heath *et al.* 1985 do). Given our arguments in Chapters 4 and 6 concerning the distinctive position of welfare professionals, it seems vital to do this. We also need to consider the crucial question as to how the sectoral effects uncovered in these surveys relate to the intra-class differences in voting patterns we have uncovered in Table 9.2. How does the public–private sector division relate to that between managerial and professional groups?

One way of probing this issue is to provide evidence of voting patterns for professional and managerial groups within the service class, broken down by their sector of employment (see Table 9.3). This provides some indications of the interplay between sector and the cultural and organisation assets. It is also a complex table to unravel. If we examine firstly the voting patterns of those in the private sector we can see that there is still a stubborn difference between the voting patterns of managers and professionals, but that the professionals are considerably more Conservative than their counterparts in the public sector. This is an interesting finding, since it is these private sector professionals who have been prominent in our analysis in Chapters 4, 6 and 7, where they were clearly distinctive as an up and coming group. They are the sort of professional specialists who, we saw, were attracted to a 'post-modern' culture. And it would appear that such a culture is consistent with a generally Conservative political orientation.

The nationalised industries reveal a considerable difference in the

Table 9.3  Sector of employment and vote, 1987 (percentages)

| | Conservative | Labour | Alliance | N = |
|---|---|---|---|---|
| | Private sector | | | |
| Managerial | 66.0 | 12.6 | 21.4 | 206 |
| Professional | 57.8 | 14.7 | 27.6 | 116 |
| Others | 40.2 | 36.4 | 23.2 | 1,114 |
| Total | 44.4 | 32.2 | 23.4 | 1,763 |
| | Nationalised industries | | | |
| Managerial | 72.7 | 9.1 | 18.2 | 22 |
| Professional | 42.9 | 14.3 | 42.9 | 21 |
| Others | 33.5 | 44.7 | 21.8 | 170 |
| Total | 38.5 | 38.0 | 23.5 | 213 |
| | Public sector | | | |
| Managerial | 39.7 | 25.9 | 34.5 | 58 |
| Professional | 36.8 | 27.3 | 35.9 | 209 |
| Others | 41.6 | 38.1 | 20.3 | 399 |
| Total | 39.9 | 33.9 | 26.4 | 666 |

Notes:
(a)  Managerial and professional SEGs defined as in Appendix 2.
(b)  Public sector is derived from a recode of V50F, categories 3, 4, 5.
Source: British General Election Survey 1987.

voting of professionals and managers. Managers are remarkably clear supporters of the Conservative Party, while professionals support the Alliance in particularly large numbers. It seems that the most likely explanation of these voting patterns must lie with the differing attitudes of these two groups to the politics of privatisation. Managers seem, by their overwhelming Conservative support, to endorse privatisation, and possibly the greater flexibility that will give them, while professionals are clearly more ambivalent.

It is, however, the public service workers who offer the most striking finding. There is very little difference in the voting patterns of managers and professionals within this group. Furthermore, both groups appear to be less likely to vote Conservative than other public sector workers from lower social classes! Clearly, there are very significant associations here between sector and vote. The reason why Heath et al. (1991) found no public–private division among managers in their analysis of the 1987 General Election is because their figures for the public sector vote are actually a misleading statistical artefact lumping together two very different groups, in the nationalised industries and the public services.

The high proportion of public service managers voting Labour and Alliance also reflects the specific type of managerial employment in the public sector, which is more likely to be of an administrative character, and is less likely to involve hierarchical decision making. In the public services, managers are more likely to have a degree (19 per cent as opposed to 9 per cent in the private sector), are more likely to have moved from a professional job to a managerial job (25 per cent of managers' first jobs were professional, compared to 16 per cent in the private sector), are slightly more likely to be female (37 per cent compared with 24 per cent in the private sector), and are less likely to be recruited from managerial backgrounds (9 per cent of public sector managers have managerial fathers, compared with 19 per cent of private sector managers). In short, we are not comparing like with like: as we indicated in Chapter 4, managers in the public sector tend to have different jobs and different backgrounds to those in the private sector, and tend to be drawn from a more 'cultured' background.

So far we have indicated the importance of the state in purely instrumental terms – as a direct employer. But there is more to it than that. Professional workers are more likely than managers to be employed in the public sector, and are also likely to have more opportunities to move into managerial jobs. We also need to consider the state's wider role in the formation and dissemination of cultural assets.

Of particular importance here is the role of education. The significance of levels of education for middle-class voting has been established in existing work. Heath *et al.* (1985) show that the proportion of the service class voting Conservative in 1983 was 42 per cent for those with degrees, compared with 60 per cent for those without 'O' levels. The same relationship holds for managers and professionals in 1987 – those with degrees being considerably less likely to vote Conservative and more likely to vote Alliance. Reliance on state education also considerably decreases the chances of voting Conservative: among professionals, 69 per cent with private education but no degree voted Conservative in 1987, compared to 54 per cent of those with a degree and private education, and only 30 per cent of those who had a degree and had only attended state schools.

The state's role in educational provision, and the significance of educational provision for the transmission of cultural assets, has a major bearing on the political alignments of different groups within the middle class. Although the figure is statistically meaningless since the sample size is so small, it is instructive to note that for professionals working in the state sector with degrees, and who had only ever attended a state school, the proportion voting Conservative falls to 28 per cent, compared to 33 per cent for Labour and 39 per cent for the Alliance ($N = 69$). An exclusive reliance by professionals on the state for education and employment is not conducive to Conservative hegemony!

The significance of education for political alignments within the middle classes raises the possibility that social mobility may also be a crucial factor in explaining the divisions we have encountered. This is indeed the type of explanation developed by Goldthorpe and G. Marshall *et al.* (1988). Let us consider the issue in some detail.

## SOCIAL MOBILITY AND THE POLITICS OF THE MIDDLE CLASSES

Goldthorpe's argument is a simple one. The service class is a class in the making, and its dramatic expansion since 1945 has led to people being recruited to it from a great variety of social backgrounds. Only a minority of current service class members had fathers in the service class, and hence it is not surprising that the service class has not yet gained a distinct set of political values.

If Goldthorpe is correct, one would expect voting differences within his service class to be related to different patterns of social mobility. Service-class members born into the service class will be more Conservative than those recruited from the lower social classes. And, indeed, there is considerable evidence supporting Goldthorpe's contention that those born into the 'service class' are more likely to vote Conservative (Robertson 1984). G. Marshall *et al.* (1988) show that 53 per cent of the present service class who had been born into the service class intended to vote Conservative, compared with 39 per cent who had been born into the working class (G. Marshall *et al.* 1988: Table 9.9). However, while there is clearly a relationship here, it is still noteworthy that the figure of 53 per cent of second generation service-class members who intend to vote Conservative still seems rather small. According to Goldthorpe this should be the part of the service class which is demographically highly formed and should be exercising its Conservative leanings, but in fact only a bare minority would vote Conservative.

In Chapter 7 we argued that it was important to break down analyses of social mobility in relation to the 'service class' into two different groups, since the professional middle class enjoyed rather better mobility chances than managerial middle class. We can take this a stage further by considering how mobility between our three middle classes appears to correlate with voting patterns, to see if the stable professional middle class, which we have argued enjoys a distinctive degree of security, has distinctive voting patterns.

Table 9.4 is startling evidence of our arguments that the professional middle class is becoming increasingly anti-Conservative. If we examine the social classes least likely to vote Conservative, it is no surprise to find that those socially immobile in other classes (the working class) are least Conservative. However, the inter-generationally stable professional middle class come a close second. Goldthorpe's idea that service class self-recruitment is conducive to Conservatism is true only for managerial groups. Second-generation managers have exceptionally high levels of Conserva-

*Table 9.4*  Voting patterns, 1987 General Election, by types of social mobility (percentages)

| Respondent's class | Father's class | Conser-vative | Labour | Liberal | N = |
|---|---|---|---|---|---|
| Managerial | Managerial | 74.0 | 6.0 | 20.0 | 50 |
| | Professional | 65.5 | 10.3 | 24.1 | 29 |
| | Self-employed | 75.6 | 4.9 | 19.5 | 41 |
| | Others | 56.4 | 19.0 | 24.6 | 158 |
| Professional | Professional | 39.1 | 23.2 | 37.7 | 69 |
| | Managerial | 46.2 | 5.8 | 48.1 | 52 |
| | Self-employed | 53.3 | 18.3 | 28.3 | 60 |
| | Others | 43.3 | 27.8 | 28.9 | 194 |
| Self-employed | Self-employed | 70.9 | 9.1 | 20.0 | 55 |
| | Managerial | 78.6 | 14.3 | 7.1 | 14 |
| | Professional | 61.5 | 15.4 | 23.1 | 13 |
| | Others | 56.9 | 23.5 | 19.6 | 102 |
| Others | Others | 35.1 | 42.1 | 22.9 | 1,360 |
| | Managerial | 60.0 | 16.0 | 24.0 | 125 |
| | Professional | 53.6 | 18.8 | 23.5 | 85 |
| | Self-employed | 56.1 | 24.9 | 19.0 | 221 |
| N = | | 44.9 | 31.1 | 23.9 | 2,628 |

*Source*: British General Election Survey 1987.

tive support (74 per cent), but second-generation professionals actually have considerably below average levels of Tory support (39 per cent). Indeed, if you are a professional you are more likely to vote Conservative if you come from a working-class background than from a professional one. There are also relatively high levels of support for the Labour Party among second-generation professionals.

Among managers, there is some relationship between social mobility and voting. The managers least likely to vote Conservative and most likely to vote Labour do indeed come from a non-middle-class background. The voting patterns of those managers from self-employed backgrounds are, however, very similar to those who come from managerial backgrounds, reinforcing our point that there is greater similarity between the managerial and the self-employed than Heath *et al.* (1985) suggest.

Those professionals most likely to vote Conservative and least likely to vote Labour also have managerial fathers. The similarity in the voting patterns of second-generation professionals and those recruited from outside the middle class is, however, striking. It suggests that a 'mature' professional class is not drawn to the Conservative Party. The second-generation self-employed also have an increased propensity to vote Conservative, and it is particularly clear that those downwardly mobile out of the middle class are likely to be much more noticeable Conservative supporters.

It seems that we must conclude that an examination of the relationship between social mobility and voting indicates that there are important relationships at work, but – as we would expect – they differ fundamentally between managerial and professional groups. While Goldthorpe's expectations about the increasing Conservatism of the service class caused by self-recruitment seem true for managerial workers, they do not appear to be true for professional workers. To repeat our striking finding, it is simply not the case that 'mature' professionals are especially likely to vote Conservative: it is actually true that they are somewhat less likely to vote Conservative than is the electorate as a whole![2]

## THATCHERISM AND THE MIDDLE CLASSES

Our analysis so far used a snapshot study of the 1987 General Election in order to show, prima facie, how the sorts of divisions we have pointed to in this book make more sense of middle-class political fragmentation than other studies. This is all very well in terms of developing an abstract understanding of class and voting. However, we clearly need to go further, in order to address the vital issue of historical change, and in order to move away from a focus on voting patterns alone. We need to contextualise and develop our argument.

The first task here is to develop a greater historical awareness of the *novelty* of these patterns. The point to emphasise is that the patterns revealed in the 1987 General Election appear to indicate a major rupture in the historical association between the Conservative Party and the professional middle classes that has existed since the nineteenth century and was still apparent in the 1950s.

There are, inevitably, problems in demonstrating this due to the lack of appropriate evidence, though we are helped by the existence of one of the better historical studies of the middle classes, a survey of middle-class voting patterns carried out between 1945 and 1951 (Bonham 1953). This and other studies demonstrate that from at least the nineteenth century the professional middle class has been the pillar of the Conservative Party. Vincent's (1967) study of pollbook evidence shows that professionals were the most distinctive of all social groups in their degree of support for the Conservatives (Vincent 1967: 23), with two-thirds voting Tory – a higher proportion than the 'gentlemen' listed. Morris's more recent analysis of Leeds pollbooks confirms this, with 60 per cent of professionals voting Tory in 1832 when their candidate won just 34 per cent of the vote (Morris 1990).

This association should cause no surprise. We saw in Chapter 3 how the professional middle classes emerged as a result of state intervention, hand in hand with the Anglican establishment, and the appeal of the party of

Church and State was therefore apparent. Bonham's work shows clearly enough how this relationship endured until after 1945, being especially clear in the 1951 General Election. According to his survey, 78 per cent of higher professionals voted Conservative in that year, the highest of any of the middle-class groups he enumerates, although the lower professionals (teachers, nurses, journalists, etc.) were considerably less partisan towards the Tory Party. But, as we have seen, by 1987 the professional middle class, especially the 'mature' second-generation professional middle class, had lost any distinctive Conservative leanings, being much more likely to vote Alliance.

On the other hand, the politics of the petite bourgeoisie has swung in the other direction. As Vincent (1966) has shown, in the Victorian period they were the backbone of the Liberal Party, being attracted by its appeals to thrift, self-reliance and its attacks on state corruption and the establishment (see also Nossiter 1975; Joyce 1980). As the Labour Party developed after 1880, and as working-class mutualist organisations began to threaten the role of the self-employed, their politics began to change. Nonetheless, Bonham's survey shows that in 1945 only 47 per cent of small businesses (but 63 per cent of 'middle businesses', many of whom were also self-employed) supported the Conservatives, lower than most other middle-class groups, and a number of studies have shown how small business owners would often tend to be influenced by wider community politics, supporting left-wing politics in working-class areas, for instance (MacIntyre 1981; Savage 1987b: 59–60). It would appear that the election of the 1945 Labour Government had a major impact in uniting the petite bourgeoisie behind the Conservative Party. According to Bonham, 64 per cent supported the Tories in 1951, and in 1964, the date of the first British General Election Survey, 74 per cent voted Tory (Heath *et al.* 1985: Table 3.2).

Managerial voting patterns have also swung, less dramatically, to the Conservatives. In 1945 less than half voted Tory, but this increased to 65 per cent by 1951 and, as we have seen, was around 60 per cent in 1987, when the overall Tory vote was much smaller.

The evidence does suggest that there has been a significant transformation of middle-class political allegiances since 1945. Until the Second World War – and beyond – the professionals were clearly the most Conservative inclined of the middle classes, but they are now the least. The reasons for this, we contend, lie in the changing politics of the Conservative Party and its relationship to the state. 'Thatcherism' marks a particularly important moment here.

The significance of 'Thatcherism' lies in its re-constitution of Conservatism. The Tory Party before the 1970s was a party concerned to defend and legitimate the state. This is not to say that it always supported public spending: to give only one example, in the inter-war years the National Government which it dominated presided over serious cuts in public benefits. Rather, it supported the strategic role of the state in maintaining tradition and hierarchy, and after its return to office in 1951 this led to its support for most of the Labour Government's reforms which increased the role of the state in economic management and welfare provision. Thatcherism, however, marked an end to Tory support for this 'social democratic' Butskellite consensus which centred on the common support for a welfare state, and moved towards a market-oriented, anti-statist politics, seen by some as linked to the development of a 'Post-Fordist' economy (Jessop *et al.* 1988). Since we have argued that the state has been centrally involved in middle-class formation in Britain, such a move cannot but have profound ramifications for middle-class politics, as we shall now discuss.

It is, however, striking that most commentaries on Thatcherism have been largely silent on this issue, and have occasionally produced contradictory arguments. The most thorough analysis is that provided by Jessop *et al.* in a number of publications (1984, 1985, 1987, 1988, 1990). They point to the way in which Thatcherism is related to 'the complex relations among the dominant classes and the structural crisis in the state' (Jessop *et al.* 1984: 47). The novelty of Thatcherism lay in its espousal of a 'two nations' politics over the traditional 'one nation' politics of older Conservatives – a shift related to its use of a 'productivist' ideology counterposing the worthiness of those producing marketable goods and services with the unworthiness of those dependent upon the state.

This formulation of Thatcherism is not wrong, but evades the crucial question under review here: the role of the middle classes in all this. They initially suggested that the 'two nations' strategy cut across class lines, and hence divided the middle classes. 'Thatcherism presents an image of social division based on a *single, vertical* cleavage stretching from top to bottom of society which opposes the productive to the parasitic' (Jessop *et al.* 1984: 51). Hence the state-employed middle classes might be seen as parasitic, but private sector managers might be seen as productive. And indeed, in line with this argument, Jessop *et al.* refer to the way in which some of the middle classes – those whom Thatcherism regards as parasitic – might become progressive political forces (Jessop *et al.* 1984: 53). In later works, however, Jessop *et al.* relate their argument to the idea of 'Post-Fordism', and see the 'two nations' as being constituted by the post-Fordist distinction between core and peripheral workers (e.g. Jessop *et al.* 1987: 108–9). In this formulation it would appear that all the middle classes, largely 'core' workers, are part of the Thatcherite constituency, and indeed they note that 'numerically the principal beneficiaries (of Thatcherism) are the new service class ... and semi-skilled private-sector manual workers' (Jessop *et al.* 1990: 96). They do not appear to feel the need to distinguish groups within the 'service class' here.

Jessop *et al.* hence appear to see all the middle classes as the beneficiaries of Thatcherism, though it is not clear whether they see them as active supporters of it. But they do make a great deal of the role of the petite bourgeoisie in developing Thatcherism: indeed they appear to be the crucial actors in some of Jessop *et al.*'s work.

> The political and ideological context for Thatcherism is the revolt of the petite bourgeoisie, small and medium capital, and even sections of the working class against the economic and social impact of the Keynesian welfare state.
>
> (Jessop *et al.* 1984: 58)

This stress is repeated in their later work (e.g. 1987) and relates to their arguments about the Thatcherite productivist ideology, where the entrepreneurial self-employed are seen as the archetypal producers.

This idea that the petite bourgeoisie are a crucial force behind the emergence of Thatcherism is one found elsewhere. Elliot *et al.* (1988) in particular emphasise the role of this class in promoting New Right ideas in the 1970s. They claim that from the mid-1970s a number of organisations representing petit bourgeois interests were formed which begin to develop considerable political clout, especially within the Tory Party. These included the National Federation of the Self-Employed, the Association of Self-Employed People, the National Association of the Self-Employed and the Independent Business Persons Association. The new Thatcherite Tory Party attempted to harness such undercurrents by setting up a 'Small Business Bureau' in the 1970s.

All these views hence see the Thatcherite project as in some ways enhancing the relationship between the middle classes and the Tory Party. And, for this reason, they are all fundamentally incorrect. For Thatcherism has witnessed a considerable loss of support from all the middle classes from Conservatism, a point borne out by Table 9.5.

Table 9.5 compares the proportions of particular social classes voting for each of their parties with the popularity of the parties among the electorate as a whole, in two different general elections, 1974 and 1987.

*Table 9.5* Propensities to vote for three major parties, broken down by social class, 1974 and 1987*

|  | Conservative | | Labour | | Alliance | |
|---|---|---|---|---|---|---|
|  | 1974 | 1987 | 1974 | 1987 | 1974 | 1987 |
| Managerial | +51 | +36 | −39 | −55 | −7 | +4 |
| Professional | +28 | − | −33 | −30 | +46 | +39 |
| Petite bourgeoisie | +87 | +47 | −70 | −49 | −5 | −25 |
| Other | −19 | −10 | +19 | +17 | −7 | −5 |

* The difference between the percentage of the given class voting for the stated party and the percentage of the electorate voting for that party expressed as a percentage of the latter.

*Source*: British General Election Survey 1987

The figures indicate that in 1987 the proportion of all middle-class groups likely to vote Tory was lower than that of other classes. It should be added here that the 1974 election was one in which the Tories captured a very small proportion of the middle-class vote compared to the 1960s (Heath *et al*. 1985: Table 3.2), and if we had selected the 1970 General Election as a benchmark the figures would be yet more striking. But even disregarding this, it is easy to see that in 1974 the professional middle class were 28 per cent more likely to vote Conservative than the electorate as a whole, but by 1987 they were no more likely to vote Tory than the electorate as a whole. The other middle-class groups still tended towards the Tories, but to a lesser degree than in 1974.

Even the petite bourgeoisie – regarded as the bastions of Thatcherism – have less pronounced Conservative leanings in 1987 compared to their support for the 1974 Heathite Tory Party. This might reflect the fact that the influx into self-employment – especially from former manual workers – might dilute the Conservative politics of the self-employed. If we only examine the second-generation self-employed, however, there is still little evidence to support the idea that there is a fundamental change in petit bourgeois politics: 69 per cent of the second-generation self-employed voted Tory in 1974, and 71 per cent in 1987. As Heath *et al*. (1985) show, the petite bourgeoisie has been consistently Tory since the 1960s, and Thatcherism is not distinctive in the degree to which it harnesses their electoral support.

It would appear then that in electoral terms alone Thatcherism has had the effect of reconstituting Tory support on lines which rely less on the middle classes: a development of major historical importance. Now we should not overemphasise the speed of change: in 1974, 42 per cent of the Conservative vote was from the middle classes, which had fallen to only 38 per cent by 1987, though it is important not to forget that in the same years the middle class increased in size from 28 per cent of the electorate to 31 per cent. Nonetheless, we would contend, the trend is revealing.

These findings are consistent with the older interpretation of Thatcherism developed by Stuart Hall. He saw Thatcherism as a form of 'authoritarian populism' (Hall and Jacques 1983). There were a number of inconsistencies in this account (Jessop *et al*. 1984), but these largely reflected the piecemeal development of the concept, and its basic contours are easy to discern. As a result of British economic decline, the declining legitimacy of the social democratic consensus and the resumption of the 'New Cold War', the British state was in crisis by the mid-1970s (see Leys 1985; Barnett 1984; Gamble 1988; Cochrane 1989). The state, rather than being the solution to Britain's economic weaknesses and social problems, was increasingly defined by Thatcherism as the cause of them. Thatcherism was hence an attempt to mobilise a populist coalition against the state, and could be seen as a form of 'passive revolution' in which elements within the dominant classes mobilised the dominated classes by drawing upon a populist refrain in order to put through its own hegemonic project which would reduce state intervention and restore market sovereignty.

The important emphasis in Hall's account is the notion that Thatcherism implicitly evoked a set of interests that could be mobilised against the social democratic consensus, and hence *against the middle-class interests enmeshed in the state*. The attack on the state is also an attack on the main axis of middle-class formation. Let us develop this point by considering in greater depth the ideological project of Thatcherism and the response of the middle classes to it.

Hall's concept of authoritarian populism runs the risk of oversimplifying the many complex and sometimes contradictory strands of Conservative rhetoric and policy in the 1980s. Heath *et al.* (1985) argue for a two-dimensional view of ideological mobilisation in the 1980s, with one axis being based around class values and the other being around liberal values. They argue that while Conservatism has shifted popular opinion towards market-based economic policy (support for privatisation, opposition to trades unions and so forth), it has singularly failed to turn back the growing degree of support for liberal values. There have been considerable decreases in support for the death penalty, and for opposition to equal opportunities for women and blacks since the 1970s. Yet, as Heath *et al.* also admit, there is a third axis which fits uneasily into their two-dimensional map, concering degrees of support for the welfare state and welfare spending. Here, against the Thatcherite emphasis, there appear to have

*Table 9.6* Ideological views and the middle classes, 1987 (percentages)

| In agreement with | Managerial | Professional | Petite bourgeoisie | Other | All SC |
|---|---|---|---|---|---|
| More nationalisation | 8 | 16 | 9 | 17 | 15 |
| More privatisation | 48 | 31 | 47 | 26 | 30 |
| Government should regulate trades unions more | 57 | 46 | 67 | 49 | 51 |
| Women's rights have not gone far enough | 42 | 48 | 36 | 41 | 42 |
| (women only) | 57 | 55 | 39 | 42 | 47 |
| Gay rights have not gone far enough | 4 | 13 | 7 | 7 | 8 |
| Government should support private education | 45 | 34 | 48 | 35 | 36 |
| Government should spend less on defence | 35 | 47 | 32 | 38 | 38 |
| Government should increase taxes, spend more | 43 | 52 | 36 | 47 | 47 |
| Government should not decrease spending | 46 | 55 | 35 | 35 | 38 |

been considerable increases in support for the greater funding of state services.

Table 9.6 takes a selection of attitude questions from the 1987 British General Election Survey. The first grouping probes economic issues, the middle grouping examines liberal attitudes, and the final grouping relates to welfare spending. Table 9.6 reveals quite starkly the polarisation between the professional middle class on the one hand, and the petite bourgeoisie on the other. With the single exception of attitudes towards nationalisation, the professional middle class are the least Thatcherite on all issues, while the petite bourgeoisie are by some margin the most Thatcherite.[3]

The professional middle classes, however, still come out as supporters of economic liberalisation, tending to support privatisation and trades union reform. This is not surprising: we saw in Chapter 4 that they have on balance benefited from the expanding job opportunities brought about by economic restructuring, and they have also gained from owner-occupation. But it is also clear that the professional middle class's distinctiveness increases in issues concerned with state welfare. These are the very issues that we have argued are crucial for middle-class formation, especially in the field of educational provision which is the key site for the transmission of cultural capital. For similar reasons managerial workers tend towards the petite bourgeoisie on most issues, but on those concerned with state welfare they move closer to the professional middle classes. As we have argued above, the crucial weakness of organisation assets lies in the fact that they cannot be stored independently of the organisation in which they are produced, and hence the main means of inter-generational transmission of class advantage takes place by the children of managers performing well at school and gaining educational credentials. This is consistent with their support of state welfare which is in marked contrast with their generally Thatcherite support of privatisation and trades union regulation.

The use of an attitude survey is not a perfect vehicle on which to test our arguments concerning class formation and political alignments, but it does seem to be the case that the findings of this survey are at the very least consistent with the arguments we have been developing. We shall now take stock of our arguments by considering in greater detail the politics of the professional middle classes.

## NEW SOCIAL MOVEMENTS AND THE MIDDLE CLASSES

It will not have escaped the attention of some readers that the arguments we have developed bear some resemblance to the ideas of the 'new class' developed by Gouldner (1979) and the Ehrenreichs (1979). It seems clear to us that the professional middle class, relying upon cultural capital, does not share current Conservative beliefs outside the realm of purely economic issues, and that the evidence we have quoted suggests that this trend is becoming more, rather than less, intense. It is therefore appropriate that we conclude this chapter by considering the extent to which the political trends we have outlined may mean that the professional middle class becomes a major social force for progressive political change in the future.

The exponents of the 'new class' idea do indeed argue along these lines. For Gouldner (1979: 88), 'the new class is the most progressive force in modern society and is a centre of whatever human emancipation is possible in the foreseeable future'. The progressive nature of the politics of this class is frequently illustrated by reference to its involvement in 'new social movements', especially the environmental movement (Cotgrove and Duff 1980; Cotgrove 1982, Morrison and Dunlop 1986; Eckersley 1989) and the peace movement (Parkin 1967; Day and Robbins 1987; Mattausch 1987).

It is, however, by no means clear that the simple fact of middle-class membership of these new social movements is of particular significance. As we have suggested above, middle-class activists are involved in all forms of legitimate politics, and it is probable that they are also heavily involved in more Conservative causes: the 'New Right', for instance, gains some support from professional academics. Furthermore, Gouldner's own account of the reasons for the progressive nature of the new classes is problematic. He argues that the 'new class' is immersed in the 'culture of critical discourse' where 'claims and assertions may not be justified by reference to the speaker's social status' and which hence engenders context-independent beliefs which underpin radical action. Yet our perspective, derived from Bourdieu, would argue against such an idealist view, and would argue that these forms of discourse are still related to practices which enhance the distinction of the speakers concerned, and hence cannot be assumed to be purely progressive.

Equally, Ingleheart's (1971) argument that the greater childhood security of the 'new class' allows it to put forward a post-materialist politics seems suspect: many of the radical 'new class' will have been brought up in working-class families given the extent of social mobility into it. Finally, and most fundamentally of all, it is not adequate to explain 'new social movements' as forms of interest-based political movements, since the issues they address are not the remit of any one class, and most opinion surveys, for instance, show that there is a general consensus on many of the points at stake. It would, for instance, be totally inappropriate to regard feminism as a middle-class movement, even if many feminists are indeed middle class. It is wrong to regard 'new social movements' as forms of middle-class politics: the more telling question is whether middle-class involvement in these movements is likely to be of benefit in pursuing the objectives of those movements.

It is in this respect that the significance of spatial mobility should be acknowledged (see also Savage 1988a; Dickens 1988; Bagguley *et al*. 1990). The most crucial development here is the growing salience of owner-occupied housing and the fact that, as we saw in Chapters 5 and 7, the middle classes are becoming more spatially 'sorted' by household type. How does this affect patterns of interaction between the middle classes and local residents? Does it allow the middle classes to participate in what Urry (1981) called 'local social movements' as they become increasingly concerned with their housing and spatial environment?

Until recently views have been strongly influenced by the work of Newby (1980) who argued against such a cosy picture. Newby stressed how middle-class 'offcomers' in rural areas had frequently been in tension with local residents, even when they tried to take an interest in local affairs. Newby's account has become the standard one, which is echoed in urban contexts by Wright's pointed statement that 'people live in different worlds, even though they share the same locality' (quoted in Thrift 1987: 253).

One of the implications of this argument is that the middle classes bring with them a new, national culture, and that genuine local traditions and cultures die and are replaced by 'invented' ones. The actual evidence for such a development is, however, mixed. One way of considering the issue is to examine the extent of spatial variations in middle-class voting behaviour. If this tends to be invariant throughout the country, this would suggest that the middle classes are indeed not receptive to their local milieux, but if it does vary then this would appear to be evidence that the middle classes are influenced by their neighbours as well as vice versa.

Conventional accounts do argue that middle-class politics is subject to relatively little local variation. Miller (1977) shows that the proportion of employers and managers in any constituency is the best guide to its voting patterns, up to the 1970s, a fact which indicates that employers and managers are a 'core class' that tends to vote the same way everywhere, regardless of spatial context. Heath *et al*. (1985: 86) show that regional variations in the voting of the 'salariat' appear to have declined: in 1964, 24 per cent voted Labour in the North, compared to 10 per cent in Scotland. By 1983 the differential had declined from 14 percentage points to 7: 18 per cent voted Labour in the Midlands, and 11 per cent in the South.

This evidence is, however, problematic, and partly because it is based around Labour voting, and partly because it examines the voting of the 'salariat', which as we have seen confuses the issue. Johnston *et al*. (1989) have presented more useful evidence, by comparing spatial variations in voting between 1979 and 1987. They show that in terms of Conservative voting, both professional and managerial groups continue to show less spatial variation than any other class. Nonetheless, this variation did increase between 1979 and 1983 (Johnston *et al*. 1989: Table 5.2). Furthermore, there was, by 1987, considerably more local variation in their support for the Labour Party than any other class, indicating a growing spatial sensitivity. And they also indicate a professional and managerial movement away from the Conservative Party in many of those regions where hostility to the Government was particularly well entrenched (Merseyside, Strathclyde: see Johnston *et al*. 1989: Table 5.8), an indication that these classes were 'swinging into line' with their neighbours.

The evidence from 'conservation movements' is more contradictory, however. The rise of these movements does appear to relate strongly to the growing significance of owner-occupation in the middle classes. In many cases these do appear to be directly concerned with middle-class instrumental interests. Short *et al*. (1986) carried out intensive research on these groups in Berkshire, and classified 43 per cent of the active groups there as 'stoppers', concerned primarily with protecting local areas from further development. Slightly more than one-third (37 per cent) were 'getters', who wanted to enhance local facilities, the remaining 20 per cent falling between.

According to Short *et al*. (1986: 125) the core activists in these groups were 'either housewives' (21 per cent) or white-collar workers, with the largest single group (47 per cent) being professional or managerial workers. Professional groups were, however, more likely to be 'stoppers', accounting for 80 per cent of the membership, while the 'getters' were dominated by people with mixed occupational status. Furthermore, owner-occupiers dominated the 'stoppers', while the tenure of the 'getters' was more mixed. Short *et al*. (1986: 227) hence argued that 'the voice of the stoppers is the voice of the middle aged owner occupiers seeking to protect their physical and social environment. This group is strong in the other two types of residences but it is not the only one.'

This testifies to the instrumental, selfish motivation for middle-class involvement in conservation politics, where attempts to develop the area for residents come second to a defensive politics designed to preserve their privileged position. However, there are other views here. In their study of the politics of planning in Lancaster, Bagguley *et al*. (1990) show how political conflicts over attempts to redevelop the town have led to divisions within the local service class. Not all of them took a narrowly instrumental line, and the professional middle classes working in the public sector were indeed generally critical.

The mistake is to assume that middle-class politics is based along a class axis in which they are lined up against the working class. In fact, middle-class political actions can also be seen as concerned with battles within the middle classes to translate assets or to distinguish themselves from other middle-class groups. In this case it may be possible for specific middle-class groups to form alliances with working-class groups more easily than with other middle classes. It cannot be assumed that there is a simple division between middle-class 'offcomers' and working-class locals. The divisions within the middle classes are bound to complicate this picture, and some groups within the middle classes may be critical of what other groups are doing.

# 10

# CONCLUSIONS

In this book we have adopted a realist approach to the study of social class. This realist approach distinguishes the causal powers of certain abstract social entities from the contingent conditions under which these causal powers may be realised in actual social life. Applied to the study of social class we have argued that assets specifying relations of exploitation can be seen as causal entities, but that it is not possible to 'read off' social classes as actual social collectivities from these causal powers alone, without taking into account a range of contingent factors. The general advantage of this perspective, we would maintain, is that it allows us to recognise the complexity of processes of middle-class formation without collapsing into empiricist description. Furthermore, it allows us to develop a 'dynamic' approach to class analysis in which class assets can have varying effects as they are drawn upon in different contexts, and they can also be translated into other assets. These class assets define the terrain on which class collectivities form, rather than specify the nature of social class *per se*. How actual classes form as distinct social groups will depend on context, and salient social-class divisions in one area may not be apparent in another. The concept of social class, in our terms, is not a totalising one.

As a result, we argue that it is not possible to tell how the middle classes form as social collectivities on the basis of, for instance, change in the labour or housing market alone. Nor is it helpful to argue that there are a definite number of social classes, each with clear boundaries around them. In this conclusion we shall draw together the threads of our argument to show how processes of middle-class formation are changing in contemporary Britain. In order to substantiate our arguments we firstly consider the respective importance of the three middle-class assets we have identified and the changing contextual conditions under which their causal powers may operate. We then move on to argue for the historic centrality of the division between a professional and managerial middle class in Britain. We show, however, that current trends may undermine this division and replace it with a broad split between a professional and propertied middle

211

class. While making this argument we also criticise the view that a unified 'service class' might become more significant, and we conclude by speculating on future developments.

## THE RESTRUCTURING OF CLASS ASSETS

We have argued that middle-class formation is based around three types of asset, each with rather different causal powers. To recap, property assets offer the most robust base for the emergence of social-class collectivities and long-term class stability since, as well as allowing the accumulation of capital, they can be readily stored and transmitted. Cultural assets can be stored readily in the form of cultural capital, but need to be deployed in a particular context in order to be used to produce economic rewards. Finally, organisation assets are highly context dependent and cannot be stored, but they do allow superordinates to exploit the labour of subordinates, and so can in certain contexts allow exploitative relationships to produce rewards for those in superior positions in organisational hierarchies.

Many previous writers considering changes to the middle class have focused extensively upon its increasing bureaucratisation (e.g. Mills 1951; Whyte 1957), and this emphasis still surfaces in more recent work. Goldthorpe (1980: 256) has maintained that 'the basis of the service class is an essentially bureaucratic one'. This view is also endorsed by Abercrombie and Urry (1983: 119) who state that 'service class places are places within bureaucracies and are likely to become increasingly so'. We believe that this stress is misplaced, since the dominant economic and social trend is the declining significance of bureaucratic hierarchies in economic organisations. While it remains true that many professionals and managers continue to work within large organisations, the type of work they do and the career strategies they use seem to be departing from those associated with older bureaucratic hierarchies. Organisations decreasingly use managerial hierarchies to structure their activities, but attempt to introduce forms of market mechanism instead. This has a profound impact on the structure of managerial careers. Of particular note here is the growing inter-organisational mobility, even for managerial workers who had previously tended to progress through an internal labour market. In our view it is the declining significance of organisation assets that is of major significance in altering the terrain on which middle-class formation takes place in the contemporary period.

In contrast, the efficacy of cultural assets has grown in recent years. As we saw in Chapter 6, however, there are two rather different types of cultural asset. First, and most important, is the old cultural distinctiveness associated with the public sector middle class where there is a close reliance on traditional forms of 'high culture', such as classical music, art, literature and so forth. Set against this is the new conspicuous extravagance of the private sector professionals, who indulge in new types of sport and fitness regimes along with exotic holidays and luxury consumption. The growing salience of cultural assets in general bears testimony to a growing demand for educated labour. While historically cultural assets have been legitimated and deployed in and through the state, the changes associated with 'Post-Fordism' – flexibility, niche production and so forth – have allowed cultural assets to be deployed through the market as firms externalise activities and draw on the labour of specialists. As a result, the importance of the state as the sole guarantor of cultural capital is now less central as these assets gain currency in the capitalist marketplace.

The significance of property for middle-class formation has traditionally been played down by writers (Mills 1951) arguing that, as the rural peasantry and small businesses declined and as property was centralised in a few hands, so property became of marginal significance for the middle classes. However, we believe that this picture is no longer valid. As owner-occupation has spread and long-term house price inflation has been sustained, petty property assets may have become a more prominent axis for class formation in contemporary Britain. In the later nineteenth century property was important for a specific sector of the petite bourgeoisie, but today its significance has become more widespread. Owner-occupation has allowed access to capital gains, particularly for middle-class groups, and has created new avenues for entrepreneurial activity. In addition it has allowed the transmission of wealth between generations. Furthermore, the long-term decline of self-employment has also been reversed in recent years (Wright and Steinmatz 1989), and petty property ownership is of major significance for many groups of middle-class people.

We have argued that two particular social factors exercise a crucial role in affecting the causal properties of these respective assets. These are, firstly, gender and household relationships and, secondly, the nature of state intervention.

On the first point, differing assets can be combined within households, and will so affect the strategies of the individuals concerned. In our view a radical distinction between class and gender inequality cannot be sustained (see, further, Savage and Witz 1991). Social classes are gendered and the resources of gender inequality may be used to construct social-class divisions. Historically a common set of patriarchal gender inequalities in which women were subordinated to domestic labour in the conventional 'middle-class' family, was a crucial factor leading towards middle-class unification. Hence, insofar as a cohesive 'service class' grouping might emerge, one vital precondition of this is the way in which common patriarchal practices might unify otherwise disparate middle-class groups (see also Savage and Witz 1991).

In view of this argument the increasing numbers of women in 'middle-class' employment is of major significance at diversifying the range of middle-class household types in existence. It is of course possible to exaggerate the incursion of women into middle-class employment. As we saw in Chapters 4 and 7, women have largely moved into 'niche' jobs from which promotion is difficult, and generally are found in the more marginal and less secure forms of middle-class employment. Nonetheless, the changes should not be dismissed as entirely cosmetic. Two pieces of evidence indicate that the influx of women into middle-class employment is of major significance. We saw in Chapter 7 that the proportion of women downwardly mobile from middle-class to other employment between 1971 and 1981 was actually smaller than the equivalent proportion of men. We also saw in Chapter 4 that salary levels for middle-class women were rising faster, in the 1980s, than they were for equivalent groups of middle-class men.

The expansion of women into middle-class employment has eroded the dominance of the nuclear family with a full-time housewife as the major household type among the middle classes. Today the association between being middle class and having a respectable, conventional family life, is simply not in evidence for large groups of middle-class employees. The 'conventional' middle-class family is now of marginal significance: only around one-quarter of middle-class households have a husband in middle-class employment and a full-time housewife.

Evidence is accumulating that the growing number of women in middle-class employment is of major social significance. To recite some of our findings in this book, it would appear that middle-class women are forcing changes in the housing market (through their prominent role in gentrification processes), that they have differing – generally more radical – political attitudes than equivalent men, and that there is a not insignificant group of single women who have achieved a relatively high income. Table 7.10 suggests that around 30 per cent of single women in middle-class employment earned over £20,000 in 1987.

Furthermore, in the case of 'dual career households' a new opportunity arises for assets to be combined within one household, so considerably increasing the scope of middle-class diversity. It is therefore not surprising that many stereotypes of the contemporary middle classes explicitly make reference to household rather than employment circumstances – notions such as 'dinkies' (double income no kids), 'yuppies' (young urban professionals), and 'woopies' (well-off older professionals). While these are all crude stereotypes they suggest the significance of differing household arrangements in specifying different types of middle-class group. However, we should emphasise that this point does not imply that gender inequality within the household is breaking down – there is very little evidence for that – but simply that the entry of some women into types of middle-class employment is leading to a growing diversity of middle-class strategies.

Secondly, the state is of central importance to processes of middle-class formation, both in terms of employing diverse middle-class groups, and also in protecting middle-class privilege. We have argued that it has historically played a particularly important role in legitimating cultural assets and in providing direct employment to large numbers of professional workers. The restructuring of the state, as a result of the changing nature of capitalism – especially the initiatives of the Conservative governments in the 1980s – has been of major importance in shifting the role of the state from one based around direct intervention in economic management and social welfare to one based around underwriting market provision. This change cannot but have major implications for middle-class formation.

Of particular importance is the changing role of the state in guaranteeing the reproduction of cultural capital through its role in the education system and in cultural provision more generally. We saw in Chapter 6 how the 'cultured' middle classes are becoming increasingly fractured between those based on an 'ascetic', and a 'post-modern' culture. This split, we argue, reflects the fact that state support is not the only way by which cultural assets can now be legitimated. Increasingly cultural assets can be legitimised through their role in defining and perpetuating consumer cultures associated with private commodity production. Those receptive to the post-modern lifestyle increasingly look to the market to legitimate and reward their cultural assets.

As we showed in Chapter 4, however, the professional middle classes have managed to deflect or avoid any major challenge to their numerical importance within the public sector. Nonetheless, the need to defend their position in a more direct way has had an impact on their cohesiveness and political allegiances.

## MIDDLE-CLASS FORMATION IN MODERN BRITAIN

There have, then, been a number of far-reaching changes that are likely to affect processes of middle-class formation – the emergence of specific social collectivities among people drawing upon middle-class assets. Of particular relevance here is to consider whether the long-standing tripartite division between the professional, managerial and petit bourgeois middle class has been redrawn.

The historical importance of the way by which the British professional middle class has carved out its dominant niche is shown in much of this book. The early formation of the professional middle class, their association with aristocratic culture and their close relationship to the state gave them a particularly prominent position. As a result, the managerial middle classes, when they emerged in the course of the twentieth century, developed as a supine, subordinated group, dependent upon their employers and unable to engage in significant collective action. The petite bourgeoisie remained even more marginal, though they continued to retain a distinctive economic presence in certain sectors.

To what extent has the historical pattern been modified by recent changes? There is abundant evidence throughout much of this book which indicates the continued depth and salience of the division between professional and managerial groups. In terms of career mobility it is clear that professional workers enjoy greater security and recruit more selectively than any other group. They are more successful in transmitting their occupational position to their children than are other middle-class groups. The managerial middle class, on the other hand, are more fluid, and more likely to recruit from outside, and to be demoted in the course of their work-life.

We have seen how the managerial middle classes fail to share in the cultural distinctiveness of professional workers. They have few distinctive consumption patterns and appear to exhibit a lifestyle based on what Whyte (1957) has termed 'inconspicuous consumption'. And while both managerial and professional middle classes are overwhelmingly owner-occupiers, it would appear that the more dramatic changes in inner-city housing are linked to the growing prominence of young, single, professionals.

In political alignments the divisions between professionals and management is also clear. The professional middle classes, backbone of the Conservative Party for over a century, are now becoming increasingly alientated from it. This is not to say that they are drawn automatically to the Labour Party, but their endorsement of the politics of centre parties and new social movements suggest that they are a dynamic force in shaping the future political landscape. Managers, on the other hand, remain more allied to the Conservative Party. This relates to the changing role of the state in middle-class formation, which we have discussed above.

Nonetheless, there are three pieces of evidence that might be used to support the idea that a more unified 'service class', in which professionals and managers merge their different identities, may emerge. Firstly, Goldthorpe's stress on the significance of the inter-generational mobility of managerial children into professional jobs (and, to a lesser extent, of professionals into managerial jobs in the course of their work-life). Secondly, more households may be composed of partners drawn from professional and managerial employment, so allowing the two assets to be combined, in a sense. And finally, Chapters 5 and 8 showed that professionals and managers both tended to live in owner-occupied housing.

These three points all have their counters, however. On the first point,

Chapter 7 shows that the children of professionals – and especially their daughters – are generally more likely to maintain a middle-class position. Furthermore, it seems that there is a growing divergence in the educational attainments of the children of professionals and managers. Whereas thirty years ago the different levels of attainment between these two groups was of marginal importance, in recent years they appear to be of much greater significance. The processes by which managers' children trade in their fathers' organisation assets for their own educational credentials may be under threat.

On the second point we should not exaggerate the extent to which managerial and professional work are combined in specific households. Table 7.9 shows that around 10 per cent of managerial men live with professional women, and 14 per cent of professional men live with managerial women. Only 7 per cent of female managers live with professional men though 15 per cent of professional women live with managerial men. Arguably of greater signficance than these figures are those for managers and professionals of both sexes – but particularly women – living alone. In these circumstances households are not likely to serve to unify managers with professionals!

Finally, while it is true that both managers and professionals are both overwhelmingly concentrated in owner-occupation there is some evidence that the types of areas in which they live are rather different. In particular, it appears that it is the professionals who are especially likely to be gentrifiers. Similarly, it seems that the migratory practices of professionals and managers are diverging: professionals remain highly spatially mobile between regions, but managers do not.

For these reasons we would insist that any notion that a 'mature' service class may become a salient social grouping in the near future is wrong. The trends largely operate in the other direction, towards a deepening of the split between professionals and management. We saw in Chapter 9 how this political division appears to have intensified in the 1980s, and the cultural fragmentation, discussed in Chapter 6, seems equally clear.

However, this is not to claim that there are no important new developments at all. Two trends seem particularly apparent. The first is the decline of managers as any sort of a cohesive social grouping. As the significance of organisation assets declines, so managers increasingly attempt to trade in these assets for cultured or propertied ones, and hence tend to take their cues from other social groupings. As we saw in Chapter 9, the politics of the managerial middle classes can best be seen as squeezed between that of the professional middle classes and the small business class. On the one hand, they tend to be drawn to the Conservative Party because of their endorsement of capitalist enterprise, while on the other they still support public welfare spending since the particular insecurity that organisation assets convey may make state provision of direct importance to them. Of particular note here is educational provision, the main channel by which managerial children retain middle-class position.

The second development is the apparent significance of the new professional middle class working in the private sector and attracted to a 'post-modern' culture. This group has expanded rapidly in numbers in the 1980s and its income has risen more quickly than any other group (see Table 4.5), and is now much higher than any other middle-class group. For this reason Bourdieu's characterisation of this as a new petite bourgeoisie is unhelpful, because this group comprises established as well as more recent professions. Lash's emphasis on the 'post-industrial middle class' might be of more accuracy here. Whatever this group is called, it is clear that there is enough firm sociological evidence to suggest that the 'yuppie' is not simply a media stereotype alone. The yuppie does appear to exist, and to be engaging in forms of social activity that increasingly marks it out from the public sector professional middle class in which it had its origins.

The rise of this new group might be evidence for a new division within the middle classes, between a public sector, professional, increasingly female, middle class on the one hand, opposed to an entrepreneurial, private sector, propertied middle class on the other. This latter group might include the self-employed, some managerial groupings, and the private sector professionals. Historically, we have argued, the professional middle class lorded over the rest: today managerial and private sector professionals may be shifting from its sphere of influence and may be joining the previously marginalised petite bourgeoisie in a more amorphous and increasingly influential private sector middle class. Certainly, in terms of political alignments the public sector professional middle class is increasingly isolated from other middle-class groupings and is attracted to a more radical politics.

These last paragraphs have been speculative, but what is beyond doubt is that the struggles of the middle classes to secure their own position through maximising the assets on which they draw will have major implications both for political conflicts, and on economic change. Any government will have to come to terms with competing middle-class interest groups with very different relationships to, and expectations of, the state. Equally, the types of strategies pursued by middle-class workers will be of major economic significance in affecting the types of policies and organisational structures that firms can implement. In this respect, social change in the 1990s and into the next century will continue to be structured by the sorts of conflicts and divisions we have outlined in this book.

# APPENDIX 1

# WHAT IS CLASS ANALYSIS?

A major problem confronting any attempt to analyse the contemporary middle classes is that the very status of class analysis itself is uncertain. This appendix is designed to explain to the reader the theoretical reasoning for our specific approach to class analysis. In view of the now extensive debates concerning the status of class analysis we felt it necessary to show how our approach relates to other versions, but since we did not want to clog up our actual text with the sort of discussion that not all readers would find interesting, we decided to leave these arguments to an appendix.

This appendix is largely concerned with indicating how the framework we develop in Chapter 1 compares with other versions of class analysis. It discusses the limitations of work associated with the quantitative tradition in class analysis, and indicates how a more useful approach can be derived from drawing upon the historians, examining issues of class formation.

## CLASS ANALYSIS AND QUANTITATIVE ANALYSIS

Much contemporary research in class analysis takes the form of examining the relationship between a class schema and one or more 'dependent' variables. People are normally allocated to a class position on the basis of their occupation. Such an approach has produced valuable empirical research. Goldthorpe's account of *Social Mobility and the Class Structure in Modern Britain,* first published in 1980, has become a classic study, which uses a rigorous classification of social classes to analyse processes of social mobility and their impact on class formation. It has led on to the most sophisticated attempts yet to carry out comparative research on class structures and processes in industrial nations (the CASMIN project: see Goldthorpe 1987: Ch. 11; Muller 1990).[1] Goldthorpe's study has also encouraged other researchers to use a sophisticated system of classifying people to classes in order to probe various facets of division and inequality. The studies of class and educational performance (Halsey *et al.* 1980), of

219

class and politics (Heath *et al.* 1985), and of the contemporary salience of social class (G. Marshall *et al.* 1988) are examples here.

Yet against this record of apparent sophistication and progress, the very basis of class analysis has been severely criticised in the past decade. There are many lines of attack, but three stand out. Firstly, it has been argued that class analysis is inherently deterministic and cannot properly appreciate the complex processes behind the formation of social action and identity (Furbank 1985). In one of the most insightful of these critiques Lockwood (1988) has argued that class analysis does not possess a coherent theory of social action. In a detailed exposition of Marxist accounts of class, Lockwood argues that class analysis presupposes a simplistic instrumental form of social action. People act to defend or advance their class interests, and hence class theory has no ability to explain forms of action that are not related to instrumental behaviour of this sort. Secondly, a feminist critique has indicated the androcentric notions at the very basis of class theory – the idea that class can be measured in terms of the male head of household, the idea that the labour market rather than the household is the prime site of social inequality, and so on (see Crompton and Mann 1986). And finally, some researchers argue that class itself is becoming a less salient social cleavage and that it is becoming more important to consider other sources of social division – for instance, those arising out of consumption processes (e.g. Pahl 1989; Saunders 1990; Dunleavy 1979).

These two apparently contrasting developments are, however, two sides of the same coin. The coin in question is the growing association between quantitative cross-sectional survey research and class analysis. In the past decade class analysis has become the 'jewel in the crown' of quantitative research. But it is our contention that the hegemony of quantitative class analysis has exacerbated many long-standing problems in class analysis and has hence allowed a powerful critique to expose some of these weaknesses. Let us demonstrate this point by considering some of the characteristics of quantitative class analysis.

There is a long-standing tradition of quantitative research applied to issues of social stratification – sometimes referred to as the 'political arithmetic' tradition (Halsey *et al.* 1980). It traces a line of descent from the 'social inquirers' of the nineteenth century – Booth and Rowntree – to Hall-Jones, Glass, and in its contemporary phase to the researchers based at Nuffield College, Oxford, notably Goldthorpe (1980), and Halsey *et al.* (1980). What is striking, however, is the fact that this quantitative approach to class analysis has become dominant in the past decade. Former critics of survey-based research, such as Gordon Marshall, who in 1983 argued that 'research energies and resources should be channelled in the direction of intensive, longitudinal ethnography in which different aspects of consciousness are located firmly in the context of class practices' (G. Marshall 1988: 121), five years later helped write a book on *Social Class in Modern*

*Britain* which demonstrated the salience of social class largely through the application of log linear modelling techniques to cross-sectional survey data. Theorists of class, such as Erik Olin Wright (1985), have argued for their conceptualisations entirely through the results of survey data using quantitative analysis. A recent book developing new quantitative methods does so entirely in relation to the debate on class (Pawson 1989). Even the work of Pierre Bourdieu, which is explicitly opposed to a classificatory approach to class analysis, has been largely absorbed into English language work as if he is providing another type of class schema (e.g. Lash and Urry 1987).

There are four main problems in adopting a quantitative approach to class analysis. They do not necessarily disable quantitative analysis *per se*: they only apply to the versions practised in the 1980s, of which log linear modelling is the most important (Goldthorpe 1980; Halsey *et al.* 1980; G. Marshall *et al.* 1988; Heath *et al.* 1985). Many researchers working within the quantitative framework are developing techniques to overcome some of the problems we discuss below – for instance, in developing longitudinal techniques, rather than those based on cross-sectional data (see Lieberson 1985). We therefore consider them in order of importance, with those easiest to rectify being discussed first.

Perhaps the most obvious problem is the 'pragmatic temptation', where theoretical decisions are made on pragmatic grounds. This problem is particularly acute when log linear modelling is used, since this requires reasonably large cell sizes in order to produce meaningful results. Hence, however distinctive a particular social class might appear to be, if it only has a small number of members, it cannot be used in analysis. The best-known instance of this problem is that the Nuffield class schema does not recognise the existence of a 'capitalist class' (Penn 1981; Ahrne 1990; Kelley 1990). Because the capitalist class is so small in absolute terms it is very difficult to gain sufficient representatives from it in a random survey, and hence impossible to analyse reliably through techniques of log linear modelling.

The pragmatic factor also surfaces in the issue of gender and class. Feminists have argued that the practice of measuring social class in terms of the male head of household cannot be theoretically justified (Acker 1973; Stanworth 1984; Walby 1986). Savage and Witz (1991) have discussed this issue in more detail elsewhere, but here it is pertinent to simply point out that the conventional approach to class analysis is much easier to manage than any of the alternatives that do attempt to incorporate women. Rather than complicated 'joint class' measures, it is possible to use the occupation of the male head of house alone as an index of class position. Nonetheless, although it might make analysis more laborious, it is perfectly possible to recognise the need to use different 'units of class' within quantitative work (e.g. Britten and Heath 1983; Arber *et al.* 1986).[2]

The second problem concerns the analysis of historical change. There are severe problems in handling change over time in contemporary quantitative research. In some research historical change is regarded as a sort of 'noise' which needs to be excluded from the analysis. Thus much of the Nuffield research on social mobility attempts to control for historical occupational change (see Payne 1987a) in order to assess whether 'mobility regimes' change over time. Yet it might very well be objected that this very procedure excludes the most crucial changes from the analysis (as Payne 1987a argues). And there have been no attempts to devise a historical class schema, where different occupations are allocated to differing social classes in various historical periods to reflect their changing social position.

But the problem goes further than this. The standard analysis of social mobility compares class of parent – usually father – when the respondent was young, with the contemporary class of the respondent. This, therefore, has an explicit temporal dimension and, it might be assumed, allows historical analyses. But as Sorenson argues,

> the destinations observed in a typical mobility table, then, are not destinations, but observations of a set of locations for people at different stages in their career ... fathers have sons at different ages and at different stages in their careers ... career processes and the basic co-ordinates of the mobility process are confounded in the standard mobility tables. So are period changes in social structure.
> (Sorenson 1986: 77–8)

In short, while people are actually engaged in a variety of career trajectories, standard social mobility research 'freezes' individuals at one point in time.[3] Attempts to analyse social class historically by using quantitative techniques are hence fraught with problems. These are being addressed in contemporary endeavours; Sorenson, for instance, calls for a refinement, rather than abandonment of the quantitative approach. But on top of this there is a third problem, which is more fundamental. This concerns the issues raised by Lockwood (1988) and Hindess (1987).

Hindess argues that class analysis involves relating diverse social practices to a social class basis, while also attempting to recognise their 'relative autonomy'. The result Hindess claims is a vacillation between determinism and voluntarism. Much the same point is made by Lockwood (1988), who argues that Marxists either reduce social action to instrumental motivations based on class interest, or adopt a voluntaristic, idealist account where social action is autonomous of a class base. These problems – of structure and agency – are long standing, but the critique is much more cogent against types of class analysis based on quantitative research. Here 'independent variables' (social classes) are separated from 'dependent variables' (educational performance, voting patterns and so forth) and the relationship between them measured through statistical procedures. As a result, a division between 'determining' and 'determined' factors is maintained in the very research procedure adopted, which hence exposes the research to the critique of being unable to demonstrate the precise causal, determining links between social class and other social phenomena.

This relates to the final problem. Conceptual issues cannot be easily separated from operational issues. Since social class has to be directly measured in order that its influence over other social practices may be precisely gauged, it is of vital theoretical importance that the various social classes can be precisely defined and grouped. As Marsh (1986) shows, the most common strategy here is to see classes as groupings of occupations, a procedure that has been best established in the Nuffield class schema. But the point to establish here is that disputes over 'boundary problems' therefore become endemic in such research (see Abercrombie and Urry 1983; Pawson 1989). Rather than leading to attempts to probe the nature of social classes, the dynamics of class conflict and so forth, research gets bogged down with questions of 'who fits into what class' (see Abercrombie and Urry 1983; Crompton 1989). Any attempt to re-theorise class leads to a reconceptualisation of which occupations are to be put into various social classes (see Pawson 1989: 257ff). Existing class categorisations are hence made redundant and discarded as new ones are introduced. Research becomes focused around narrow sets of issues to establish which class schema is the most statistically powerful (notably G. Marshall *et al.* 1988), as the effectiveness of class schemas is judged according to the respective power of statistical measures of association.

We do not accept the view that the ultimate test of a particular theory of class is to be evaluated in this way. It is not clear why one should prefer a class schema because it correlates best with other social practices, as measured through survey analyses. As Lieberson (1985) demonstrates, the idea that the best explanation of a specific phenomenon can be reduced to the amount for which its variation can be accounted, is fallacious. As Lieberson (1985: 115) argues, 'it is premature to think about variability in an event before knowledge is developed about the fundamental cause of the event itself. Explanation of a variable's variation should not be confused with an explanation of the event or process itself.' The claim of theoretical realism is to stress that a social entity's causal powers still exist even if they are never actually exercised!

More generally one might want to claim that it is only in certain historical events, or in certain social situations, that class divisions become important, and that in many everyday practices social class might not be that salient. We endorse the realist view that classes should be seen as entities (Sayer 1984) with certain causal powers, but that these causal powers can only be revealed through their effects. Since the existence of these effects will depend upon a variety of contingent, contextual conditions, there is no reason why one should expect these class effects to appear routinely in survey research.

Goldthorpe, to his credit, recognises the salience of this general point, and insists that the significance of a particular theory of social class should not be gauged simply by the extent to which it accounts for the statistical variance in other social phenomena (see Goldthorpe 1983, 1984).[4] Such caution is thrown to the wind in the more recent accounts of Marsh (1986), G. Marshall *et al.* (1988), Marshall (1990a), Pawson (1989, 1990) and Marshall and Rose (1990). G. Marshall *et al.* (1988), for instance, argue that Goldthorpe's class schema is more robust than that developed by the American Marxist Erik Olin Wright, largely on the basis that the former is more statistically robust. Statements such as 'Goldthorpe's theory certainly better explains class identification and voting intentions than does that of Wright' (Marshall and Rose 1990: 265) conflates correlation with explanation. Goldthorpe's class schema may provide a better association with voting than does Wright's, but this does not demonstrate its explanatory superiority.

It is for this reason that our preferred approach is to start with the issue that Goldthorpe puts at the heart of his class analysis: 'how far classes have formed as relatively stable collectivities' (Goldthorpe 1984: 491). This approach is primarily concerned with the importance of class formation, about the way in which social classes form as collectivities and hence may have vital historical effects. In order to probe this issue we need to consider the historical analysis of social class.

The study of class formation is largely associated with Marixst historical writers. These writers, including Hilton, Hill, Hobsbawm, and especially E.P. Thompson, tend to use the concept in a very different way to those in the quantitative tradition (see the overview in Kaye 1984). Here the focus is on class as a dynamic historical force, which has a crucial role in affecting patterns of social development. A major source of difference with the first tradition is that while the quantitative writers attempt to establish the importance of class in terms of its measurable impact on routine social events for an individual (educational performance, career prospects, etc.), the historians are concerned with the importance of class as manifested in decisive historical situations. The fact that class divisions are not always evident in routine social life would not for them be an over-riding critique since they would emphasise the significance of class when they matter historically.

The historical tradition was highly productive between the 1950s and 1970s. E.P. Thompson's *The Making of the English Working Class* (1963), E.J. Hobsbawm's *Labouring Men* (1964), Rodney Hilton's *Bond Men Made Free* (1973), and others were all concerned to show how social class groups actively caused historical change, and that there were no purely economic forces of development that operate independently of social actors. This work produced distinctive 'class struggle' interpretations of many historical events, perhaps the best known of which was the debate about the transition from feudalism to capitalism (e.g. Hilton 1976). It also had a major impact outside historical writing alone, and through its impact on associated writers such as Raymond Williams its concerns fed through to writers associated with cultural studies (e.g. Hall *et al.* 1977). By conceiving class analysis in this way the Marxist historians were able to sidestep issues such as the boundary problem, since it did not really matter who was in a particular class. Rather than worry about how social classes could be measured and operationalised, the historians were more concerned to probe the social, cultural and political practices of given classes. And while none of the historians was influenced by theoretical realism, it is these sorts of inquiries that more usefully force us to think about the causal powers of social classes, and the types of contexts in which they might operate. Similarly, although as Kaye (1984) shows all the Marxist historians grappled with issues of determinism, their solutions were more flexible and they were not wedded to a definition of class based on narrow occupational measures.

Yet, while quantitative analyses of class have continued to prosper in the 1980s, the historical approach to class analysis has largely disappeared, and there is no longer a recognisable Marxist historiography of social class. The reasons for this relate to the growing sensitivity of historians to the issues of 'imposing' modern western European concepts of class into other periods. In a particularly trenchant critique William Reddy attacked the Marxist historians for imposing concepts of class onto groups of people who in fact were motivated by very different concerns such as liberty (Reddy 1987). Former Marxists such as Jones (1983) similarly argued that historical work had to be sensitive to the languages and discourses of particular historical periods, and the language of class has no especial priority or importance. Yet for our purposes the vital point is that even if this invalidates the approach for other historical periods, it does not discredit it as applied to the contemporary world.

A greater problem was the failure of the Marxist historical tradition to leave any clear conceptual tools to aid future research. The scepticism of all the Marxist historians towards 'theory' made them suspicious of abstractions (notably Thompson 1978), and as a result they left no easy legacy that could guide other writers. Even though Kaye (1984) argues that they did make a distinct conceptual contribution to what he terms 'class-struggle analysis' the actual specifics of this remain obscure.

The one exception to this, we would contend, is the concept of class formation. For E.P. Thompson, the vital issue is to show how classes form themselves. In the case of the English working class, 'the working class did not rise like the sun at an appointed time. It was present at its own making' (Thompson 1963: 9). This notion of class formation is also important since

225

it allows a dialogue with the quantitative tradition to ensue, since Goldthorpe (1980) and Wright (1978) also develop the concept of class formation in their work.

It would appear then that the most useful way forward is to adopt an approach to class analysis that sees its purpose as being to understand the way in which social classes are formed as social collectivities and, hence, how they might have an impact on processes of historical change. In this book we are interested in showing how understanding the middle classes helps to throw light on contemporary processes of economic and social change. Our study of the middle classes allows us to indicate how and in what ways middle-class formation make a difference to processes of contemporary social change.

## CLASS FORMATION

The concept of class formation, which we place centre stage, is, however, a problematic one. It is widely used not only by historians but also by sociologists, but in a way we would distance ourselves from. In its contemporary application, class formation is usually understood as being in relation to the class structure, or to a system of class positions (see Wright 1978; Goldthorpe 1980; G. Marshall *et al*. 1988). This formulation owes much to Giddens' idea of class structuration, which refers to the 'modes in which economic relationships become translated into non-economic social structures' (Giddens 1973: 105)

There are differences in the way that the distinction between class structure and class formation is used by different writers (see G. Marshall *et al*. 1988). It seems to us that the fundamental similarity of approach is more striking than any specific points of difference. For both Goldthorpe and Wright, class positions are economically defined, though the precise way depends on how they conceptualise the economic. Class positions are hence related to the place people occupy in the social division of labour: a Marxist such as Wright (1978, 1985) puts forward a different set of class positions to a neo-Weberian such as Goldthorpe (1980). Nonetheless these are differences of degree since the architecture of Wright's and Goldthorpe's account – the key distinction between class structure and class formation – is common to them both.

If class structure refers to the system of positions in the division of labour, class formation, on the other hand, tends to refer to the way in which these groups of people who occupy a common place in the social division of labour may form as a social collectivity on the basis of these positions. As G. Marshall *et al*. (1988) point out, Wright does not develop a particularly developed account here. Goldthorpe's clearer conceptualisation (1980) argues that there are two crucially important types of class formation: 'socio-demographic' and 'socio-political'. The former is linked

226

to patterns of social mobility, Goldthorpe's point being that the more likely it is that individuals stay in one class position in the course of their own life the more likely it is that they will develop a strong sense of class. The latter concerns the way in which political parties may help organise social classes into collectivities through their actions.

Implicitly or explicitly, the use of the distinction between class structure and class formation has parallels with Poulantzas' distinction between 'places' and 'persons'. Class structures examine the class places, i.e. the sorts of occupations or economic positions that fall into particular classes, while class formation examines the type of people who occupy the class places, and the way in which they might become 'attached' to particular places. The distinction assumes that it is possible to detect a set of economically defined class positions, and then examine the sorts of people who fill those class positions as two analytically separate tasks.

But as feminists (e.g. Crompton 1989) have shown, this distinction is in practice untenable. Some positions are defined by the very gender of the people doing the job, and the class place cannot be specified independently of the people filling them. As Pringle (1989) shows, it is not possible to define the job of a 'secretary' without recourse to its gendered characteristics as a female occupation. Many aspects of the secretary's job, such as her 'servicing' role for male bosses, cannot be understood independently of the job's gendered nature. Much the same point has been made by writers examining the relationship between race and class. Attempts to argue that racial groups fit into class positions 'contingently' fail to show that the nature of the position tends to change if a particular racial group moves into it (see the overview by Anthias 1990, and more generally Savage and Witz 1991).

Going on from this there is a very real problem in explaining patterns of historical change. It is very difficult to integrate a theory of class based on a synchronic examination of class positions into an account of diachronic historical change. As G. Marshall *et al.* (1988: 84) point out, it tends to lead to a mode of class analysis in which the structure of class positions is taken as given and is not itself subject to inquiry. This means that it is not clear how class analysis might explain the historical formation of social class positions. Given our insistence on the purpose of class analysis as being able to explain patterns of historical change, it is vital that the changing structure of class positions is itself the subject of critical scrutiny.[5] It is noteworthy that E.P. Thompson explicitly denies the possibility of being able to 'stop the clock' in order to analyse class structure: 'if we stop history at a given point, then there are no classes but simply a multitude of individuals' (Thompson 1963: 11). While Sewell (1990) is right to maintain that it is possible and valuable to 'freeze' the historical process in order to examine classes and class formation at a given time, we should always remember that such a procedure is provisional, and should simply be used to throw light on the wider historical change.

But there is a key point here: the very separation of (synchronic) class position from (diachronic) class formation may actually prevent any adequate analysis of the historical dynamics of class formation being developed. As soon as attention is focused on historical processes it becomes impossible to specify distinct class positions. This is because attention is necessarily refocused away from the positions themselves to the processes that structure these class positions. Hence, the critique developed by G. Marshall *et al.* (1988) is more radical than they realise, since it undermines the foundation of Goldthorpe's enterprise.

This point can best be illustrated through reference to developments in the sociology of the professions. Older approaches to the sociology of the professions operated with a set of principles quite similar to the distinction between class position and class formation. Professional 'positions', as it were, could be singled out by the possession of certain traits or qualities which defined professional occupations, and then it was possible to see how 'professional formation' – the development of professional associations and so forth – might take place on the basis of these positions (see Carr-Saunders and Wilson 1933 and Millerson 1965 for examples).

The seminal critique of Johnson (1972) argued that professionalism could not be distilled into a series of traits, since professions were historically specific. 'A profession is not then an occupation, but a means of controlling an occupation' (Johnson 1972: 45). The important research questions involve the examination of processes of 'occupational control', not a sterile adjudication of which occupations are to be regarded as professions and which are not. Hence, rather than first drawing up a set of class positions and then seeing whether class formation takes place on the basis of these, it seems more valuable to consider how classes form as social collectivities, and then, if necessary, investigate how this process of class formation might affect the occupational order (see Crompton 1990c).

We would hence argue, following Holmwood and Stewart (1983), that the distinction between class structure and class formation is a mark of 'explanatory failure'. Holmwood and Stewart see the existence of unintegrated and unintegratable theoretical components (such as that between class structure and class formation) as a mark of an unproductive theory which needs to be replaced by one better able to provide an integrated account. The solution to these problems, we believe, is to adopt a more historical account of class formation, as advocated by Przeworski (1977). He sees the process of class formation as the process of organisation, disorganisation and reorganisation of class positions. It is hence, in his terms, theoretically prior to, and determinant of, the structure of class positions – if by this we mean sets of occupations and forms of employment. This is precisely the way in which the sociology of the professions has proceeded since Johnson's influential work. Attention has centred around the historical processes by which professional groups develop and sustain claims to privileged positions within the social division of labour (e.g. Larson 1977). And this is also the way in which class formation is understood in the Marxist historical tradition, as an examination of the way in which social classes are formed economically, socially and politically.

For these reasons class analysis is best seen as concerned with issues around class formation. Our development of this argument takes places in Chapter 1.

# APPENDIX 2

# SOCIO-ECONOMIC GROUPS

We use socio-economic groups (SEGs), aggregated in various ways, to provide class groupings for analysis. Unless otherwise stated these are calculated on the basis of current or last job, and include the retired, domestic workers and unemployed, on the basis of their most recent employment.

Here we provide a full listing and indicate how they are conventionally grouped to approximate to the Nuffield class schema.

| *Nuffield class* | | *Socio-economic group* |
|---|---|---|
| 1 | Upper service | 1.1 Employers in industry, commerce, etc. – large establishments. |
| 1 | Upper service | 1.2 Managers in central and local government, industry, commerce, etc. – large establishments. |
| 4 | Petit bourgeois | 2.1 Employers in industry, commerce, etc. – small establishments. |
| 2 | Lower service | 2.2 Managers in industry, commerce, etc. – small establishments. |
| 1 | Upper service | 3 Professional workers – self-employed. |
| 1 | Upper service | 4 Professional workers – employees. |
| 2 | Lower service | 5.1 Ancillary workers and artists. |
| 2 | Lower service | 5.2 Foremen and supervisors – non-manual. |
| 3 | Intermediate non-manual | 6 Junior non-manual workers. |
| 3 | Intermediate non-manual | 7 Personal service workers. |
| 5 | Supervisory | 8 Foremen and supervisors – manual. |
| 6 | Skilled manual | 9 Skilled manual workers. |
| 7 | Unskilled manual | 10 Semi-skilled manual workers. |
| 7 | Unskilled manual | 11 Unskilled manual workers. |

230

| 4 | Petit bourgeois | 12 | Own account workers (other than professional). |
| 4 | Petit bourgeois | 13 | Farmers (employers and managers). |
| 4 | Petit bourgeois | 14 | Farmers (own account). |
| 7 | Unskilled manual | 15 | Agricultural workers. |
| 6 | Skilled manual | 16 | Members of armed forces. |
| | | 17 | Inadequately decribed. |

We use SEGs in our secondary analysis of two surveys:

*British General Election Survey*

This survey was carried out in the three months following the General Election 1987. In England, Wales, and Scotland south of the Caledonian canal, 3,826 respondents were interviewed.

The principal investigators were A.F. Heath, R.M. Jowell, and J.K. Curtice.

In Chapter 9 we also refer to analyses we carried out using the 1974 British General Election Survey. This was a sample of individuals in 200 constituencies: 2,164 interviews were carried out in England, and 1,170 in Scotland.

*The OPCS Longitudinal Study*

The LS links together the census records of 1.096 per cent of the population between 1971 and 1981. Our analysis of the data is based around grouping individuals into OPCS Socio-Economic Groups (SEGs).

In our use of this study we take all individuals (men and women) as the unit of analysis unless otherwise specified.

*Unlike* our analysis of the BGES we do distinguish the unemployed, who are excluded from the SEG listings.

There is a problem in classifying jobs by SEG using the LS since classification procedures were changed between 1971 and 1981. This might increase the apparent extent of mobility since people in the same jobs might appear to have moved between classes because their jobs were reclassified. However:
– Our checks show that only a few people appear to have been affected in this way.
– Most changes are between neighbouring SEGs (for instance, SEG 1.2 and 2.2) and are unlikely to undermine our conclusions; and relatively few occupations were moved into or out of the middle classes as a whole.
– For men, the petite bourgeoisie lost 0.5 per cent as a result of the changes, for middle-class employees they gained 0.3 per cent, the manual working class was increased by 1.3 per cent, and the routine white-collar workers

declined by 1.2 per cent. For women, the petite bourgeoisie declined by 0.2 per cent, middle-class employees by 0.1 per cent, manual workers gained by 1 per cent and routine non-manual workers declined by 0.8 per cent.

# APPENDIX 3

# THE BRITISH MARKET RESEARCH BUREAU'S 'TARGET GROUP INDEX'
## Classification of occupations

The BMRB's (1988b) research findings are based on self-completion questionnaires received from a representative sample of adults who have been previously contacted by random location methods in approximately 3,500 sampling points throughout Great Britain. Occupations, as discussed in Chapter 6, are categorised by the TGI as follows.

*Government* (Figure 6.2)
National government
Local government

*Education, health, welfare* (Figure 6.2)
Teacher in higher education
Other teachers
Other in education
Medical/dental practitioner
Other medical (nursing, physiotherapy, etc.)
Welfare, social services
Minister of religion

*Arts, sports* (Figure 6.2)
Author/writer/journalist
Artist/designer
Actor/musician
Sportsman

*Managers* (Figure 6.4)
Construction
Manufacturing
Transport, utilities, mining
Retail, distribution

Hotels, catering
Farm manager
Office manager

*Professionals* (Figure 6.4)
Legal professions
Financial professions
Personnel/industrial relations
Economist/statistician
Computing/data processing
Marketing/advertising/public relations
Sales/purchasing

# NOTES

## CHAPTER 3 – THE HISTORICAL FORMATION OF THE BRITISH MIDDLE CLASSES

1 The small-scale character of British economic development has been stressed by, amongst others, Samuel (1977), Berg (1985), and Behagg (1979).
2 Though Rubinstein does present some evidence that lawyers were also part of the wealthy bloc compared to the industrialists.
3 The role of governesses would be worth considering here. The high proportion of women school teachers is a further point to be borne in mind. For a literary illustration of the role of women in transmitting cultural capital – in this case from mothers to sons – D.H. Lawrence, *Sons and Lovers*, comes immediately to mind.
4 It may well be possible to re-interpret the Weiner thesis in order to argue that the anti-industrial ethic is a professional rather than an aristocratic one. This, however, falls outside the province of this book.
5 Thanks to David Vincent for raising this point.

## CHAPTER 4 – THE CONTEMPORARY RESTRUCTURING OF THE MIDDLE CLASSES

1 This debate about 'proletarianisation' rambles on, and Goldthorpe (1990) continues to criticise it. It has never been the only Marxist approach to the middle classes, however (see Abercrombie and Urry 1983: Ch. 5), and there are few contemporary proponents of the thesis. As Crompton argues, 'it might seem reasonable to suggest that there is little point in continuing the argument' (Crompton 1990b: 98).
2 A particularly clear account of these issues is to be found in Bagguley *et al.* (1990), Chapter 1, where they distinguish three approaches on this issue.
3 In this respect it is important to recognise that many of the changes discussed by Lash and Urry (1987) have proved to be short-term ones in the early/mid-1980s, and have not continued more recently. This includes the decline of national collective bargaining, counter-urbanisation, the decline of class voting and so forth. This shows that for all their insights the book fails to distinguish necessary from contingent changes brought about by capitalist restructuring.
4 By conventional career paths they mean those where the respondents believe they have made 'steady progression' or 'rapid upward moves' within their

organisation or profession, where 'I have done much the same kind of job throughout my life and my career has consisted in doing it better', or where 'my current career is just beginning and I am finding my way'. Self-directed career paths are those where 'my career has consisted of moves designed to broaden my experience in a variety of settings while making progress towards a career goal', where 'my career has consisted of one or more changes in fields as I searched for a better fit between myself and my work role', or where 'my career has consisted mainly of choices based on personal interests rather than on ambition'.

5   The question asked was: 'How likely are you to change jobs in the next 12 months?' Thirteen per cent said it was very likely that they would stay in the same post but have a major change in work duties; 7 per cent thought it very likely that they would move to another post within the company; 6 per cent thought it very likely they would be promoted; 10 per cent thought it very likely they would move to a different employer; and 4 per cent thought they would be made redundant.

## CHAPTER 5 – THE HOUSING MARKET AND THE MIDDLE CLASSES: CLASS TENURE AND CAPITAL ACCUMULATION

1   This point is especially ironic since elsewhere (1989) Saunders has criticised Goldthorpe (1987) for over-emphasising 'relative' social mobility over the absolute patterns. This critique is exaggerated anyway, but it is noteworthy that in his own work Saunders is clearly not immune from sheltering behind statistical artefacts, rather than drawing attention to the basic patterns revealed by the data.

## CHAPTER 6 – CULTURE, CONSUMPTION AND LIFESTYLE

1   Of course it is possible that these figures reflect two different groups within the sample with very different consumption patterns. It is, however, unlikely that this is the case since one would expect this to cancel out any distinct patterns. Nonetheless, we would repeat our argument that ethnographic work would be needed to substantiate the arguments developed in this chapter, and elsewhere in the book.

2   The BMRB also asked a question which asked respondents to rate the relative importance of career and family.

## CHAPTER 7 – SOCIAL MOBILITY AND HOUSEHOLD FORMATION

1   This distinction is perhaps confusing because absolute rates are analysed not by absolute numbers, but by percentages (i.e, $x$ per cent of class $a$ is from class $a$, $y$ per cent from class $b$, etc.). This differs from relative rates since the percentages of different absolute rates are compared using odds ratios. For Goldthorpe's classic statement of his approach see (1980: Ch. 1).

2   Other examples might include Therborn's argument that levels of unemployment are related to the political priorities of differing national governments,

which themselves might relate to the types of social and political conflict in differing countries (Therborn 1986b).

3 We have chosen not to carry out more sophisticated analyses for reasons partly developed in Chapter 1, but also relating to the fact that we wanted to use absolute figures in order to describe the basic patterns.

4 These figures are based on a recalculation from marginal totals provided in these tables and hence may not be exact.

5 Goldthorpe did carry out a 'follow up inquiry' which recorded full job histories of some men, but the sampling for this was done on the basis of their inter-generational mobility, concentrating on those men who had stayed in the service class, or who had experienced long-range mobility in and out of it. The data appear to indicate a considerable degree of career mobility, but are not syste-matically presented by Goldthorpe.

## CHAPTER 8 – REGIONAL CONTEXT AND SPATIAL MOBILITY

1 Though it is clear that evidence has been collected on this issue, and some research carried out using the data (see Coté 1983 and Payne *et al.* 1982). This research has not been widely publicised or developed, however.

2 In this chapter we use the terms middle-class employee and service class interchangeably.

3 A Location Quotient records the importance of a particular element in a particular region by means of the ratio of the regional percentage to the percentage for England and Wales as a whole. Thus an LQ of 1.00 means that the regional percentage is the same as the national one; an LQ of 2.00 means that the regional percentage is double the national one, and so forth.

4 It would have been useful to have broken down the 'service class' grouping into professional and managerial ones in Tables 8.2 and 8.3, but unfortunately this proved impractical.

## CHAPTER 9 – CLASS FORMATION AND POLITICAL CHANGE

1 In this and subsequent tables we have not distinguished SEG 1.1 from SEG 1.2. As is apparent from Chapter 5, there are very few people in SEG 1.1, and since both SEG 1.1 and 1.2 are included in the 'service class' by the Nuffield class schema there seemed to be no need to distinguish them (unlike SEG 2.1, 2.2).

2 This is not to say, of course, that the professional middle classes are less Thatcherite than the working class. Our amorphous category 'others' does not distinguish differing classes.

3 Again, we should point out that if 'others' are decomposed into differing social classes then some of them may prove to be less Thatcherite.

## APPENDIX 1

1 This is only the best known of a number of important international projects, such as that organised by Erik Wright. See G. Marshall *et al.* (1988) for further details. See also Therborn (1986a: 98ff) for a brief survey of other European work.

2 This point was brought home partly as a result of Mike Savage's involvement in an analysis of social class and housing tenure mobility. See Savage *et al.* (1991).

3 This point may seem to ignore the fact that Goldthorpe has explicitly declared the need for a 'trajectory' account of class positions, which has been hailed by his supporters (G. Marshall *et al.* 1988) as a mark of his superiority of his approach over that of Wright. However, it remains unclear to us how Goldthorpe's class schema has actually been influenced by this stated commitment: it is not raised in his discussion of his class schema (Goldthorpe 1987: Ch. 2). And, it is unclear what a class schema that was based upon people's trajectories would actually look like, since it would seem to problematise any attempt to identify employment relationships independently of the people who occupy them. We return to this point presently.

4 Though it would appear that Goldthorpe is prepared to trumpet the value of statistical association when it supports his class schema: hence his claim that the Nuffield schema, 'will "work" better in more clearly showing up variation in social attitudes and action' (than Wright's) (Goldthorpe 1990: 408).

5 Though G. Marshall *et al.* (1988) seem to misunderstand Goldthorpe on this point. They quote Goldthorpe as saying, 'it is in no way the aim of class analysis to account ... for a structure of class positions' (p 84). However, Goldthorpe only claims that they should not be accounted for in functionalist terms (Goldthorpe 1983). Rather, Goldthorpe's position seems to be that no worthwhile theory of the structuring of class positions can be developed, since there are no general, historical, tendencies in society. While, strictly speaking, this is true, this does not rule out the sort of enterprise essayed by Lash and Urry (1987), however, where accounts of general social trends can be used to explore differences between patterns of historical change in different countries, as much as their similarities.

# REFERENCES

Abel, R.L. (1989), 'Between market and state: the legal profession in turmoil', *The Modern Law Review*, 52, 3, 285–325.

Abercrombie, N. and Urry, J. (1983), *Capital, Labour and the Middle Classes*, London: George Allen and Unwin.

Abramson, P.R. (1972), 'Inter-generational social mobility and partisan choice', *American Political Science Review*, 66, 4, 1291–1294.

Acker, S. (1973), 'Women and social stratification: a case of intellectual sexism', *American Journal of Sociology*, 78, 4.

Acton Society Trust (1956), *Management Succession*, London.

Aglietta, M. (1979), *A Theory of Capitalist Regulation: the US Experience*, London: New Left Books.

Ahrne, G. (1990), 'Class and society: a critique of John Goldthorpe's Model of Social Classes', in Clark *et al.* (eds).

Alban-Metcalfe, B.M. and Nicholson, N. (1984), *The Career Development of British Managers*, London: BIM.

Allen, J. (1988a), 'Fragmented firms, disorganised labour', in Allen and Massey (eds).

Allen, J. (1988b), 'The geographies of services', in D. Massey and J. Allen (eds), *Uneven Redevelopment*, London: Hodder and Stoughton.

Allen, J. (1988c), 'Towards a post-industrial economy?', in Allen and Massey (eds).

Allen, J. and Massey, D. (eds) (1988), *The Economy in Question*, London: Sage.

Althauser, R.P. and Kalleberg, A.L. (1981), 'Firms, occupations and the structure of labour markets: a conceptual analysis', in I. Berg (ed.), *Sociological Perspectives on Labour Markets*, New York: Academic Press.

Anderson, P. (1963), 'Origins of the modern crisis', *New Left Review*, 23.

Anderson, P. (1987), 'The figures of descent', *New Left Review*, 161, 20–77.

Anthias, F. (1990), 'Race and class revisited: conceptualising race and racisms', *Sociological Review*, 38, 1, 19–42.

Arber, S., Dale, A. and Gilbert, G.N. (1986), 'The limitations of existing social class classifications for women', in A. Jacoby (ed.), *The Measurement of Social Class*, London: SRA.

Armstrong, P. (1987), 'Engineers, management and trust', *Work, Employment and Society*, 1, 4, 421–440.

Atkinson, J. (1984), 'Manpower strategies for flexible organisations', *Personnel Management*, August.

Bagguley, P., Mark-Lawson, J., Shapiro, D., Urry, J., Walby, S. and Warde, A. (1990), *Restructuring: Place, Class and Gender*, London: Sage.

Ball, M. (1978), 'British housing policy and the housebuilding industry', *Capital and Class*, 4, 78–99.

Ball, M. (1981), 'The development of capitalism in housing provision', *International Journal of Urban and Regional Research*, 5, 145–177.

Ball, M. (1983), *Housing Policy and Economic Power: the Political Economy of Owner Occupation*, London: Methuen.

Barlow, J. (1989), 'Regionalisation or geographical segmentation: developments in London and South East Housing Markets', in M. Breheney and P. Congdon, *Growth and Change in a Core Region*, London: Pion.

Barlow, J. (1990), 'Who plans Berkshire? the land market, house price inflation and developers', *Centre for Urban and Regional Studies Working Paper*, No. 72, University of Sussex.

Barlow, J. and Duncan, S. (1989), 'The use and abuse of housing tenure', *Housing Studies*, 3, 4.

Barlow, J. and Hamnett, C. (1987), *Flat Conversions Project Technical Report*, mimeo, available from authors.

Barlow, J. and Savage, M. (1986), 'Conflict and cleavage in a Tory heartland', *Capital and Class*, No. 31.

Barnett, C. (1984), *The Collapse of British Power*, London: Alan Sutton.

Baron, J.N., Davis-Blake, A. and Bielby, W.T. (1986), 'The structure of opportunity: how promotion ladders vary within and among organisations', *Administrative Science Quarterly*, 31, 248–273.

Barton, T. and Doring, H. (1986), 'The social and attitudinal profile of the Social Democratic Party: note on a survey of the 1982 Council for Social Democracy', *Political Studies*, XXXIV, 2, 296–305.

Bauman, Z. (1988), 'Is there a postmodern sociology?', *Theory, Culture and Society*, 5, 217–237.

Becher, H.W. (1984), 'The social origins and post-graduate careers of a Cambridge intellectual elite', *Victorian Studies*, 97–124.

Bechhofer, F. and Elliot, B. (1976), 'Persistence and change: the petite bourgeoisie in industrial society', *European Journal of Sociology*, XVII, 74–99.

Beckett, J.V. (1984), 'The pattern of landownership in England and Wales 1660–1880', *Economic History Review*, 37, 1–22.

Beckett, J.V. (1986), *The Aristocracy in England, 1660–1914*, Oxford: Oxford University Press.

Behagg, C. (1979), 'Custom, class and change in the trade societies of Birmingham', *Social History*, 4.

Bell, C. (1969), *Middle Class Families*, London: Routledge and Kegan Paul.

Benjamin, W. (1973), 'The work of art in the age of mechanical reproduction', in *Illuminations*, London: Fontana.

Benson, J. (1982), *The Penny Capitalists*, London: Croom Helm.

Berg, M. (1985), *The Age of Manufactures 1700–1820*, London: Fontana.

Berlanstein, L.C. (1988), 'Managers and engineers in French Big Business of the 19th century', *Journal of Social History*, 22, 2, 211–236.

Bernstein, B. (1975), 'Class and pedagogies: visible and invisible', in *Class, Codes and Control*, Vol. 3, London: Routledge & Kegan Paul.

Bhaskar, R. (1975), *A Realist Theory of Science*, Leeds: Leeds Books.

Birch, S. and McMillan, B. (1971), *Managers on the Move*, London: BIM.

Blau, P. and Duncan, O.T. (1967), *The American Occupational Structure*, New York: Wiley.

Blumin, S. (1989), *The Emergence of the Middle Class: Social Experience in the American City*, Cambridge: Cambridge University Press.

# REFERENCES

BMRB (1988a), *A Plain Man's Guide to the TGI*, London: British Market Research Bureau.

BMRB (1988b), *Your Lifestyle*, London: British Market Research Bureau.

Boddy, M. (1980), *The Building Societies*, London: Macmillan.

Boddy, M. *et al.* (1986), *Sunbelt City: a Study of Economic Change in Britain's M4 Corridor*, Oxford: Clarendon.

Boltanski, L. (1985), *Cadres: the Making of a Class*, Cambridge: Cambridge University Press.

Bonham, J. (1953), *The Middle Class Vote*, London: Gee.

Bourdieu, P. (1984), *Distinction*, London: Routledge & Kegan Paul.

Bourdieu, P. (1990), *In Other Words*, Cambridge: Polity.

Bourdieu, P. and Boltanski, L. (1982), 'Change in social structure and change in the demand for education', in S. Giner and M.G. Archer (eds), *Contemporary Europe: Social Structure and Cultural Patterns*, London: Routledge & Kegan Paul.

Bourdieu, P. and Passeron, J. (1977), *Reproduction in Education, Society, and Culture*, London: Sage.

Bover, O., Muellbauer, J. and Murphy, M. (1988), 'Housing, wages and UK labour markets', Discussion Paper No. 268, Centre for Economic Policy Research.

Bowley, M. (1966), *The British Building Industry*, Cambridge: Cambridge University Press.

Braverman, H. (1974), *Labour and Monopoly Capital*, New York: Monthly Review.

Briggs, A. (1960), 'The language of class', in A. Briggs and J. Saville (eds), *Essays in Labour History*, Vol. 1, London: Macmillan.

Britten, N. and Heath, A. (1983), 'Women, men and social class', in E.Gamarnikow *et al.* (eds), *Gender, Class and Work*, London: Heinemann.

Brown, R. (1982), 'Work histories, career strategies and the class structure', in A. Giddens and G. MacKenzie (eds), *Social Class and the Division of Labour*, Cambridge: Cambridge University Press.

Bruce, A., Buck, T., Coyne, J. and Wright, M. (1990), 'Incentives for senior managers: share options and buy outs', in G. Jenkins and M. Poole (eds), *New Forms of Ownership*, London: Routledge.

Burnett, J. (1986), *A Social History of Housing, 1815–1985*, London: Methuen.

Burrage, M. (1990a), 'Beyond a sub-set: the professional aspirations of manual workers in France, the United States and Britain', in M. Burrage and R. Torstendahl (eds), *Professions in Theory and History*, London: Sage.

Burrage, M. (1990b), 'Introduction: the professions in sociology and history', in M. Burrage and R. Torstendahl (eds), *Professions in Theory and History*, London: Sage.

Burris, V. (1989), 'New directions in class analysis', in E.O. Wright and others, *The Debate on Classes*, London: Verso.

Burrows, R. (1990), 'A socio-economic anatomy of the British petty bourgoisie', in R. Burrows (ed.), *Deciphering the Enterprise Culture*, London: Routledge.

Bury, M.O. (1973), 'Graduates into industry', in H. Greenaway and G. Williams (eds), *Patterns of Change in Graduate Employment*, London: Society for Research in Higher Education.

Calvert, P. (1982), *The Concept of Class*, London: Hutchinson.

Cannadine, D. (1980), *Lords and Landlords: the Aristocracy and the Towns 1774–1967*, Leicester: Leicester University Press.

Carchedi, G. (1977), *On the Economic Identification of Social Classes*, London: Routledge & Kegan Paul.

Carr-Saunders, A.M. and Wilson, P.A. (1933), *The Professions*, Oxford: Oxford University Press.

Carter, B. (1985), *Capitalism, Class Conflict and the New Middle Class*, London: Routledge and Kegan Paul.

Castells, M. (1983), *The City and the Grassroots*, London: Edward Arnold.

CBI (1988), *Special CBI Survey of Housing Needs in the South East*, London: CBI.

Chandler, A.D. (1977), *The Visible Hand*, Harvard: Harvard University Press.

Child, J. (1986), 'Information technology and the service class', in K. Purcell, S. Wood, A. Waton and S. Allen (eds), *The Changing Experience of Employment*, London: Macmillan.

Clark, D.C. (1966), *The Industrial Manager: His Background and Career Pattern*, London: Business Publications.

Clark, J., Modgil, C. and Modgil, S. (eds) (1990), *John H. Goldthorpe: Consensus and Controversy*, London: Falmer.

Clegg, S. (1989), *Fameworks of Power*, London: Sage.

Clegg, S. (1990), *Modern Organisations*, London: Sage.

Clegg, S., Boreham, P. and Dow, G. (1986), *Class, Politics and the Economy*, London: Routledge & Kegan Paul.

Clements, R.V. (1958), *Managers: a Study of Their Careers in Industry*, London: George Allen and Unwin.

Cochrane, A. (1989), 'Britain's political crisis', in A. Cochrane and J. Anderson (eds), *Politics in Transition*, London: Sage.

Cohn, S. (1986), *The Process of Occupational Sex-Typing: the Feminisation of Clerical Labour in Great Britain*, Philadelphia: University of Philadelphia Press.

Coleman, D.C. (1969), *Courtaulds: An Economic and Social History*, Vol. 1, Oxford: Oxford University Press.

Connor, S. (1989), *Postmodern Culture*, Oxford: Blackwell.

Cooke, P. (1983), *Theories of Planning and Spatial Development*, London: Hutchinson.

Coombes, M., Champion, T. and Munro, M. (1990), 'House price inflation and local labour market influences in Britain', in J. Allen and C. Hamnett (eds), *Housing and Labour Markets*, London: Unwin Hyman.

Copeman, G. (1958), *Leaders of British Industry*, London: Gee.

Copeman, G. (1959), *The Role of the Managing Director*, London: Business Publications.

Corrigan, P. and Sayer, D. (1985), *The Great Arch*, Oxford: Blackwell.

Coté, G. (1983), *Moving On: Area, Migration and Socio-Economic Attainment in Sociological Perspective*, Oxford University, D.Phil. thesis.

Cotgrove, S. (1982), *Catastrophe or Cornucopia: The Environment, Politics and the Future*, Chichester: Wiley.

Cotgrove, S. and Duff, A. (1980), 'Environmentalism, middle class radicalism and politics', *Sociological Review*, 28, 2, 333–351.

Coulson-Thomas, C. (1988), *The New Professionals*, British Institute of Management.

Craig, P. (1986), 'The house that jerry built? Building societies, the state and the politics of owner occupation', *Housing Studies*, 1, 87–108.

Crewe, I. (1986), 'On the death and resurrection of class voting: some notes on "How Britain Votes"', *Political Studies*, 34, 620–638.

Crewe, I. and Sarlvik, B. (1981), *Decade of Dealignment*, Cambridge: Cambridge University Press.

Crockett, G. and Elias, P. (1984), 'British managers: a study of their education, training, mobility and earnings', *British Journal of Industrial Relations*, XXII.

Crompton, R. (1986), 'Women and the "service class"', in R. Crompton and M. Mann (eds), *Gender and Stratification*, Cambridge: Polity.

Crompton, R. (1989), 'Class theory and gender', *British Journal of Sociology*, 40, 4.

## REFERENCES

Crompton, R. (1990a), 'Professions in the current context', *Work, Employment and Society*, 3, 2.

Crompton, R. (1990b), 'Goldthorpe and Marxist theories of historical development', in Clark *et al.* (eds).

Crompton, R. (1990c), 'The service class', Paper presented at BSA Conference, University of Surrey.

Crompton, R. and Jones, G. (1984), *A White Collar Proletariat?*, London: Macmillan.

Crompton, R. and Mann, M. (eds) (1986), *Gender and Stratification*, Cambridge: Polity.

Crompton, R. and Sanderson, K. (1990), *Gendered Jobs and Social Change*, London: Unwin Hyman.

Curran, J. (1990), 'Rethinking economic structure: exploring the role of the small firm and self-employment in the British economy', *Work, Employment and Society*, mimeo.

Curran, J. and Blackburn, R.A. (1990), *Changes in the Context of Enterprise*, mimeo.

Dahrendorf, R. (1959), *Class and Class Conflict in an Industrial Society*, London: Routledge and Kegan Paul.

Davidoff, L. and Hall, C. (1987), *Family Fortunes*, London: Methuen.

Davis, C. (1983), 'Professionals in bureaucracies: the conflict thesis revisited', in R. Dingwall and C. Lewis (eds), *The Sociology of the Professions*, London: Macmillan.

Day, G. and Robbins, D. (1987), 'Activists for peace: the social basis of a local peace movement', in C. Creighton and M. Shaw (eds), *The Sociology of War and Peace*, London: Macmillan.

Deeks, R. (1972), 'Educational and occupational histories of owner managers and managers', *Journal of Management Studies*, 9, 2.

Delphy, C. (1977), *The Main Enemy*, London: Women's Resource Centre.

Dent, M. (1990), 'Professionalism, educated labour and the state: hospital medicine and the new managerialism', paper given at BSA Conference, University of Surrey.

Devis, T. (1983), 'People changing address: 1971 and 1981', *Population Trends*, 32.

Dex, S. (1987), *Women's Occupational Mobility*, Basingstoke: Macmillan.

Dex, S. (1988), *Women's Attitudes towards Work*, London: Macmillan.

Dickens, P. (1988), *One Nation? Social Change and the Politics of Locality*, London: Pluto.

Dickens, P. and Savage, M. (1988), 'The Japanization of British industry? Examples from a hi-tech region', *Industrial Relations Journal*, 19.

Doeringer, P. and Piore, M. (1971), *Internal Labour Markets and Manpower Analysis*, Lexington, Mass.: Heath.

Drewry, G. and Butcher, T. (1988), *The Civil Service Today*, Oxford: Blackwell.

Duman, D. (1982), *The Judicial Bench in England 1727–1875: the Reshaping of a Professional Elite*, London: Royal Historical Society.

Duncan, S. (1990), 'Do house prices rise that much? A dissenting view', *Housing Studies*, 5, 195–208.

Dunleavy, P. (1979), 'The urban bases of political alignment: social class, domestic property ownership and state intervention in consumption processes', *British Journal of Political Science*, 9.

Dunleavy, P. (1980), 'The political implications of sectoral cleavages: the growth of state employment: Part 1, The analysis of production cleavages', *Political Studies*, 28.

Eckersley, R. (1989), 'Green politics and the new class: selfishness or virtue?', *Political Studies*, 37, 2, 205–223.

Edgell, S. (1980), *Middle Class Couples*, London: George Allen and Unwin.

Edgell, S. and Duke, V. (1986), 'Radicalism, radicalisation and recession: Britain in the 1980s', *British Journal of Sociology*, 37, 4.

Edwards, P.K. (1987), *Managing the Factory*, Oxford: Blackwell.

Ehrenreich, B. and Ehrenreich, J. (1979), 'The professional–managerial class', in P. Walker (ed.), *Between Labour and Capital*, New York: Monthly Review.

Elbaum, B. and Lazonick, W. (1986), *The Decline of the British Economy*, Oxford: Clarendon.

Elliot, B., McCrone, D. and Bechhofer, F. (1988), 'Anxieties and ambitions: the petite bourgeoisie and the new right', in D. Rose (ed.), *Social Stratification and Economic Change*, London: Hutchinson.

Engel, A.J. (1983), *From Clergyman to Don: the Rise of the Academic Profession in Nineteenth Century Oxford*, Oxford: Clarendon.

Erikson, C. (1959), *British Industrialists: Steel and Hosiery 1850–1950*, Cambridge: Cambridge University Press.

Evans, A. (1990), *Speculative Housebuilding in the 1980s: Flexible Design and Flexible Production?*, University of Sussex, mimeo.

Farmer, M. and Barrell, R. (1981), 'Entrepreneurship and government policy', *Journal of Public Policy*, 1, 307–332.

Featherstone, M. (1982), 'Lifestyle and consumer culture', *Theory, Culture and Society*, 1, 18–33.

Feinstein, C. (1965), *Domestic Capital Formation in the United Kingdom 1920–1938*, Cambridge: Cambridge University Press.

Felstead, A. (1990), 'A chance to be your own boss: the myths or reality of franchise ownership', in G. Jenkins and M. Poole (eds), *New Forms of Ownership*, London: Routledge.

Fieghen, G.L. and Reddaway, W.B. (1981), *Companies' Incentives and Senior Managers*, Oxford: Oxford University Press.

Fielding, A.J. (1989), 'Inter-regional migration and social change: a study of south east England based upon the Longitudinal Study', *Transactions of the Institute of British Geographers*, 14, 24–36.

Fielding, A.J. and Savage, M. (1987), 'Social mobility and the changing class composition of south east England', *University of Sussex Working Paper in Urban and Regional Studies*, No. 60.

Finch, J. (1983), *Married to the Job*, London: Heinemann.

Fleming, M. (1966), 'The long term measurment of construction costs in the UK', *Journal of the Royal Statistical Society*, 129, 534–556.

Flynn, R. (1990), 'Managing markets: consumers and producers in the NHS', paper presented at BSA Conference, University of Surrey.

Foreman-Peck, J. (1985), 'Seedcorn or chaff? New firm formation and the performance of the inter war economy', *Economic History Review*, 8, 3.

Forrest, R. and Murie, A. (1989a), 'The affluent homeowner: labour market position and the shaping of local histories', in N. Thrift and P. Williams (eds), *Class and Space*, London: Routledge.

Forrest, R. and Murie, A. (1989b), 'Differential accumulation: wealth, inheritance and housing policy reconsidered', *Policy and Politics*, 17.

Forrest, R. and Murie, A. (1990), 'Housing markets, labour markets and housing histories', in J. Allen and C. Hamnett (eds), *Housing and Labour Markets*, London: Unwin Hyman.

Forrest, R., Murie, A. and Williams, P. (1990), *Home Ownership: Differentiation and Fragmentation*, London: Unwin Hyman.

Foster, J. (1974), *Class Struggle in the Industrial Revolution*, London: Methuen.

Fox, A. (1974), *Beyond Contract: Work, Power and Trust Relations*, London: Faber.

# REFERENCES

Friedson, E. (1986), *Professional Powers*, Chicago: University of Chicago Press.

Furbank, P.N. (1985), *The Idea of Social Class*, Oxford: Oxford University Press.

Fyfe, G. (1990), *A Trojan Horse at the Tate: the Chantry Bequest and the State*, mimeo, University of Keele.

Gallos, J.V. (1989), 'Exploring women's development: implications for career theory, practice and research', in M.B. Arthur *et al.* (eds), *Handbook of Career Theory*, Cambridge: Cambridge University Press.

Gamble, A. (1988), *The Free Economy and the Strong State: the Politics of Thatcherism*, Basingstoke: Macmillan.

Garrard, J., Jary, D., Goldsmith, M. and Oldfield, A. (1978), *The Middle Class in Politics*, London: Saxon House.

Gauldie, E. (1974), *Cruel Habitations: a History of Working Class Housing 1780–1914*, London: Allen and Unwin.

Giddens, A. (1973), *The Class Structure of the Advanced Societies*, London: Hutchinson.

Gill, A.A. and Lockyer, K.G. (nd), *The Career Development of the Production Manager*, London: BIM Occasional Paper No. 17.

Glass, D.V. (ed.) (1954), *Social Mobility in Britain*, London: Routledge & Kegan Paul.

Glassner, B. (1989), 'Fitness and the post modern self', in *Journal of Health and Social Behaviour*, 30, 180–191.

Gleave, D. and Sellens, R. (1984), 'An inquiry into British labour market processes', ESRC Report, Environment and Planning Committee, No. 3.

Glucksmann, M. (1990), *Women Assemble*, London: Routledge.

Goldthorpe, J. (with Llewellyn, C. and Payne, C.)(1980), *Social Mobility and the Class Structure in Modern Britain*, Oxford: Clarendon.

Goldthorpe, J. (with Llewellyn, C. and Payne, C.)(1987), *Social Mobility and the Class Structure in Modern Britain* (2nd edn), Oxford: Clarendon.

Goldthorpe, J. (1982), 'On the service class: its formation and future', in A. Giddens and G. MacKenzie (eds), *Social Class and the Division of Labour*, Cambridge: Cambridge University Press.

Goldthorpe, J. (1983), 'Women and class analysis: in defence of the conventional view', *Sociology*, 17.

Goldthorpe, J. (1984), 'Women and class analysis: a reply to the replies', *Sociology*, 18, 491–499.

Goldthorpe, J. (1990), 'A Response', in Clark *et al.* (eds).

Goode, W.J. (1963), *World Revolution and Family Patterns*, London: Collier-Macmillan.

Gouldner, A. (1957–58), 'Cosmopolitans and locals: towards an analysis of latent social roles', *Administrative Science Quarterly*, Part 1 in vol. 1, 2 and Part 2 in vol. 2, 2.

Gouldner, A. (1979), *The Future of the Intellectuals and the Rise of the New Class*, London: Macmillan.

Gourvish, T.K. (1987), 'British business and the transition to a corporate economy: entrepreneurship and management structures', *Business History*, 6, 2.

Gowan, P. (1987), 'The origins of the administrative elite', *New Left Review*, 162.

Greenaway, H. (1973), 'The impact of educational policies', in H. Greenaway and G. Williams (eds), *Patterns of Change in Graduate Employment*, London: Society for Research into Higher Education.

Guerrier, Y. and Philpott, N. (1978), *The British Manager: Careers and Mobility*, London: BIM.

Gunn, S. (1988), 'The "failure" of the Victorian middle class: a critique', in J. Wolff and J. Seed (eds), *The Culture of Capital: Art, Power and the Nineteenth Century Middle Class*, Manchester: Manchester University Press.

Gyford, J. (1985), *The Politics of Local Socialism*, London: George Allen and Unwin.

Habbakuk, H. (1962), 'Fluctuation in house building in Britain and the US in the nineteenth century', *Journal of Economic History*, 22, 198–230.

Hakim, C. (1987), 'Current trends in the flexible workforce', *Employment Gazette*, 95, 11, 549–560.

Hakim, C. (1989), 'Self-employment in Britain: recent trends and current issues', *Work, Employment and Society*, 2, 4, 421–450.

Hall, C. (1990), 'The tale of Samuel and Jemima: gender and working class culture in nineteenth century England', in H. Kaye and K. McLelland (eds), *E.P. Thompson: Critical Perspectives*, Cambridge: Polity.

Hall, D. (1975), *Occupations and the Social Structure*, New Jersey: Prentice-Hall.

Hall, D. and Amado-Fischgrund, D. (1971), *Survey of British Managers*, London: Business Publications.

Hall, P., Breheney, M., McQuaid, R. and Hart, D. (1987), *Western Sunrise: the Genesis and Growth of Britain's Major Hi-tech Corridor*, London: Allen and Unwin.

Hall, S. *et al.* (1977), *Resistance through Rituals*, London: Hutchinson.

Hall, S. and Jacques, M. (1983), *The Politics of Thatcherism*, London, Verso.

Hallet, R. (1990), 'Privatisation and the restructuring of a public utility: a case study of British Telecom's corporate strategy and structure', in G. Jenkins and M. Poole (eds), *New Forms of Ownership*, London: Routledge.

Halsey, A., Heath, A. and Ridge, J.M. (1980), *Origins and Destinations*, Oxford: Clarendon.

Ham, C. (1985), *Policy Making in the NHS*, London: Macmillan.

Hamnett, C. (1984), 'Housing the two nations: socio-tenurial polarization in England and Wales 1961–1981', *Urban Studies*, 21, 3, 389–405.

Hamnett, C. (1986), 'The changing socio-economic structure of London and the South-East', *Regional Studies*, 20, 5, 391–406.

Hamnett, C. (1988), 'Regional variations in house prices and house price inflation 1969–1988', *The Royal Bank of Scotland Review*, No. 159, 29–40.

Hamnett, C. (1989), 'Consumption and class in contemporary Britain', in C. Hamnett *et al.* (eds), *The Changing Social Structure*, London: Sage.

Hamnett, C. (1990), 'Labour markets, housing markets and social restructuring in a global city: the case of London', in J. Allen and C. Hamnett (eds), *Housing and Labour Markets*, London: Unwin Hyman.

Hannah, L. (1976), *The Rise of the Corporate Economy*, London: Methuen.

Hardiman, S. (1990), 'Capitalism and Corporatism: the political economy of advanced capitalist societies', in Clark *et al.* (eds).

Harmer, M. and Hamnett, C. (1990), 'Regional variations in housing inheritance', *Area*, 22.

Harries-Jenkins, C. (1970), 'Professionals in organisations', in J.A. Jackson (ed.), *Professions and Professionalism*, Cambridge: Cambridge University Press.

Harrison, S. (1988), *Managing the National Health Service*, London: Chapman and Hall.

Harvey, D. (1982), *The Limits to Capital*, Oxford: Blackwell.

Harvey, D. (1989), *The Condition of Post-Modernity*, Oxford: Blackwell.

Heath, A. (1981), *Social Mobility*, London: Fontana.

Heath, A. (1987), 'Trendless fluctuation: relative class voting 1964–83', *Political Studies*, XXXV.

Heath, A., Curtice, J. and Jowell, R. (1991), *Understanding Political Change*, London: Pergamon.

Heath, A., Jowell, R. and Curtice, J. (1985), *How Britain Votes* (1st edn), London: Pergamon.

Heller, T. (1978), *Restructuring the Medical Profession*, London: Croom Helm.

Hennock, E.P. (1973), *Fit and Proper Persons: Ideal and Reality in 19th Century Urban Government*, London: Edward Arnold.

Hilton, R. (1973), *Bond Men Made Free*, London: Methuen.

Hilton, R. (ed.) (1976), *The Transition from Feudalism to Capitalism*, London: New Left Books.

Hindess, B. (1967), *The Decline of Working Class Politics*, London.

Hindess, B. (1987), *Politics and Class Analysis*, Oxford: Blackwell.

Hobsbawm, E.J. (1964), *Labouring Men*, London: Weidenfeld.

Hobsbawm, E.J. (1968), *Industry and Empire*, London: Penguin.

Holmans, A. (1986), 'Flow of funds associated with house price purchase for owner occupation in the UK, 1977–1984, and equity withdrawal for house purchase finance', *Government Economic Service Working Paper*, No. 92, London: Dept of Environment.

Holmans, A. (1990), 'House prices: changes through time at national and sub-national level', *Government Economic Service Working Paper*, No. 110, London: Dept of Environment.

Holmes, G. (1982), *Augustan England: Professions, State and Society 1680–1730*, London: Allen and Unwin.

Holmwood, J. and Stewart, A. (1983), 'The role of contradictions in modern theories of stratification', *Sociology*, 17.

Honeyman, K. (1982), 'Elites in British history', *Social History*, 7, 3.

Honneth, A. (1986), 'The fragmented world of symbolic forms: reflections on Pierre Bourdieu's sociology of culture', *Theory, Culture and Society*, 3, 3.

Ingham, G. (1986), *Capitalism Divided: The City and Industry in British Social Development*, London: Macmillan.

Ingleheart, I. (1971), 'The silent revolution in Europe: intergenerational change in post-industrial societies', *American Political Science Review*, 991–1017.

Jackson, A. (1973), *Semi-detached London: Suburban Development Life and Transport 1900–1939*, London: Allen and Unwin.

Jackson, P. (1991), 'Mapping meanings', in *Environment and Planning A*, 23, 2.

Jager, M. (1987), 'Class definition and the aesthetics of gentrification', in Smith and Williams (eds).

Jameson, F. (1984), 'Postmodernism, or the cultural logic of late capitalism', *New Left Review*, 146.

Jessop, B., Bonnett, K., Bromley, S. and Ling, T. (1984), 'Authoritarian populism, two nations, and Thatcherism', *New Left Review*, 147, 32–60.

Jessop, B., Bonnett, K., Bromley, S. and Ling, T. (1985), 'Thatcherism and the politics of hegemony: a reply to Stuart Hall', *New Left Review*, 153, 87–101.

Jessop, B., Bonnett, K., Bromley, S. and Ling, T. (1987), 'Popular capitalism, flexible accumulation and left strategy', *New Left Review*, 165, 104–122.

Jessop, B., Bonnett, K., Bromley, S. and Ling, T. (1988), *Thatcherism, a Tale of Two Nations*, Cambridge: Polity.

Jessop, B., Bonnett, K. and Bromley, S. (1990), 'Farewell to Thatcherism? Neo-Liberalism and "New Times"', *New Left Review*, 179, 81–102.

Johnson, J.H., Salt, J. and Wood, P. (1974), *Housing and the Migration of Labour in England and Wales*, London: Saxon House.

Johnson, T. (1972), *Professions and Power*, London: Macmillan.

Johnson, T. (1982), 'The state and the professions: peculiarities of the British', in A. Giddens and G. MacKenzie, *Social Class and the Divison of Labour*, Cambridge: Cambridge University Press.

Johnston, R., Pattie, C. and Allsop, A. (1989), *A Nation Dividing?*, London: Longman.

Jones, G.S. (1983), *Languages of Class*, Cambridge: Cambridge University Press.

Joyce, P. (1980), *Work, Society and Politics*, Brighton: Harvester.

Kanter, R. (1977), *Men and Women of the Corporation*, New York: Basic.

Kanter, R. (1984), 'Variations in managerial career structures in high technology firms: the impact of organisational characteristics on internal labour market patterns', in P. Osterman (ed.), *Internal Labour Markets*, Cambridge, Mass.: MIT Press.

Kaye, H. (1984), *The British Marxist Historians*, Cambridge: Polity.

Keat, R. and Urry, J. (1975), *Social Theory as Science*, London: Routledge & Kegan Paul.

Kelley, J. (1990), 'The failure of a paradigm: log linear models of social mobility', in Clark *et al.* (eds).

Kelsall, R.K. (1955), *Higher Civil Servants in Britain*, London: Routledge & Kegan Hall.

Kemp, P. (1982), 'Housing landlordism in late nineteenth century Britain', *Environment and Planning A*, 14, 1437–1447.

Kemp, P. (1987), 'Aspects of housing consumption in later nineteenth century England and Wales', *Housing Studies*, 2, 1, 3–16.

Klein, R. (1984), 'The politics of ideology vs the reality of politics', *Millbank Memorial Fund Quarterly Health and Society*, 62, 1.

Kocka, J. (1990), '"Burgertum" and professions in the nineteenth century: two alternative approaches', in M. Burrage and R. Torstendahl (eds), *Professions in Theory and History*, London: Sage.

Larson, M.S. (1977), *The Rise of Professionalism: a Sociological Analysis*, Berkeley: The University of California Press.

Larson, M.S. (1990), 'In the matter of experts and professionals, or how impossible it is to leave nothing unsaid', in R. Torstendahl and M. Burrage (eds), *The Formation of Professions*, London: Sage.

Lash, S. (1990), *The Sociology of Post-Modernism*, London: Routledge.

Lash, S. and Urry, J. (1987), *The End of Organised Capitalism*, Cambridge: Polity.

Law, C. (1981), *British Regional Development since World War 1*, London: Methuen.

Le Grand, J. and Goodwin, R.E. (1987), *Not Only the Poor: the Middle Class and the Welfare State*, London: Unwin Hyman.

Leadbeater, C. (1989), 'Boomtown blues', *Marxism Today*, October, 20–23.

Lee, G. (1981), *Who Gets to the Top? A Sociological Study of Business Executives*, Aldershot: Gower.

Leggatt, T. (1978), 'Managers in industry: their background and education', *Sociological Review*, 26, 807–825.

Levenson, B. (1961), 'Bureaucratic succession', in A. Etzioni (ed.), *Complex Organisations*, New York: Holt, Rinehart and Winston.

Levitt, R. (1976), *The Re-organised National Health Service*, London: Croom Helm.

Lewis, R. and Maude, A. (1953), *The English Middle Classes*, London: Penguin.

Leys, C. (1985), *Politics in Britain*, London: Verso.

Leyshon, A., Thrift, N. and Twommey, C. (1988), 'South goes north? The rise of the British financial centre', *Working Papers in Producer Services*, University of Bristol.

Leyshon, A. and Thrift, N. (1989), 'South goes north? The rise of the British provincial financial centre', in J. Lewis and A. Townsend (eds), *The North/South Divide*, London: Paul Chapman.

Lieberson, S. (1985), *Making It Count*, Berkeley: University of California.

Lockwood, D. (1988), 'The weakest link in the chain: some remarks on the Marxist theory of action', in D. Rose (ed.), *Social Stratification and Economic Change*, London: Hutchinson.

MacAdams, J. (1987), 'Testing the theory of the new class', *Sociological Quarterly*, 28, 1, 23–49.

MacIntyre, S. (1981), *Little Moscows*, London: Croom Helm.

Mallet, S. (1975), *Essays on the New Working Class*, St Louis, Miss.: Telos Press.

Marcuse, P. (1990), 'Housing markets and labour markets in the quartered city', in J. Allen and C. Hamnett (eds), *Housing and Labour Markets*, London: Unwin Hyman.

Marsh, C. (1986), 'Social class and occupation', in B. Burgess (ed.), *Key Variables in Sociological Investigation*, London: Routledge & Kegan Paul.

Marshall, G. (1987), 'The politics of the new middle classes: history and predictions', paper given at 1988 BSA Conference, University of Edinburgh.

Marshall, G. (1988), 'Some remarks on the study of working class consciousness', in D. Rose (ed.), *Social Stratification and Economic Change*, London: Hutchinson.

Marshall, G. (1990a), 'John Goldthorpe and class analysis', in Clark *et al.* (eds).

Marshall, G. (1990b), *In Praise of Sociology*, London: Unwin Hyman.

Marshall, G., Newby, H., Rose, D. and Vogler, C. (1988), *Social Class in Modern Britain*, London: Unwin Hyman.

Marshall, G. and Rose, D. (1986), 'Constructing the (W)right classes', *Sociology*, 20, 3.

Marshall, G. and Rose, D. (1990), 'Out-classed by our critics?', *Sociology*, 24, 2.

Marshall, J. (1989), 'Revisioning career concepts: a feminist invitation', in M.B. Hall *et al.* (eds), *Handbook of Career Theory*, Cambridge: Cambridge University Press.

Marshall, J.N. and others (1988), *Services and Uneven Development*, Oxford: Oxford University Press.

Martin, R. (1988), 'Industrial capitalism in transition: the contemporary re-organisation of the British space economy', in D. Massey and J. Allen (eds), *Uneven Redevelopment*, London: Hodder and Stoughton.

Martindale, H. (1938), *Women Servants of the State 1870–1938*, London: George Allen and Unwin.

Mason, C. *et al.* (1989), 'Explaining recent trends in new firm formation in the UK: some evidence from South Hampshire', *Regional Studies*, 23, 4, 331–346.

Massey, D. (1984), *Spatial Divisions of Labour*, London: Methuen.

Massey, D. (1988a), 'What's happening to UK manufacturing', in Allen and Massey (eds).

Massey, D. (1988b), 'Uneven development: social change and spatial divisions of labour', in D. Massey and J. Allen (eds), *Uneven Redevelopment*, London: Hodder and Stoughton.

Massey, D. and Meegan, R. (1979), *The Anatomy of Job Loss*, London: Methuen.

Mattausch, J. (1987), 'The sociology of CND', in C. Creighton and M. Shaw (eds), *The Sociology of War and Peace*, London: Macmillan.

Mayhew, H. (1971), in E. Yeo and E.P. Thompson (eds), *The Unknown Mayhew*, London: Penguin.

Maywald, K. (1954), 'An index of building costs in the United Kingdom 1845–1938', *Economic History Review*, 7, 187–203.

Melrose-Woodman, J. (1976), *Profile of the British Manager*, London: BIM.

Merrett, S. (1979), *State Housing in Britain*, London: Routledge & Kegan Paul.

Merrett, S. and Gray, F. (1982), *Owner Occupation in Britain*, London: Routledge & Kegan Paul.

Merton, R.K. (1961), 'Bureaucratic structure and personality', in A. Etzioni (ed.), *Industrial Man*, London: Penguin.

Miles, A. (1990), 'Lower middle class mobility in England, 1839–1914', paper to Conference on Social Mobility in European History, Florence.

Miller, W. (1977), *Electoral Dynamics*, London: Macmillan.

Millerson, G. (1965), *The Qualifying Associations*, London: Routledge & Kegan Paul.

Mills, C. (1988), 'Everyday life on the upslope: the postmodern landscape of gentrification', *Society and Space*, 6, 2, 151–172.

Mills, C. Wright (1951), *White Collar*, New York: Oxford University Press.

Mohan, J. (1988), 'Spatial aspects of health care employment in Britain: 1. Aggregate trends', *Environment and Planning A*, 20, 7, 7–23.

Morgan, D. (1969), 'The social and educational background of Anglican bishops: continuities and change', *British Journal of Sociology*, 20, 2, 295–310.

Morris, R.J. (1990), *Class, Sect and Party: the Making of the Middle Class in Leeds 1820–1850*, Manchester: Manchester University Press.

Morrison, D.E. and Dunlop, R.E. (1986), 'Environmentalism and elitism: a conceptual and empirical analysis', *Environmental Management*, 10, 5, 581–589.

Moss, M. and Hume, J.R. (1986), *Shipbuilders to the World: 125 years of Harland and Wolff, Belfast 1861–1986*, Belfast: Blackstaff.

Muller, W. (1990), 'Social mobility in industrial nations', in Clark *et al.* (eds).

Murphy, R. (1988), *Social Closure: the Theory of Monopolization and Exclusion*, Oxford: Clarendon Press.

Newby, H. (1980), *Green and Pleasant Land*, London: Penguin.

Nicholson, P. and West, M. (1988), *Managerial Job Change*, Cambridge: Cambridge University Press.

Noble, D. (1977), *America by Design*, New York: Knopf.

Nossiter, N.J. (1975), *Influence, Opinion and Political Idiom in Reformed England: Case Studies from the North East 1832–1874*, Brighton: Harvester.

Offe, C. (1985), *Disorganised Capitalism*, Cambridge: Polity.

Offe, C. and Wisenthal, H. (1980), 'Two logics of collective action: theoretical notes on social class and organisational form', in M. Zeitlin (ed.), *Political Power and Social Theory*, Greenwich, Connecticut: Jai.

Offer, A. (1981), *Property and Politics 1870–1914: Landownership, Law and Urban Development in England*, Cambridge: Cambridge University Press.

Oliver, P., Davis, I. and Bentley, I. (1981), *Dunroamin: the Suburban Semi and its Enemies*, London: Barrie and Jenkins.

Otley, C. (1970), 'Social origins of British Army officers', *Sociological Review*, 18, 2, 213–240.

Outhwaite, W. (1987), *New Philosophies of Social Science*, Basingstoke: Macmillan.

Owen, D. and Green, A. (1984), 'The spatial manifestation of the changing socio-economic composition of employment in manufacturing', CURDS Discussion Paper, No. 56.

Pahl, J. and Pahl, R. (1971), *British Managers and their Wives*, London: Allen Lane.

Pahl, R. (1989), 'Is the emperor naked? Some questions on the adequacy of sociological theory in urban and regional research', *International Journal of Urban and Regional Research*, 13, 4.

Parkin, F. (1967), *Middle Class Radicalism*, Cambridge: Cambridge University Press.

Parkin, F. (1979), *Marxism and Class Theory: a Bourgeois Critique*, London: Routledge & Kegan Paul.

Parry-Lewis, J. (1965), *Building Cycles and Britain's Economic Growth*, London: Macmillan.

# REFERENCES

Parsons, D. and Hutt, R. (1981), 'The mobility of young graduates', *IMS Working Paper*, No. 26, University of Sussex.

Parsons, T. (1959), 'The social structure of the family', in R. Amsden (ed.), *The Family: its Functions and Destiny*, New York: Harper and Row.

Pawson, R. (1989), *A Measure for Measures*, London: Routledge.

Pawson, R. (1990), 'Half truths about bias', *Sociology*, 24, 2.

Payne, G. (1987a), *Mobility and Change in Modern Societies*, London: Macmillan.

Payne, G. (1987b), *Employment and Opportunity*, London: Macmillan.

Payne, G., Payne, J. and Chapman, T. (1982), *Regional Variations in Social Mobility*, paper to Advancement of Science Annual Meeting.

Penn, R. (1981), 'The Nuffield class categorization', *Sociology*, 15, 265–271.

Peppercorn, G. and Skoulding, G. (1987), *Profile of British Industry – The Manager's View*, London: BIM.

Perkin, H. (1968), *The Origins of Modern English Society*, London: Routledge & Kegan Paul.

Perkin, H. (1989), *The Professionalisation of English Society 1880–1980*, London: Routledge.

Peterson, M. (1978), *The Medical Profession in Mid Victorian London*, Berkeley: University of California Press.

Pfeffer, J. and Cohn, Y. (1984), 'Determinants of internal labour markets in organisations', *Administrative Science Quarterly*, 29, 550–572.

Pfeil, F. (1988), 'Post modernism as a "structure of feeling"', in C. Nelson and L. Grossberg (eds), *Marxism and the Interpretation of Culture*, Basingstoke: Macmillan.

Pickvance, C. (1987), 'The crisis of local government in Britain: an interpretation', in M. Gottdeiner (ed.), *Cities in Stress: a new look at the urban crisis*, Beverly Hills: Sage.

Pinch, S. (1989), 'The restructuring thesis and the study of public services', *Environment and Planning A*, 21, 7, 905–926.

Piore, M. and Sabel, P. (1984), *The Second Industrial Divide*, New York: Basic.

Podmore, D. and Spencer, A. (1986), 'Gender in the labour process: the case of men and women lawyers', in D. Knights and H. Willmott (eds), *Gender and the Labour Process*, Aldershot: Gower.

Pollard, S. (1962), *The Development of the British Economy 1914–50*, London: Arnold.

Pollard, S. (1985), 'Capital exports 1870–1914: harmful or beneficial?', *Economic History Review*, 38, 489–513.

Pollert, A. (1988), 'The flexible firm: fixation or fact?', *Work, Employment and Society*, 2, 3, 281–316.

Pond, C. (1989), 'The changing distribution of income, wealth and poverty', in C. Hamnett, L. McDowell and P. Sarre (eds), *The Changing Social Structure*, London: Sage.

Poole, M. *et al.* (1981), *Managers in Focus*, Aldershot: Gower.

Poulantzas, N. (1975), *Classes in Contemporary Capitalism*, London: New Left Books.

Pratt, G. (1989), 'Incorporation theory and the reproduction of the community fabric', in J. Wolch and M. Dear (eds), *The Power of Geography*, London: Unwin Hyman.

Prest, W. (1987), *Professions in Early Modern England*, London: Croom Helm.

Presthus, R. (1979), *The Organisational Society* (2nd edn), London: Macmillan.

Pringle, R. (1989), *Secretaries Talk*, London: Verso.

Przeworski, A. (1977), 'Proletariat into class: the process of class formation for Karl Kautsky's "The Class Struggles" to recent controversies', *Politics and Society*, 7, 343–401.

Rajan, A. (1987), *Services: the Second Industrial Revolution?*, London: Butterworth.

Randolph, B. (1990), 'Housing markets, labour markets, and discontinuity theory', in J. Allen and C. Hamnett (eds), *Housing and Labour Markets*, London: Unwin Hyman.

Rapoport, R. and Rapoport, R.N. (1971), *Dual Career Families*, London: Penguin.

Ratansi, A. (1985), 'The end of an orthodoxy? The critique of sociology's view of Marx on class', *Sociological Review*, 33, 4.

Raynor, J. (1969), *The Middle Class*, London: Longman.

Reader, W.J. (1975), *ICI: A History*, Vol. 2, London: Oxford University Press.

Reddy, W. (1987), *Money and Liberty in Western Europe*, Cambridge: Cambridge University Press.

Reed, M. (1984), 'The peasantry of 19th century England: a neglected class?', *History Workshop*, 18, 53–76.

Robertson, D. (1984), *Class and the British Electorate*, Oxford: Blackwell.

Roper, N. (1989), 'Life histories of managers', in *Life History*.

Rose, D. (1981), 'Homeownership and industrial change: the struggle for a separate sphere', *University of Sussex Working Paper in Urban and Regional Studies*, No. 25.

Rose, D. (1988), 'A feminist perspective of employment restructuring and gentrification: the case of Montreal', in J. Wolch and M. Dear (eds), *The Power of Geography*, London: Unwin Hyman.

Rothblatt, S. (1976), *Tradition and Change in English Liberal Education*, London: Faber and Faber.

Routh, G. (1980), *Occupation and Pay*, London: Methuen.

Rubery, J. (1988), 'Employers and the labour market', in D. Gallie (ed.), *Employment in Britain*, Oxford: Blackwell.

Rubinstein, W. (1981), *Men of Property*, London: Croom Helm.

Rubinstein, W. (1986), 'Education and the social origins of elites 1880–1970', *Past and Present*, 112, 163–207.

Rubinstein, W. (1987), 'The geographical distribution of middle class income in Britain 1800–1914', in his *Elites and the Wealthy in Modern British History*, Sussex: Harvester.

Rueschmeyer, M. (1981), *Professional Work and Marriage: an East–West Comparison*, London: Macmillan.

Salt, J. (1990), 'Labour migration and housing in the UK: an overview', in J. Allen and C. Hamnett (eds), *Housing and Labour Markets*, London: Unwin Hyman.

Samuel, R. (1977), 'The workshop of the world', *History Workshop*, 3.

Samuel, R. (1983a), 'The middle class between the wars: part one', *New Socialist*, Jan./Feb., 30–36.

Samuel, R. (1983b), 'The middle class between the wars: part two', *New Socialist*, March/April, 28–30.

Sanderson, K. (1990), 'Meanings of class and social mobility: the public and private lives of women civil servants', in H. Corr and L. Jamieson (eds), *The Politics of Everyday Life*, London: Macmillan.

Sarre, P. (1989), 'Race and the class structure', in C. Hamnett *et al.* (eds), *The Changing Social Structure*, London: Sage.

Saul, S. (1962), 'House building in England 1890–1914', *Economic History Review*, 15, 119–137.

Saunders, P. (1989), *Social Class and Stratification*, Basingstoke: Macmillan.

Saunders, P. (1990), *A Nation of Homeowners*, London: Unwin Hyman.

Savage, M. (1987a), 'Spatial mobility and the professional labour market', *University of Sussex Working Paper in Urban and Regional Studies*, No. 56.

Savage, M. (1987b), *The Dynamics of Working Class Politics: the Labour Movement in Preston 1880–1940*, Cambridge: Cambridge University Press.

Savage, M. (1988a), 'The missing link? The relationship between spatial mobility and social mobility', *British Journal of Sociology*, 39, 4.

Savage, M. (1988b), 'Trade unionism, sex segregation and the state: women's employment in "new industries" in inter war Britain', *Social History*, 13, 2, 209–229.

Savage, M. (1991a), 'Managerial hierarchies and career structures: the case of Lloyds Bank 1870–1950', in P. Friedson and M. Levy-Leboyer (eds), *Business Management in Historical Perspective*, Cambridge: Cambridge University Press.

Savage, M. (1991b), 'Making sense of middle class politics: a secondary analysis of the British General Election Survey 1987', *Sociological Review*, 39, 26–54.

Savage, M., Dickens, P. and Fielding, A.J. (1988), 'Some social and political implications of the contemporary fragmentation of the service class', *International Journal of Urban and Regional Research*, 12.

Savage, M. and Fielding, A.J. (1989), 'Class formation and regional development: the "service class" in South East England', *Geoforum*, 20, 2.

Savage, M., Watt, P. and Arber, S. (1991), 'Social class, consumption divisions, and housing mobility', in C. Marsh and R. Burrows (eds), *Consumption and Class: Divisions and Change*, Basingstoke: Macmillan.

Savage, M. and Witz, A. (1991), *The Gendered Dynamics of Service Class Formation: Beyond the Women and Class Debate*, mimeo.

Sayer, R.A. (1984), *Method in Social Science: a Realist Approach*, London: Hutchinson.

Sayer, R.A. (1989), 'Post Fordism in question', *International Journal of Urban and Regional Research*, 666–695.

Scase, R. (1982), 'The petty bourgeoisie and modern capitalism: a review of recent theories', in A. Giddens and G. MacKenzie (eds), *Social Class and the Division of Labour*, Cambridge: Cambridge University Press.

Scase, R. and Goffee, M. (1989), *Reluctant Managers*, London: Unwin Hyman.

Scott, J. (1989), 'Ownership and employer control', in D. Gallie (ed.), *Employment in Britain*, Oxford: Blackwell.

Scott, J. and Griff, J. (1984), *Directors of Industry*, Cambridge: Polity.

Scott, W.R. (1966), 'Professionals in bureaucracies: areas of conflict', in H. Volmer and D. Mills (eds), *Professionalisation*, Englewood Cliffs: Prentice-Hall.

Seed, J. (1988), 'Commerce and the liberal arts: the political economy of art in Manchester', in J. Wolff and J. Seed (eds), *The Culture of Capital*, Manchester: Manchester University Press.

Sewell, W.H. (1990), 'How classes are made: critical reflections on E.P. Thompson's theory of working class formation', in H. Kaye and K. McClelland (eds), *E.P. Thompson: Critical Perspectives*, Cambridge: Polity.

Short, J., Fleming, S. and Witt, S. (1986), *Housebuilding, Planning and Community Action*, London: Routledge & Kegan Paul.

Simon, B. (1987), 'Systematisation and segmentation in education: the case of England', in D.K. Muller, F. Rigner and B. Simon (eds), *The Rise of the Modern Educational System*, Cambridge: Cambridge University Press.

Smith, A.D. (1982a), *The Ethnic Revival*, Cambridge: Cambridge University Press.

Smith, C. (1987a), *Technical Workers: Class, Labour and Trade Unionism*, Basingstoke: Macmillan.

Smith, D. (1982b), *Conflict and Compromise: Class Formation in English Society*, London: Routledge & Kegan Paul.

Smith, D.R. (1983), 'Mobility in professional occupational internal labour markets: stratification, segmentation and vacancy chains', *American Sociological Review*, 48.

Smith, N. (1981), *Uneven Development*, Oxford: Blackwell.

Smith, N. (1987b), 'Of yuppies and housing: gentrification and the urban dream', *Society and Space*, 5, 2, 151–172.

Smith, N. and Williams, P. (eds) (1987), *Gentrification of the City*, London: Allen and Unwin.

Snape, P. and Bamber, G. (1985), *Managers in Britain*, mimeo.

Sorenson, A.B. (1986), 'Theory and methodology in stratification research', in U. Himmelstrand (ed.), *The Sociology of Structure and Action: Vol. 1, Sociology, from Crisis to Science?*, London: Sage.

Stanworth, M. (1984), 'Women and class analysis: a reply to Goldthorpe', *Sociology*, 18, 159–170.

Star, L. (1991), 'The sociology of the invisible: the primacy of work in the writings of Anselm Strauss', in D. Maines (ed.), *Social Organisation and Social Processes: Essays in Honor of Anselm Strauss*, New York: de Gruyter.

Starkey, K. (1989), 'Time and professionalism: disputes concerning the nature of conflict', *British Journal of Industrial Relations*, 27, 3.

Steinmatz, G. and Wright, E.O. (1989), 'The fall and rise of the petty bourgeoisie', *American Journal of Sociology*, 94, 973–1018.

Stone, L. and Stone, J.C. (1984), *An Open Elite: England 1540–1880*, Oxford: Oxford University Press.

Storper, D. and Walker, M. (1989), *The Capitalist Imperative*, London: Methuen.

Therborn, G. (1986a), 'Class analysis: a history and defence', in U. Himmelstrand (ed.), *The Sociology of Structure and Action*, London: Sage.

Therborn, G. (1986b), *Why Some People are More Unemployed than Others*, London: Verso.

Thompson, E.P. (1963), *The Making of the English Working Class*, London: Gollancz.

Thompson, E.P. (1965), 'The peculiarities of the English', *The Socialist Register*.

Thompson, E.P. (1978), *The Poverty of Theory*, London: Merlin.

Thomson, F.M.L. (1963), *English Landed Society in the 19th Century*, London: Routledge & Kegan Paul.

Thrift, N. (1987), 'The geography of late twentieth century class formation', in N. Thrift and P. Williams (eds), *Class and Space*, London: Routledge & Kegan Paul.

Thrift, N. (1989), 'Images of social change', in C. Hamnett, L. McDowell and P. Sarre (eds), *The Changing Social Structure*, London: Sage.

Tolliday, S. (1987), *Business, Banking and Politics*, Harvard: Harvard University Press.

Tolliday, S. and Zeitlin, J. (1986), *Between Fordism and Flexibility*, Cambridge: Polity.

Torstendahl, R. (1990), 'Introduction: promotion and strategies of knowledge', in R. Torstendahl and M. Burrage (eds), *The Formation of Professions*, London: Sage.

Urry, J. (1981), 'Localities, regions and social class', *International Journal of Urban and Regional Research*, 5, 455–74.

Urry, J. (1986), 'Capitalist production, scientific management and the service class', in A.J. Scott and M. Storper (eds), *Production, Work Territory*, London: Allen and Unwin.

Urry, J. (1987), 'Some social and spatial aspects of services', *Society and Space*, 5, 5–26.

Urry, J. (1990), *The Tourist Gaze*, London: Sage.

Vincent, J. (1966), *The Formation of the Modern Liberal Party*, London: Penguin.

Vincent, J. (1967), *Pollbooks: How Victorians Voted*, Cambridge: Cambridge University Press.

Waddington, I. (1984), *The Medical Profession in the Industrial Revolution*, Dublin: Gill and Macmillan.

Walby, S. (1986), 'Gender, class and stratification: towards a new approach', in Crompton and Mann (eds).

Walby, S. (1990), *Theorising Patriarchy*, Cambridge: Polity.

Waldinger, R., Ward, R. and Aldrich, H. (1985), 'Ethnic business and occupational mobility in advanced society', *Sociology*, 19, 4, 586–597.

Walton, J.K. (1983), *The English Seaside Resort*, Manchester: The University Press.

Ward, R. (1985), 'Minority settlement and the local economy', in B. Roberts, R. Finnegan and D. Gallie (eds), *New Approaches to Economic Life*, Manchester: Manchester University Press.

Ward, S. (1988), *The Geography of Inter-War Britain: the State and Uneven Development*, London: Routledge.

Warner, L. and Ableggen, J.C. (1959), 'Occupational succession', in W.L. Warner and N.H. Martin (eds), *Industrial Man*, New York: Harper and Brothers.

Watson, W. (1964), 'Social mobility and social class in industrial societies', in M. Glucksmann and E. Devons (eds), *Closed Systems and Open Minds*, Edinburgh: Oliver and Boyd.

Weber, B. (1955), 'A new index of residential construction, 1938–1950', *Scottish Journal of Political Economy*, 2, 131–132.

Weber, M. (1978), *Economy and Society* (2 Vols), ed. by G. Roth and C. Wittich, New York: Bedminster.

Weiner, M. (1980), *English Culture and the Decline of the Industrial Spirit*, London: Penguin.

Whalley, P. (1986), *The Social Production of Technical Work*, London: Macmillan.

Whatmore, S. (1990), *Patriarchy and Farming*, London: Unwin Hyman.

Whitley, R. (1989), 'On the nature of managerial tasks and skills: their distinguishing characteristics and organisation', *Journal of Management Studies*, 26, 3, 209–224.

Wholey, D.R. (1985), 'Determinants of firm internal labour markets in large law firms', *Administrative Science Quarterly*, 30, 318–335.

Whyte, W.S. (1957), *The Organisation Man*, New York: Touchstone.

Wieck, H.C. and Berlinger, L.R. (1989), 'Career improvisation in self-designing organisations', in M.B. Hall *et al.* (eds), *Handbook of Career Theory*, Cambridge: Cambridge University Press.

Wilson, C. (1954), *The History of Unilever*, Vol. 2, London: Cassel.

Winstanley, M. (1983), *The Shopkeepers' World*, Manchester: Manchester University Press.

Witz, A. (1990), 'Patriarchy and professions: the gendered politics of occupational closure', *Sociology*, 24, 4.

Witz, A. (1991), *Professions and Patriarchy*, London: Routledge.

Wolff, J. (1988), 'The culture of separate spheres: the role of culture in 19th century public and private life', in J. Wolff and J. Seed (eds), *The Culture of Capital*, Manchester: Manchester University Press.

Wordie, J. (1983), 'The chronology of English Enclosure 1500–1914', *Economic History Review*, 36, 483–505.

Wright, E.O. (1978), *Class, Crisis and the State*, London: New Left Books.

Wright, E.O. (1985), *Classes*, London: Verso.

Wright, E.O. (1989), 'Rethinking, once again the concept of class structure', in E.O. Wright and others, *The Debate on Classes*, London: Verso.

Wright, E.O. and Steinmatz, G. (1989), 'The fall and rise of the petite bourgeoisie: changing patterns of self employment in the USA', *American Journal of Sociology*, 94, 5.

Wright, M., Coyne, J. and Mills, A. (1987), *Spicer and Pegler's Management Buy Outs*, Cambridge: Woodhead and Faulkner.

Zimmeck, M. (1988), 'The new woman in the machinery of government: a spanner in the works?', in R. McLeod (ed.), *Government and Expertise: Specialists, Administrators and Professionals 1860–1919*, Cambridge: Cambridge University Press.

Zukin, S. (1985), *Loft Living: Culture and Capital in Urban Change*, London: Radium.

# NAME INDEX

Abel, R.L. 74, 76
Abercrombie, N. 2, 8, 10, 11, 12, 20, 24, 58, 212, 223
Ableggen, J.C. 24
Abramson, P.R. 188
Acker, S. 221
Acton Society Trust 50, 51
Aglietta, M. 59, 60
Ahrne, G. 221
Alban-Metcalfe, B.M. 67
Allen, J. 59, 61, 161
Althauser, R.P. 24
Anderson, P. 36, 37, 41
Anthias, F. 227
Arber, S. 221
Armstrong, P. 55, 141
Atkinson, J. 62

Bagguley, P. 8, 62, 73, 74, 101, 109, 129, 174, 188, 208, 209
Ball, M. 81, 82, 85, 86
Bamber, G. 25
Barlow, J. 64, 80, 89, 92
Barnett, C. 204
Baron, J.N. 25
Barrell, R. 91
Barton, T. 187–8
Bauman, Z. 130
Becher, H.W. 41–2
Bechhofer, F. 46, 47
Beckett, J.V. 37, 46
Benjamin, W. 130
Benson, J. 46, 47
Berlanstein, L.C. 56
Berlinger, L.R. 62
Bernstein, B. 151
Bhaskar, R. 6

Birch, S. 67
Blackburn, R.A. 69, 70, 71
Blau, P. 159
Blumin, S. 30
BMRB 104–12, 114, 117, 119, 121, 122, 124, 125, 126, 127
Boddy, M. 64, 83
Boltanski, L. 28, 29, 42, 56
Bonham, J. 200–1
Bourdieu, P. 16–17, 28, 42, 58, 100–3, 113, 114, 115, 151, 221
Bowley, M. 82
Braverman, H. 2, 3, 58
Britten, N. 221
Brown, R. 24, 26
Bruce, A. 69
Burnett, J. 82–3
Burrage, M. 28, 38, 39
Burris, V. 15
Burrows, R. 70, 71
Bury, M.O. 72
Butcher, T. 43

Calvert, P. 5
Cannadine, D. 37
Carchedi, G. 2
Carr-Saunders, A.M. 37–8, 228
Carter, B. 2, 3, 187
Castells, M. 97
CBI 89–90
Chandler, A.D. 49, 52, 53, 56, 60
Child, J. 65, 74–5
Clegg, S. 13, 62–3
Cochrane, A. 204
Cohen, Y. 25
Coleman, D.C. 52–3
Connor, S. 128, 130

257

# SUBJECT INDEX